RECONSTRUCTING THE STATE

Why do some state-building efforts succeed when others fail? Using newly available archival sources, this book presents a reinterpretation of the rise and subsequent collapse of the Soviet state. The study explains how personal networks and elite identity served as informal sources of power that influenced state strength. *Reconstructing the State* also offers a revised explanation of how the weak Bolshevik state extended its reach to a vast rural and multiethnic periphery as well as the dynamics of the center–regional conflict in the 1930s that culminated in the Great Terror.

Gerald M. Easter is an Assistant Professor in the Political Science Department at Boston College.

CAMBRIDGE STUDIES IN
COMPARATIVE POLITICS

General Editor
PETER LANGE   Duke University

Associate Editors
ROBERT H. BATES   Harvard University
ELLEN COMISSO   University of California, San Diego
PETER HALL   Harvard University
JOEL MIGDAL   University of Washington
HELEN MILNER   Columbia University
RONALD ROGOWSKI   University of California, Los Angeles
SIDNEY TARROW   Cornell University

Series list continues on page following index.

RECONSTRUCTING THE STATE

Personal Networks and Elite Identity in Soviet Russia

GERALD M. EASTER

Boston College

CAMBRIDGE UNIVERSITY PRESS

PUBLISHED BY THE PRESS SYNDICATE OF THE UNIVERSITY OF CAMBRIDGE
The Pitt Building, Trumpington Street, Cambridge, United Kingdom

CAMBRIDGE UNIVERSITY PRESS
The Edinburgh Building, Cambridge CB2 2RU, UK   http://www.cup.cam.ac.uk
40 West 20th Street, New York, NY 10011-4211, USA   http://www.cup.org
10 Stamford Road, Oakleigh, Melbourne 3166, Australia
Ruiz de Alarcón 13, 28014 Madrid, Spain

First published 2000

Printed in the United States of America

Typeface Garamond # 3 11/13 pt.   *System* DeskTopPro$_{/\text{UX}}$® [BV]

A catalog record for this book is available from the British Library.

Library of Congress Cataloging in Publication data
Easter, Gerald, 1959–
Reconstructing the State : Personal Networks and Elite Identity in Soviet Russia /
Gerald Easter.
p.   cm. – (Cambridge studies in comparative politics)
Includes bibliographical references.
ISBN 0–521–66085–8
1. Soviet Union – Politics and government.   2. Elite (Social
sciences) – Soviet Union.   3. Policy networks – Soviet Union.
4. Central–local government relations – Soviet Union.   I. Title.
II. Series.
JN6531.E27   1999
320.8'0947'0904 – dc21   98–53579
                                                          CIP

ISBN 0 521 66085 8 hardback

to mara lynn

CONTENTS

PREFACE

The activity of the administrative apparatus poses a greater threat to Bolshevik domination than the actions of officer cadets and Kerenskii. Kerenskii can be arrested and the cadets can be shot with a gun, but the very best gun cannot replace a battered typewriter, nor can the bravest sailor replace a modest clerk in any of the departments. Without the state mechanism, without the apparatus of power, the entire activity of the new government resembles a machine without a driving belt – it goes round and round, but produces nothing.

Tribuna gosudarstvennykh sluzhashchikh, 1917

The new Soviet state will be built from the principles of scientific management and from passion and blood.

Valerian V. Kuibyshev, 1924

In November 1920, as Baron Petr Vrangel organized the final retreat of White Russia from the Crimean peninsula across the Black Sea, the fledgling Bolshevik regime turned to confront the new challenge of post-revolutionary state building. In three years of civil war, the Bolsheviks mastered the ability to employ coercion against military foes in the field and political opponents at home. Now the Bolsheviks sought to extend their influence beyond the urban industrial areas to Russia's vast rural and multiethnic periphery. But the infrastructural powers of the new state were especially weak at this time. Even Lenin had at first openly speculated that the Bolsheviks would last at best one year. In less than a decade, however, they constructed the foundation and framework of communism's command–administrative state and extended their reach across Soviet Russia's fractious and far-flung regions.

The command–administrative state was the institutional means by which Soviet Russia sped through an industrial revolution in the 1930s, defeated the Nazi war machine in the 1940s, led the way into space exploration in the 1950s, and emerged as a global superpower in the 1960s. In a century that witnessed a proliferation of newly independent nations, the core features of the command–administrative state – a single, mass-based political party and a centrally planned economy – offered would-be state builders an alternative to the capitalist West. In the reconfiguration of world politics following the Second World War, the institutional design of the command–administrative state was readily emulated by some and brutally imposed on others.

While the command–administrative state is now almost casually dismissed as a failed experiment, it only recently consumed the attention of the West as a fearsome rival. Prior to the onset of its demise in the late 1980s, a solid consensus existed among Western scholars that Soviet Russia was a "strong" state. Area specialists argued bitterly over whether the sources of state strength were to be found above in the organs of control and coercion or below in strategic bases of social support. Yet virtually no one anticipated the collapse of the state. While Russian area specialists have borne the brunt of criticism for not foreseeing the collapse, it is noteworthy that comparative political theorists fared no better in their estimations of Soviet state strength. In fact, comparative theorists from both the "modernizationist" and the "statist" perspectives had previously held up the Soviet case as a model of successful twentieth-century state building.

What were the underlying constraints on power that comparative theorists and area specialists failed to include in their assessments of state strength in Soviet Russia? This book attempts to answer this question. It argues that scholars have tended to focus on the formal aspects of the state to the detriment of its informal side. Central leadership, coercion, and, most of all, formal organization were cited as the mainsprings of state strength. Yet, the Soviet Russian state collapsed when a strong and capable leader was at the helm, its capacity to employ coercion was unsurpassed, and its bureaucratic lines of command were more stable and clearly defined than at any previous time in its history. This book suggests that the missing piece to the puzzle of state strength was informal sources of power: personal networks and elite identities. The book demonstrates how these informal elements intersected with the formal structures of the Soviet Russian state in a way that directly influenced its capacities of rule. Moreover, it shows that the seeds of state collapse can be traced back to the original Bolshevik state-building strategies. The case study reconstructs the Soviet Russian state to reveal the workings of its less often seen informal side of personal networks and elite identities.

In the constructing and reconstructing of this book, I have become aware of the ways in which personal networks thrive – not just within the state, but also in academia. It is with much gratitude that I acknowledge the informal sources of support I have received. As an undergraduate at Boston College, I was first introduced to Russian studies by Donald Carlisle, whose passion for the Byzantine world of Kremlin politics kept lecture halls packed with students precariously perched on seat edges. While studying political science at Columbia University, I had the good fortune to work with Leopold Haimson, whose masterful interpretations of the structures, conjunctures, and events in Russian history have inspired my own scholarly aspirations. I likewise benefited from the wit and wisdom of the stout-hearted members of my own graduate school *druzhina*: Buz Bishop, from whom I have learned to always go at life from the top rope; David McDonald, from whom I have come to appreciate the value of a good short game; and Burton Miller, with whom I shared many second-hand camels and holy cows. More recently, I owe an increasing debt to my surrogate advisor, Brian Silver, who first put the social science into Russian studies. His counsel and company are sometimes all that prevent me from canceling my e-mail service.

In addition, I am grateful for the support, in one form or another, that I received along the way from the following: Harley Balzer, Pete Beisada, Tom Bernstein, Seweryn Bialer, Stephen Cohen, Susan Easter, Peggy Freund, Puck N. Fritty, Mark Gelfand, Thane Gustafson, John Hazard, Bob Jackman, Peter Lange, Mary McAuley, Raymond T. McNally, Ambassador William G. Miller, Sam Mujal-Leon, Joe Rothschild, Peter Solomon, Susan Gross Solomon, V. M. Ustinov, Mark Von Hagen, and A. I. Zevelev. My research efforts were ably assisted by the staffs at the Slavic collection at Columbia University, particularly its stalwart keeper Evgenii Beshenkovskii; Perkins Library at Duke University; and the Russian Institute for the Preservation of Documents of Recent History, in Moscow. The following institutions contributed to the funding of this project: the Harriman Institute at Columbia University, the East–West Center at Duke University, the Carnegie Foundation, the Kennan Institute, the Social Science Research Council, and PepsiCo.

Ekaterinburg, Russia

INTRODUCTION: EXPLAINING STATE-BUILDING OUTCOMES AND THE SOVIET RUSSIAN CASE

Throughout the twentieth century, the Soviet Russian state was most often depicted in the West as a modern Leviathan: omnipotent, imposing, and menacing. Yet by the end of the century, this once most feared member of the world community of states had ceased to exist. In its final months, the internal weaknesses of the Soviet Russian state were exposed in a succession of dramatic events: the unraveling of the communist bloc in Eastern Europe, the inept displays of force in the non-Russian national republics, and, finally, the botched palace coup in the capital. In the end, the Soviet Russian state proved incapable of averting its own territorial demise and quietly passed into history with the stroke of a pen.

Among Western scholars, the Soviet Russian state, if not the Leviathan, was certainly assumed to possess sufficient strength to endure well into the twenty-first century. For comparative theorists, Soviet Russia had long stood as a paradigm of successful state building. Leading theorists from both the modernizationist and the statist approaches would concur that, while the means employed were undeniably harsh, the end product was a state that had effectively realized its capacity to rule. Russian area specialists, meanwhile, reinforced this image through their many accounts of the seemingly boundless capabilities of the state to employ coercion, to mobilize resources, and to recast society. The major debates among area specialists were not over strength and weakness, but over the sources of strength. One side in these debates located state strength above in the formal organs of coercion and bureaucratic control; in contrast, another side located state strength below in strategic bases of popular and elite support. For all their many disagreements, before 1989 few area specialists on either side seriously doubted the long-term survival of the state.

Thus, the sudden and unexpected collapse of the Soviet Russian state called into question the conceptual premises of state strength, which led to the widespread and ultimately mistaken assumptions about its survival. What were the underlying constraints of power that area specialists as well as comparative theorists neglected to include in their assessments of the Soviet Russian state?

This study seeks to answer this question. It argues that state strength in Soviet Russia was most often conceptualized in terms of formal sources of power, while informal sources were generally overlooked. The study does not contend that formal sources of power – coercive and bureaucratic organs – were insignificant; instead, it asserts that these formal sources were constrained by informal sources of power – personal networks and elite identity. State strength, it is argued, was determined by the constraints of power formed by the intersection of formal and informal power resources.

To demonstrate this assertion, the study directs attention away from the events of state collapse and reexamines the process of state building. The seeds of the demise of the Soviet state, it is argued, can be found in the survival strategies devised by state leaders in the early postrevolutionary period. Strategies that were successful in the short term had the unintended effect of contributing to the undoing of the state in the long term.

The study departs from standard treatments of Soviet state building in that the empirical focus is on an elite cohort, rather than central leaders or organizations. In particular, it charts the rise and fall of the new state's first generation of regional leaders. In so doing, it breaks new ground as the first Western study to focus systematically on these particular actors, who played the leading role in extending the administrative and extractive capacities of the new state to the vast rural and non-Russian periphery. The case study shows how personal network ties and elite identity among the members of this cohort served as informal power resources, which in turn had a defining influence on the process of postrevolutionary state building.

The case study is organized into three parts, which address three interrelated sets of questions concerning state building and state strength in Soviet Russia. First, who built the Soviet Russian state? How did they come to hold positions of power in the new state? What was the basis of their claim on elite status? How did they envision their role in the new state? Second, how did the intersection of informal and formal sources of power affect the development of state strength? In what ways was state strength enhanced? In what ways was it subverted? Third, how did the resulting constraints on power shape intraelite conflicts in the new state? Was it possible to redefine the existing constraints of power? If so, by what means? And how did the constraints of power influence the type of political regime that emerged in the new state?

The answers to these empirical questions provide an explanation to the larger theoretical puzzle about the underlying constraints on the state. The study asserts that it was the tendency to conceptualize power in its formal manifestations that led so many area specialists and comparative theorists to overestimate the strength of the Soviet state. Neither Soviet state building nor state collapse can be fully explained without understanding the way in which informal sources of power intersected with the formal lines of command in the state. Moreover, the reconceptualization of state strength as a manifestation of the intersection of informal and formal sources of power contributes to the ongoing effort of comparative theorists to explain cross-national variations in state-building outcomes. More specifically, the case study demonstrates the mechanism through which microlevel social structures give shape to macrolevel political institutions.

This chapter introduces the theoretical issues raised in the study, including (1) a review of the comparative state-building literature; (2) a review of the Russian area studies literature; (3) an elaboration of the theoretical framework; and (4) a discussion of the methodology.

I. STATE BUILDING AND COMPARATIVE THEORY

Two decades ago, comparative theorists refocused their attention on the state.[1] What began as an incipient challenge to the field's "behavioralist" postwar status quo soon became the new mainstream, boasting one of the most substantial bodies of literature ever produced in Western social science. Looking back on these efforts, one can discern three phases in the development of comparative state-building theory, broadly distinguished by the conceptual units of analysis. In the first phase, the advocates for "bringing the state back in" reacted against a perceived neglect by comparative theorists of the causal role of state institutional structures in determining political outcomes.[2] The state in these works was conceptualized as a relatively autonomous actor, based on the extent to which it was able to develop its own discrete interests and to act upon them apart from the interests and actions of societal actors. Thus, a strong state was one that had successfully insulated itself from society.

For many, the "statists" appeared to be staking out a claim in the field by exaggerating and polemicizing their differences with the behavioralists of the 1950s and 1960s.[3] Indeed, state capacity, even if by another name, had been a central concern of some of the best-known works of this earlier period.[4] Moreover, the statists' initial emphasis on a state-society conceptual dichotomy was targeted by critics for its "superficial" and "misleading appeal."[5]

Despite these criticisms, comparative research on the state thrived in the 1980s.[6] In the second phase, research efforts produced more nuanced conceptualizations of the state as a causal agent and greater sensitivity to the interactions between state and society. Michael Mann's influential article distinguishing a state's "despotic," or decision-making, powers from its "infrastructural," or implementation, powers provided much needed clarity to the discussion.[7] From this distinction emerged a focus on state capacities, or capabilities, which offered more concrete subject matter for analysis. Capacities referred to the "infrastructural" powers of the state, that is, the early modern state's functions of territorial administration, military coercive power, and revenue extraction as well as its later developed interventionary social and economic functions.[8]

Studies of state building sought to determine the extent to which central, or strategic, state actors were able to develop enduring institutional forms through which these functions, or capacities, could be realized.[9] Scholars measured capacity in "high-low" terms. States that developed a high capacity to perform these functions independent of society were labeled "strong" states, while states that maintained a low capacity were labeled "weak" states.[10] It was further discovered that most states, in fact, exhibited simultaneously a high capacity for performing certain functions and a low capacity for performing certain others, which in turn made problematic the application of the "strong" and "weak" concepts.[11]

By the early 1990s, it seemed as if scholarly interest in the state had finally been exhausted. New criticisms arose over the inability to explain cross-national differences in state-building outcomes. Why was it that some state-building efforts succeeded when others failed? Why were some states strong and others weak? Until this time, the tendency among state theorists was to stress Gerschenkronian macrolevel causes to explain state-building outcomes. The structure of the international environment was frequently cited as the determining force shaping state-building processes. Accordingly, the more hostile the international environment appeared to centrally located state actors, the greater the liklihood that measures would be undertaken to construct a strong state, or at least a state with well-developed coercive and extractive capacities.[12] Likewise, and often interrelated, strong states, it was argued, were more likely to emerge in societies where macrolevel socioeconomic structures acted as obstacles to industrial development.[13] But even among scholars that were generally sympathetic to the approach, these explanations were not sufficient. Barbara Geddes summed up the prevailing dissatisfaction with the literature at this time when she noted that "the short-coming of these macrolevel explanations is that they describe virtually all developing countries."[14]

In response to this situation, a third phase in comparative state theory unfolded in which scholars moved away from macrolevel concepts and sought out new areas of analysis. Scholarly interest in state building was given an added boost by world events in the late 1980s and 1990s, as a flood of new cases emerged in the wake of fallen authoritarian and communist regimes.[15] While no scholarly consensus has yet emerged from these more recent efforts, agreement does exist on the need to develop new conceptualizations of the state and state strength as units of comparative analysis. In this search, comparativists have moved in three directions: rational choice, state in society, and neodevelopment.

The "rational choice" approach has attempted to explain variations in state-building outcomes by reconceptualizing the state as a microlevel unit of analysis. The focus of inquiry is on individual leading actors, their preferences, and the structural constraints under which they operate. A major step in this direction was taken by Magaret Levi, who called for "bringing people back into the state," revenue hungry rulers to be more precise. Beginning with the premise that all state leaders share a preference to maximize income, Levi provided a wide-ranging comparative historical study which explained state-building outcomes as a consequence of the strategies calculated by leaders as the most efficient means of enhancing revenue extraction. The rational choice approach was extended further by Barbara Geddes in a study of radical political and economic reform in Latin America. Geddes posited a conceptualization of the state as a collection of politically self-interested individuals.[17] She argued that all state actors share a preference to advance their political careers. Toward this end, they are confronted by the "politician's dilemma," in which policy choices reflect the constraints of career advancement. The politician's dilemma, thus, explained the seemingly paradoxical situation in which state actors willingly undertake reforms that reduce state powers. By refocusing on leadership preferences and microlevel structural constraints, these works offer one solution to the puzzle of varying state-building outcomes.

Wary of the tendency toward reification in the "state as rational actor" approach, Joel Migdal, Atul Kohli, and Vivienne Shue have pushed the literature in another direction. They argued for a "state in society" approach in order to "disaggregate" the state as a unit of analysis and to resituate its component parts in concrete social settings.[18] The state in society approach attempts to identify the underlying social foundations of political institutions. To avoid the earlier "behavioralist" assumptions, they stress that state–society influences are interactive, not unidirectional. And to move beyond the existing conceptualizations of the state, they reconceptualize the state as a four-tiered structure, including: central leadership, central administration, regional administration, and field offices. Each tier, they argue, provides its own arena within which power struggles are waged among competing state players as well as between state and nonstate players. Ultimately, the overall "patterns of domination" in the state–societal relationship are shaped by the sum of the outcomes of the power struggles in these multilevel arenas.

In a variation on the state in society approach, Peter Evans has devised the concept of "embedded autonomy" to explain why some developmental states are more successful than others in promoting industrial growth.[19] Evans began by revising the concept of state autonomy from meaning simply the degree of insulation from societal influences to indicating instead the extent of organizational coherence and professional standards within the state bureaucracy. But autonomy alone does not lead to enhanced state capacity. He went on to stress that building state capacity requires that state actors obtain information and secure cooperation from societal actors. For this reason, he argued, capacity is enhanced when an autonomous state becomes embedded in society. Social networks are the means by which this "embedded autonomy" is achieved. People and information pass back and forth between state and society along informal network ties. The concept of embedded autonomy represents not only an advance to the state in society approach, but is likely to be considered one of the more significant contributions to have emerged from comparative state theory.

The rational choice and state in society approaches build upon the existing body of literature on comparative state theory. By contrast, the "neodevelopment" approach rejects this theoretical base. In a counterreaction to the statists, neodevelopment proponents begin with the premise that state institutional forms are shaped by societal influences. They cite the recent wave of democratic transitions as vindication of sorts of earlier political development theory. Robert Jackman has leveled the strongest attack on the conceptual foundations of comparative state theory from a neodevelopment perspective.[20] Jackman argued that the conceptualizations of state capacity in the statist literature are flawed and, as a result, provide a distorted measure of state strength. He argued that a more accurate measure of state strength was "political capacity," that is, the ability of a state to achieve its policy goals without resort to coercion or bureaucratic fiat. Political capacity indicates the extent to which state institutions are considered legitimate by society. State strength, thus, should not reflect the extent to which functions, such as revenue extraction are realized, but instead should reflect the compliance strategies employed by state leaders to carry out these functions.

This study contributes to the recent efforts to extend the explanatory reach of the state-building literature. It follows the state in society approach by uncovering the microlevel social structures from which emerge macrolevel political institutions. In so doing, a new explanation is offered for one of the most studied cases of twentieth-century state building: Soviet Russia.

II. STATE BUILDING AND SOVIET RUSSIA

The Russian revolution was notable for the relative ease by which Vladimir Lenin and his small party of radical socialists, the Bolsheviks, came to power in October 1917. The process of consolidating power in new institutional forms, however, was conflictual and prolonged. State capacities were developed incrementally over a period of two decades. Why the Soviet Russian state developed along the lines that it did remains a disputed question in Western scholarship. This debate, as old as the field itself, has produced an assortment of answers, ranging from the structural to the ideological, from the cultural to the institutional, and from the societal to the individual.

A different question, however, is why were Bolshevik state-building efforts successful? The postrevolutionary regime confronted a formidable array of obstacles. Even Lenin at first expressed doubt that the Bolsheviks could hold power for more than a year. For over two decades, Western scholars displayed a virtual consensus on the question of the success of Soviet state building. They stressed strong leaders, coercion, and, especially, formal organization.[21] According to this view, by the early 1920s, the Communist party provided a tightly organized and centralized formal structure by which the state center developed a capacity to administer Soviet Russia's vast periphery. On top of this structure sat the party's general secretary, Iosif Stalin, whose hands were firmly secured to the organizational levers of power. "The tentacles of the Secretariat," it was said, "reached the smallest territorial units throughout Russia."[22]

This depiction by area specialists of the means by which a strong state was built in postrevolutionary Soviet Russia became a paradigmatic case for comparative state theory. The conventional view was that Lenin's Bolsheviks embodied a kind of "organizational weapon" that enabled them to triumph over all manifestations of societal resistance and upon which a single-party state was successfully constructed.[23] During the 1960s and 1970s, when established democracies appeared to be increasingly "ungovernable" and transitions to new democracies were as yet unheard of, the single-party state was depicted by comparative theorists as an institutional expedient for would-be state builders in the postcolonial world.[24] Most attractive about the single-party state was the internal coherence and discipline that was presumed to exist within the organizational framework of a Leninist party. Indeed, some of the most influential studies in comparative politics over the past thirty years borrowed directly from the Soviet studies literature to support the larger claim that formal organizational structure was the key ingredient for successful state-building outcomes.

Samuel Huntington's *Political Order in Changing Societies* preceded the "return to the state" in comparative politics by a decade, but his focus on "political order" is, in fact, a study of the dilemmas encountered by new postcolonial states seeking to develop their capacities to rule. Huntington held up the Soviet case as a model of effective political institution building for other modernizing countries. Just as French absolutism and British parliamentarism had once provided exemplary institutional forms for the rest of the world, Huntington argued, the Soviet single-party state had become the institutional model for twentieth-century postcolonial states. In particular, he stressed the role played by formal organization to explain Soviet Russia's state-building outcome. "The relative success of communist states in providing political order," he wrote, "in large part derives from the priority they have given to the conscious act of political organization."[25]

More recently, Theda Skocpol's *States and Social Revolutions* has become one of the most prominent studies to come out of the "return to the state" literature. Skocpol may have differed with Huntington on a number of analytical and methodological points, but she treated the Soviet case in similar terms. She presented Soviet Russia as one of the twentieth century's most successful state-building attempts. While Skocpol stressed macrolevel international and socioeconomic structures to explain why a strong state emerged in postrevolutionary Soviet Russia, she adopted the conventional area studies argument that formal organization was the means to that end. She noted that the Communist party "consisted of hierarchically ordered cadres subject to appointment and explicit discipline by the top party leadership, thus allowing much more effective central coordination than the tsar could achieve."[26] Both Huntington and Skocpol directly cited the earlier area studies literature to support their depictions of the state-building process in Soviet Russia.[27]

Comparative state theory, however, did not keep pace with Soviet area studies. Over the past decade, new empirical investigations have revealed anything but a tightly organized and centrally coordinated party structure for well over a decade after the civil war.[28] In a comprehensive study of local politics in the 1920s, Roger Pethyridge expressed what is now the prevailing view among area specialists concerning the formal organizational structures of the new state in the periphery: "Chaos reigned. Orders arrived from higher bodies in a raw form, [t]hey were not often understood and so ignored."[29]

But if functioning centralized organizations were the exception not the norm in the Soviet periphery at this time, then a major question is left unanswered for area specialists as well as comparative theorists. How did this "infrastructurally" weak state carry out a comprehensive, state-directed campaign of radical economic transformation? This campaign incurred mass economic dislocation and social resistance, yet not only did the regime survive, but the foundations and framework were built for what became communism's command–administrative state. It was exactly in this period, when formal organizations were still weak, that the new state's capacities for territorial administration and revenue extraction were most significantly enhanced. If the earlier scholarly assumptions about formal organization were in error, then what was the missing piece to the puzzle of Soviet state building?

Among area specialists, this question provoked a debate between adherents to the conventional view, who stressed coercion and organizational forces from above, and a new generation of "revisionists," who stressed class forces from below.[30] Revisionist empirical investigations exposed the explanatory limits of the once conventional explanation of the means of Soviet state building. But the revisionsist emphasis on class forces did not form the basis of a new consensus. Commenting on what had become a theoretical impasse in the field, Mark Von Hagen observed that "the boundaries between state and society are not so neatly fixed. This is true everywhere, but it is perhaps especially clear in the Soviet Union." He urged scholars instead to explore "a large middle ground of social groups and political formations" that directly shaped the Soviet Russian state-building process.[31]

In its attempt to explain the outcome of the Soviet state-building process, this study follows Von Hagen's advice. The empirical focus is on the new state's first generation of regional leaders, who are depicted neither as agents of the state per se nor of society. Instead, they are cast as an intrastate elite cohort, who engaged in strategies of cooperation and conflict with one another as well as with other intrastate actors. The Soviet state-building process, it is argued, was ultimately shaped by these intra-elite maneuverings, which at times enhanced and at other times constrained state strength.

III. EXPLAINING STATE-BUILDING OUTCOMES: THE SOVIET RUSSIAN CASE RECONSTRUCTED

This section outlines the analytical framework and defines the concepts employed in the case study. The study offers a new explanation for Soviet Russia's state-building outcome. It is important to stress that the study does not claim that coercive and bureaucratic forces from above or social forces from below were inconsequential to the state-building process. Rather, it suggests that these elements in and of themselves do not satisfactorily explain the outcome. The study asserts that informal power resources – personal networks and elite identities – constitute the missing element that explains how the "infrastructurally" weak Soviet Russian state was able to develop its capacities for territorial administration and revenue extraction in the decade following the civil war. More specifically, it argues that the structure of network ties, as indicated by the way in which informal and formal power resources intersected, was the mechanism by which state capacities were realized in postrevolutionary Soviet Russia.

When applied to Soviet Russia, the concept of the "state" sometimes causes confusion. Soviet Russia was ruled by two parallel political structures: the Communist party bureaucracy and the governmental ministries. In Soviet parlance, the "state" (*gosudarstvo*) sometimes referred specifically to the governmental ministries, distinct from the party bureaucracy. This narrow definition has also been applied by some Western scholars. This study, however, employs the more generally accepted social science definition of the state. The state refers to the entity that makes a monopolistic claim on rule making for the population of a bounded territory. The state maintains this claim through a complex of administrative, coercive, and extractive arrangements. In this study, the state encompasses both the party bureaucracy and the governmental ministries, though the empirical focus is on regional administration in areas where the party bureaucracy played the dominant role. The study also employs conventional definitions for "state capacity" and "state strength." The study adopts Migdal's definition, according to which state capacity refers to the functions that are commonly associated with the modern state, such as territorial administration, coercion, and revenue extraction; and state strength simply refers to the extent to which these functions can be executed at the discretion of central state actors.[32]

The study examines the process of postrevolutionary state building in Soviet Russia through a case study of the center–regional relationship. Sidney Tarrow has distinguished three alternative conceptualizations of "center–regional relations" in Western social science: sociocultural, socio-economic, and political-administrative.[33] This study employs the "political–administrative" concept of center–regional relations. In this regard, the study follows along the path of previous scholars, who have enriched the comparative theoretical literature on state building through empirical investigations of the strategies and struggles of central state actors attempting to develop the capacity of territorial administration.[34]

The case study is organized into three parts, which together provide the evidence to the larger assertions about the dynamics of Soviet state building: (1) identifying the regional leaders and their informal sources of power; (2) uncovering the ways in which state capacity was enhanced as well as constrained by the intersection of informal and formal structures; and (3) explaining how the constraints of power in the center–regional relationship were redefined and, in turn, influenced the state-building outcome.

STRUCTURE AND IDENTITY IN THE POSTREVOLUTIONARY STATE

The study is unique in that it examines the state-building process through a case study of the new state's first cohort of regional leaders. Despite the prominent role these actors played in the construction of the Soviet Russian state, little is known about them in Western scholarship. The study illuminates an alternative perspective on state building by uncovering the informal power resources of this group and demonstrating how they were employed. In this study, the concept of "informal power resources" refers to the personal network ties and the elite identity of the regional leaders. Personal network ties served as a power resource in that they provided an informal social structure by which information was exchanged, resources were obtained, and collaborative actions were planned. Elite identity served as an informal power resource in that these constructed self-images served as a source of status independent of formal position. Perceptions of status among the regional leaders, in turn, influenced their preferences concerning the allocation of power and demarcation of political roles in the new state. By contrast, the concept of "formal power resources" refers to the state's bureaucratic lines of command and the organs of coercion.

Personal networks originated in the prerevolutionary underground, but became better defined and more cohesive in the civil war. The major battle fronts of the civil war gave rise to informal groups of fighter organizers, who used their personal network ties to carry out territorial conquest and political consolidation. When hostilities finally ended, these wartime networks were not dismantled but adapted to the new challenges of postrevolutionary regional administration. During the 1920s, center–regional relations were hampered by poorly developed bureaucratic lines and institutional incoherence. Consequently, the center was reconnected to the regions through personal network ties. In the regions, rival networks competed over access to and control over scarce organizational and material resources distributed by the center. Those networks that were most successful in this competition eventually came to dominate the administrative apparatus in their particular region. In the process, their network rivals in the region were either displaced or subsumed by these dominant networks. The first postrevolutionary cohort of regional leaders were members of such dominant personal networks.

The study argues that personal networks played a significantly larger role in the state-building process than has previously been recognized by Western scholars. Of course, scholars of communist systems have long been aware of the workings of personal networks within established political and institutional settings.[35] The role of personal networks in the actual process of institution building, however, has gone largely unnoticed.[36] In this study, the term "personal network" is similar to Warner and Lunt's definition of a clique: a nonkinship, informal association, within which exists group feeling and intimacy as well as group norms of behavior.[37] David Knoke has distinguished two types of political personal networks: "influence" networks, in which information is exchanged among relatively equal members, and "domination" networks, in which scarce goods are allocated in unequal relationships. Regional leaders in Soviet Russia belonged to networks that exhibited both types of network ties. They included peer type relationships of comradery, shaped by shared experiences in the underground and the civil war. Later, as network ties became enmeshed with formal organizations in the new state, they increasingly developed hierarchical type relationships of clientelism, shaped by the new state's personalized system of reward and advancement.

The second informal power resource of regional leaders was elite identity. The elite identity of the first regional leaders was a constructed image of the services they rendered to the party in its march to power. In particular, regional leaders stressed their service in the prerevolutionary underground and the civil war, portraying themselves as an elite corps of fighter organizers. Participation in these events became a source of elite status in the new Bolshevik regime for the regional leaders as well as other elite members. At this time, the old regime's sources of elite status – noble inheritance, wealth, official rank – were discredited. Since bureaucratic lines of command were not yet clearly established, elite status could not simply be an extension of formal position.

Weber described a status group as a plurality of persons, who within a larger group successfully claim a special social esteem through the appropriation of privileges and power.[39] The participants in these founding events distinguished themselves from other elite subgroups in the new state: the *intelligenty* who fled abroad after 1905, rather than continue to serve in the underground; the post-civil war party recruits, who were either too young or too late to participate in the battles of the civil war; and, the former tsarist civil servants, who despite their technical–administrative expertise were tainted by their previous political affiliations. The regional leaders believed that they had earned elite status on the basis of their past services to the party. This perception was formally reinforced by the celebratory and heroic images of these events projected by early party historians, the official mythmakers of the new state. This status image, in addition, was informally reinforced through personal network ties.

But regional leaders were not content with simply the image of elite status. They sought to consolidate their elite status through the formal trappings of state power. Regional leaders contended that the allocation of power and definition of roles in the new state should reflect their elite status. Most significantly, they attempted to secure a proprietary claim on the formal position of regional governor. It is further noteworthy that this particular source of elite status – service records – was conferred independent of the actions or opinions of central state leaders.

INFORMAL SOURCES OF POWER IN THE POSTREVOLUTIONARY STATE

The study argues that the structure of network ties provided a microlevel mechanism that directly influenced the macrolevel administrative capacities of the new Soviet state. Informal personal network ties intersected with the formal bureaucratic lines of command in the new state. As a result of this intersection of informal and formal structures, state strength was both enhanced and constrained. This statement is not a contradiction, if Mann's conceptual distinction between "infrastructural" and "despotic" state powers is taken into consideration.[40]

The infrastructural powers of the state refer to the capacity to implement policy. State strength in this context is indicated by the extent to which state policies are fulfilled. If a state is routinely capable of administering its territory, extracting resources and employing coercion, then it is considered to be an "infrastructurally" strong state. But all states do not employ the same means to realize their capacities of rule.[41] The varying means by which policies are fulfilled signify the character of a state's infrastructural powers. In a rich comparative study of early modern state building, Thomas Ertman identified two infrastructural types: "bureaucratic" and "patrimonial."[42] A bureaucratic infrastructure resembles a Weberian rational–legal arrangement, distinguished by "a set of standard operating procedures subject to the strictures of a formalized, impersonal administrative law." In this system, the agents of the state are selected on the basis of expertise, and mechanisms exist for their routine removal from office. By contrast, a patrimonial infrastructure refers to a personalistic arrangement, distinguished by the appropriation of state resources by those entrusted with their use. In this system, the agents of the state are selected on the basis of patronage, and mechanisms exist to assure their proprietary claim on office.

In postrevolutionary Soviet Russia, the organizational, financial, and human resources necessary to construct a "bureaucratic" state infrastructure were sorely lacking. In their absence, the new state's capacity for territorial administration was realized through a "patrimonial" infrastructure. More specifically, personal network ties became the means by which the state center was reconnected to the regions. Regionally based personal networks provided an informal social structure along which information was exchanged, resources were allocated and activities were coordinated.

The widespread existence of personal networks in the regions, however, did not in itself ensure the development of a capacity for territorial administration. The study contends that the structure of network ties – the way in which informal network ties intersected with formal bureaucratic lines – influenced state capacity.[43] Two structural features of network ties are especially significant in this regard: the reach of network ties and the location of core network members. First, are network ties limited in reach, mainly concentrated in a host region, or do they extend across the physical or institutional boundaries of the host region? Second, are core network members confined to a host region, or have they relocated to the state center or another strategic position outside the host region? The structure of network ties is outward if they exhibit cross-regional reach and core network members relocate to the center. The structure of network ties is inward if they exhibit a limited reach and core network members remain within a host region. Outwardly structured network ties provide an informal mechanism by which a state's capacity for territorial administration may be enhanced. By contrast, inwardly structured network ties diminsh a state's capacity for territorial administration.

In postrevolutionary Soviet Russia, the inward structure of network ties at first hindered the development of a capacity for territorial administration. In the course of the 1920s, however, this situation was reversed and an outward structure was established: network ties displayed a cross-regional reach and core network members relocated to the center. Network ties provided an informal social structure along which information was exchanged, resources were allocated and activities were coordinated. By such means, the administrative reach of the new Soviet state was extended across its rural and multiethnic periphery. And, the infrastructural power of the Soviet Russian state was strengthened. But the character of infrastructural power in the new state was patrimonial, not bureaucratic, which in turn acted as a constraint on the state's despotic powers.

The despotic powers of the state refer to the rule-making process: Who participates in the process? What is the nature of their participation? Who makes rules for whom? What checks exist on those empowered to make rules? The answers to these questions reveal the character of a state's despotic powers, or its regime type. In Soviet Russia, the character of despotic power of course indicated an authoritarian regime type, but which variant of authoritarianism was not determined until the end of the 1930s. At that time, the places of ruler and elite in the state's rule-making process were finally resolved after nearly a decade of conflict.

In Soviet Russia, the extensive use of personal networks to develop the infrastructural powers of the state had the unintended effect of creating constraints on the state's despotic powers. The despotic powers of the state were formally located in the central offices of the party and governmental bureaucracies; more specifically, in the office of the party's general secretary. But in relations with regional leaders, the center's formal powers were distorted by informal power resources. The central location of core network members provided regional leaders with informal access to the rule-making process. The cross-organizational reach of network ties effectively restrained the enforcement and checking mechanisms of the state center. Moreover, the center was dependent on the regional leaders and their personal network ties to administer the periphery. Finally, the identity of the regional leaders as an elite status group reinforced their belief that they should be included in the rule-making process.

The intersection of informal and formal structures created an underlying constraint on despotic power, defining the parameters of interaction between central and regional actors. In this regard, the constraints of power can be regarded as a kind of institutional arrangement within the new state.[44] But central state leaders were not content with this arrangement. They strove to redefine the constraints of power in such a way that they could more fully realize their claim on the state's despotic powers, which soon provoked intrastate conflict.

INTRASTATE CONFLICT AND THE CONSTRAINTS OF POWER REDEFINED

The constraints of power in the new state were exposed during the 1930s, when central and regional actors clashed over the implementation of agricultural collectivization. If only formal power resources had been operative at the time, central leaders would not have had to engage the regional leaders in this protracted conflict. But in the first half of the decade, the informal power resources of the regional leaders effectively checked the center's formal power resources. At this time, Stalin vented frustration at the constraints on the despotic powers of the state center. Regarding the personal network ties of regional leaders, he complained that "in selecting cadres for their personal devotion, these comrades evidently want to create conditions which make them independent from the center."[45] He also attacked the elite identity of the regional leaders, when he railed against "people who rendered famous services in the past, people who have become grand princes, people who consider that Party decisions and Soviet laws are not written for them, but for idiots."[46]

But the center–regional conflict of the 1930s was more than a dispute about policy implementation. It was a clash over the institutionalization of power and status between ruler and elite in the new state. The resolution of this intrastate conflict had a direct influence on the outcome of Soviet Russia's state-building process. Central and regional actors envisioned alternative regime types for the new state.

In the center, Stalin sought to construct a bureaucratic absolutist state. In this type, the despotic powers of the state would remain personalized and unchecked. The rule-making process would resemble medieval court politics. The ruler's personal discretion would dictate rule-making procedures. Participation in the process and the allocation of power would indicate who was in favor in Stalin's court. But to realize such a system of despotic power, it was deemed necessary to transform the character of infrastructural power from patrimonial to bureaucratic. The system of administration would be depersonalized, rationalized, and checked. For the agents of state administration, power and status would be allocated strictly in accordance with the formal bureaucratic lines of command.

By contrast, regional leaders sought to construct a protocorporatist regime type. In this type, the overriding concern of regional leaders was to eliminate the arbitrariness of despotic power. The rule-making process would be rationalized and checked. Regional leaders wanted to be included in the state's rule-making process, especially in matters directly relating to their areas of responsibility. In this way, despotic power would be formally shared by the elite, or corporate, bodies within the state. By creating procedural checks on despotic power, the regional leaders hoped to consolidate the patrimonial system of infrastructural power. They asserted a proprietary claim on their formal position as regional governors as well as a patronage claim on other strategic state offices within their jurisdiction. They wanted discretionary power over their internal affairs, including the distribution of organizational and financial resources. They wanted the means of state administration to remain personalized in order to ensure the survival of their political machines.

In the early 1930s, the underlying constraints of power defined the parameters of interaction between center and regional leaders. Neither side at this time was able to realize its preferred regime type. In mid-decade, however, both central and regional leaders made attempts to move outside the existing constraints to achieve their ends. In these efforts, regional leaders failed, while central leaders were ultimately successful. By the late 1930s, the constraints of power were redefined so that the formal bureaucratic and coercive powers of the center could be employed routinely in their conflict with the regions. As a consequence, a regime type emerged that more closely resembled Stalin's vision of a bureaucratic absolutist state than the regional elite's protocorporatist state.

IV. ABOUT THE CASE STUDY

The case study focuses on the first generation of regional leaders in the postrevolutionary Soviet state. They are referred to collectively in this study as the *Provincial Komitetchiki*. The Provincial Komitetchiki oversaw the major agricultural and grain-producing regions from the second half of the 1920s until the second half of the 1930s. During this time, they were charged with the task of developing the state capacity for territorial administration across the rural and non-Russian periphery. They led the campaigns to collectivize agriculture, thereby providing the state with the means for direct revenue extraction from the countryside. But their reign as regional leaders proved shortlived. In the 1930s, the Provincial Komitetchiki found themselves embroiled in a conflict with central leaders, which by the end of the decade led to their political and physical demise.

In early Western writings, the Provincial Komitetchiki were most often depicted as Stalin's henchmen or unwitting pawns.[47] Over the past twenty years, this view has been displaced by one that to a greater extent recognizes the autonomy of regional leaders in relations with the general secretary.[48] Indeed, some scholars now maintain that it was the Provincial Komitetchiki who drove Stalin to adopt a radical policy course in the early 1930s.[49] Despite a growing recognition of their importance, the Provincial Komitetchiki have never been the subject of a focused investigation and have remained an obscure group in Western historiography.

In Soviet historiography, the Provincial Komitetchiki were virtually erased from the pages of party history in the second half of Stalin's reign. They were officially rehabilitated during the revision of party history in the early 1960s.[50] For more than twenty years, the Provincial Komitetchiki were cast as state heroes and the victims of Stalin's machinations. Known as the "Leninist Old Guard," their rehabilitation had been motivated by Nikita Khrushchev's effort to confine the blame for the violent excesses of the 1930s on Stalin and a circle of his closest collaborators without impugning the integrity of the command–administrative state. The current wave of historical revision in post-Soviet Russia is again reassessing the role of the Provincial Komitetchiki. These recent depictions present a more critical view of the Provincial Komitetchiki, which at times resembles the earlier Western treatments.[51]

This case study is the first systematic investigation of the Provincial Komitetchiki in Western scholarship. It rejects both the once pervasive Western caricature of the Provincial Komitetchiki as henchmen, the more recent caricature as instigators, and the long-held Soviet caricature as heroes. Instead, the study builds on an observation made by Stephen Cohen over twenty years ago: "As administrators and politicians, they were most often associated with the general secretary. Most of them, however, were not his mindless political creatures, but independent-minded leaders in their own right."[52]

The term "Provincial Komitetchiki" was not used by these actors to refer to themselves. It has been coined here since it incorporates two salient traits about the cohort. First, its members, prior to joining the party, during the underground years, in the civil war and in state service, remained provincial actors. In the late 1920s and early 1930s, they emerged as a subgroup within the new state elite, located at the upper stratum of regional administration. At this time, they served as the intermediary link between the state center and the rural provinces. Second, this cohort emerged from a much larger prerevolutionary group of underground committee workers, or *komitetchiki*. The social and political experiences of the komitetchiki were distinct from the older founding generation of party workers as well as the younger postrevolutionary generation. This distinction became an enduring feature of the identity of the members of this cohort.

Most of the Provincial Komitetchiki remained party committee workers throughout their careers. In their tenure as regional leaders, they occupied the formal position of first secretary of the regional party committees. This study, however, stresses two informal features of the Provincial Komitetchiki: personal network ties and elite identity. In their rise to power and in their subsequent conflict with central state actors, personal network ties and elite identity provided the informal power resources of the Provincial Komitetchiki.

The study attempts to uncover the personal network ties and to specify their modes of influence in order to provide a new perspective on the state-building process in postrevolutionary Soviet Russia. Network analysis helps to identify the microlevel social relations that exist within a macro-level social or institutional complex. According to Barry Wellman and S. D. Berkowitz, "network analysis is neither a method nor a metaphor, but a fundamental intellectual tool for the study of social structures."[53] Network analysis has grown over the past three decades in Western social science. First elaborated by British anthropologists in the 1950s and 1960s, it challenged existing theories of "mass society" by studying the sociological effects of urban in-migration.[54] In the 1970s and 1980s, network analysis gained prominence among Amercian sociologists who used new quantitative techniques to reveal the underlying social ties beneath the "hidden hand" in a variety of economic markets.[55] In political science, network analysis has been employed with success to describe community-level power structures[56] and to explain policy-making processes.[57] These studies, however, tend to focus on network ties in established institutional settings; it is far less common to see network analysis used to study processes of political institution building.

A standard form of network analysis is utilized in the case study to distinguish several of the personal networks that existed within Soviet Russia's postrevolutionary state elite. The study attempts to uncover the network ties of the Provincial Komitetchiki. Network ties are determined by two criteria: (1) evidence of a working relationship (one or more years) in at least one of three milieux (prerevolutionary underground, civil war, postwar regional administration); and/or (2) evidence of friendship or family relationship.[58] Relational data on the Provincial Komitetchiki are drawn from the following source materials: personal correspondences, autobiographical statements, official personnel files, published memoirs, secondary biographies, and histories.[59] The study also employs the concept of core network members to describe those individuals with the greatest number of direct ties among the entire membership.[60] Core network members are crucial figures, playing the role of intermediary between the central and regional leaders.

The study also attempts to reconstruct the elite identity of the Provincial Komitetchiki. In this effort, the study relies to a large extent on autobiographical materials (personal memoirs and personal questionnaires) submitted by the Provincial Komitetchiki to the Society of Old Bolsheviks. These materials were solicited by the Society when considering an applicant for membership. The Society of Old Bolsheviks served as a kind of fraternity for the prerevolutionary veterans of the party. Membership, more than anything else, conferred status. The society's membership, at first, was small and exclusive, encompassing mainly the pre-1905 intellectuals. Most of the Provincial Komitetchiki did not join the Society until the late 1920s and early 1930s. For the Provincial Komitetchiki, membership in the Society of Old Bolsheviks was a form of validation of their services rendered to the party and their perceived elite status.

These autobiographical materials have not been used previously in scholarly analysis of the postrevolutionary state elite. They have only recently been made available to Western scholars through the opening of the long closed Communist party archives.[61] These source materials are not used in the case study to reproduce a "realistic" depiction of the life experiences of the Provincial Komitetchiki. Rather, they represent a constructed image of an ideal type of party worker. For this reason, it is more accurate to describe the self-image projected in these autobiographies as an "elite" identity, instead of a social identity. The autobiographies emphasize politically desirable personal qualities, social backgrounds and service attributes, which were surely tailored to accommodate an officially sanctioned model. But it was precisely the ability of the Provincial Komitetchiki to conform to such a model that supported their claim on elite status in the new state. For this reason, the collective portrait of the Provincial Komitetchiki assembled from these materials provides an illuminating glimpse into the value culture of the postrevolutionary state elite.

The case study that follows is organized into three analytically separate parts. Part I includes two chapters, which focus on the postrevolutionary elite. Chapter 2 sketches a collective biographical portrait of the Provincial

Komitetchiki, emphasizing the informal political and social structures that shaped their rise to power in the new state. Chapter 3 outlines the elite identity of the Provincial Komitetchiki, focusing on their images of self, service and state. Part II includes two chapters, which direct attention to the ways in which informal personal network ties intersected with formal organizational command lines in the new state. Chapter 4 demonstrates how personal network ties were used to extend the administrative reach of the new state to the regions using a case study of the Transcaucasian network. Chapter 5 examines how personal network ties among the regional leaders became a constraint on central state leaders. Part III includes two chapters, which focus on the center–regional conflict that unfolded in the 1930s. Chapter 6 examines the center–regional conflict through a case study of collectivization and the crisis it caused for regional administration. Chapter 7 shows how the constraints of power caused by the intersection of informal and formal strucures were redefined by central leaders, leading to the fall of the Provincial Komitetchiki. A concluding chapter summarizes the findings of the case study and discusses their implications for comparative state-building theory.

PART I

STRUCTURE AND IDENTITY IN THE POSTREVOLUTIONARY STATE ELITE

2

ANATOMY OF A REGIONAL ELITE: THE RISE OF THE PROVINCIAL KOMITETCHIKI

Who built the Soviet Russian state? While Western scholarship has produced a rich literature on leadership politics, organizational development and social processes, surprisingly few studies exist that direct attention to the state elites. Of the many excellent works on postrevolutionary politics, the first generation of state elites appear more often as supporting cast than as the focus of investigation.[1] This study examines a select group of Bolsheviks, who, after the civil war, rose from the lower ranks of local administration to become the new state's first cohort of regional leaders. They are collectively referred to as the Provincial Komitetchiki. In the command chain of the postrevolutionary state, the Provincial Komitetchiki occupied the connecting link between the state center and the territorial political–administrative apparatus.

This chapter introduces the Provincial Komitetchiki. It sketches a collective biography, outlining the sociopolitical circumstances that influenced their formation and ascent to power. While the study marks the first focused investigation of the postrevolutionary regional leadership, it is by no means the first attempt to analyze the postrevolutionary state by investigating the center–regional relationship. Accordingly, the chapter begins with a brief survey and critique of the existing literature on center–regional relations and regional leaders. A second section discusses the rise of personal networks in postrevolutionary regional administration. This section is followed by an overview of intraparty cleavages and the power struggles of the 1920s. The final section draws a biographical sketch of the individuals who composed the Provincial Komitetchiki. In so doing, a preliminary answer is offered for the question: Who built the Soviet Russian state?

I. CENTER–REGIONAL RELATIONS AND REGIONAL LEADERS IN THE SOVIET RUSSIAN STATE

For more than six decades, the subject of center–regional relations attracted the attention of the foremost analysts of Soviet Russia. Their efforts sustained a vigorous debate over the sources and dynamics of power in the Soviet state. This literature produced four distinct approaches: social forces, unilateral organizational, inefficient organizational, and patron–client.

The center–regional relationship was first addressed by Leon Trotsky in the 1930s, as part of a larger effort to explain within a Marxist framework his own political defeat, the rise of Stalin, and the subsequent evolution of Soviet socialism. In Trotsky's well-known thesis, he argued that Stalin was carried to the heights of power on the crest of a Thermidorian wave of bureaucratization that overtook the Bolshevik party in the years following the civil war.[2] According to this "apparat as social force" approach, the flow of power between center and regions moved in an upward direction so that state policies reflected the interests of the bureaucratic elite. Stalin's autonomy was minimized in relation to the elite and his leadership victory trivialized as mere historical anecdote.[3] Trotsky depicted the regional leadership as the very embodiment of the bureaucratic degeneration of the once revolutionary Bolshevik party into a stratum of petit-bourgeois clerks.[4]

Next, during the 1950s and 1960s, Western scholars developed the all-encompassing concept of totalitarianism as an interpretative framework for understanding the Soviet experience. In a reversal of Trotsky's thesis, the totalitarian model identified a downward moving dynamic in center–regional relations, as in the command chain of a formal organization. At the top of the structure sat General Secretary Iosif Stalin, who by the mid-1920s was said to be in firm control of the organizational levers. Regional leaders lacked autonomy in this approach. They were dismissed as compliant servitors, faithfully executing the orders of their superiors. For nearly two decades, the totalitarian-inspired "unilateral organizational" approach dominated area studies.[5]

Despite their opposing premises, the "social forces" and the "unilateral organizational" approaches were vulnerable to similar criticisms. First, both approaches identified a unidirectional flow of power – a social force moving from bottom to top or a bureaucratic force moving from top to bottom. They rejected the notion of an interactive dynamic between central and regional leaders. Trotsky argued that "Stalinism was above all else the automatic work of the impersonal apparatus on the decline of the revolution."[6] Robert Daniels, meanwhile, stated that the relationship between the center and the regional leadership was not determined by "the magic of personal politics," but instead was based on "organization and its manipulation" and thus "depersonalized."[7] Second, these approaches downplayed the role of regional leaders, portraying them as one dimensional characters. Trotsky described the provincial leaders as pusillanimous careerists.[8] The "unilateral organizational" approach was no less derisive, employing such labels as "Stalin's faithful lieutenants" and "small men raised up by Stalin."[9] Third, each approach underestimated the propensity for competing centers of power within the institutional structures of the state. While Trotsky described a pervasive social force infusing the state with a "petit bourgeois" persona, totalitarian adherents emphasized the monolithic character of the party–state.

Empirical investigations, however, rendered a more complex view of the relationship between center and regions. These studies exposed the conceptual weaknesses of the "social forces" and the "unilateral organizational" approaches. As a result, a less rigid variant of an organizational approach evolved in the Western literature. Accordingly, the relationship between center and regions in principle remained embedded in a command–organizational structure, however, in practice the structure frequently broke down, revealing a less than omnipotent center. The earliest and still outstanding example of this "inefficient organizational" approach was Merle Fainsod's case study of the Smolensk region. Fainsod worked within the framework of the totalitarian model, but he treated it more as an ideal type than an actual state of affairs. He described the center–regional command chain as an "undependable apparatus," providing limited space for autonomous action from regional leaders.[10]

Several influential contributions to the field built upon the "inefficient organizational" approach. Although covering a later period, Jerry Hough's study of provincial party leaders and industrial management offered a richly detailed reconceptualization of the flow of power between center and regions, demonstrating how bureaucratic shortcomings provided an even wider area of autonomy for regional leaders than Fainsod had proposed.[11] J. Arch Getty advanced the discussion still further through a reexamination of the bureaucratic origins of the great purges of the 1930s. Although Getty rejected the premises of totalitarianism, his depiction of a "disordered organization," featuring protective circles, personal fiefdoms and petty indulgences, was consistent with the "inefficient organizational" approach.[12] Subsequent empirical studies confirmed that bureaucratic malfunctioning, informal cooperation and intrastate conflict represented the norm, not the exception, in center–regional relations.[13] By the 1980s, the "inefficient organizational" approach had become the field's dominant model of center–regional relations.

Still another approach was developed in the Western literature, which sought to explain center–regional relations by focusing on personalistic, rather than bureaucratic structures. This patron–client approach depicted mutual flows of power between center and regions. Regional leaders were portrayed as autonomous politicians, engaged in a process of acquiring and trading resources beyond the center's control. The patron–client approach was first advanced by T. H. Rigby in a seminal article explaining the rise of Stalin and the subsequent evolution of leadership politics.[14] Rigby argued that in the early 1920s regional administration was dominated by informal cliques held together by personal ties that eventually became centered around organizationally powerful party secretaries acting as patrons. When Stalin moved into the secretarial apparatus he was able to exploit these regionally based cliques for his own advantage by assuming the role of supra-patron. Building on Rigby's work, Graeme Gill attempted to explain not just the rise of Stalin but the very essence of the Stalinist state in terms of an ongoing tension between personalistic and institutional structures.[15] He developed the concept of "patrimonial institutionalism" to highlight the way in which patronage networks, not bureaucracy, connected the center to the regions in the period following the civil war. Subsequent efforts by the center to construct a reliable formal organizational chain, he argued, were impeded by the pervasiveness of informal patron–client ties across regional officialdom.

Since the 1980s, the patron–client approach has gradually gained greater acceptance as an alternative to the "inefficient organizational" approach. The patron–client and inefficient organizational approaches, of course, are not mutually exclusive. Indeed, the works of Hough and Gill could easily be categorized as hybrid models, combining aspects of both approaches. Each approach recognized the existence of mutual flows of power, intrastate conflict and the autonomy of regional leaders. They differed, however, on the underlying source of these phenomena. The "inefficient organizational" approach attributed them to the limitations of formal organizational structures. By contrast, the patron–client approach attributed them to the persistence of informal social structures. I put the distinction in the form of a question: Was the basis of the autonomy of regional leaders a by-product of the center's bureaucratic shortcomings, or was it intrinsic to the web of personalistic relations of the regional leaders?

The patron–client approach serves as an analytical point of departure for recent attempts to understand better the way in which informal social structures intersected with and reshaped formal organizational structures in communist states.[16] As part of that effort, this study builds on the research findings of Rigby and Gill to contribute an alternative explanation of postrevolutionary state building.

Rigby's analysis of patronage networks to explain Stalin's leadership victory in the 1920s illuminated the informal side of power in the new state and the interactive dynamic in center–regional relations. But his analysis was less successful in explaining why the chief patron in the center eventually destroyed his clients in the provinces in the 1930s. When Rigby returned to the subject in a later article he argued that those closest to Stalin in fact were much less likely to fall victim to the purges.[17] But in his rejoinder, Rigby equivocated over who was a client. The regional leaders, who were explicitly identified as clients in the first article, were no longer considered as such in the response. Gill's work convincingly demonstrated how patron–client networks substituted for formal organization in regional administration in the 1920s. But his conclusion that personal networks ultimately undermined the state-building process is based on a narrow view of institution building. Informal and formal structures are described as mutually exclusive phenomena. Moreover, Gill's analysis of the center–regional conflict wrings out the politics and the people from the story. It focuses on the "internal coherence" of political institutions, but overlooks the intense factional battles over access to and control of organizational resources.[18]

In an attempt to extend the explanatory reach of the patron–client literature, this study advances three innovations: (1) elite identity as a source of autonomy of regional leaders, (2) alternative types of personal networks, and (3) personal networks as a means of facilitating state capacity. First, the study, like Rigby and Gill, argues that personal network ties provided regional leaders with an informal power resource independent of the center. The study further posits that regional leaders shared an elite identity that was based on a romanticized image of their participation in the major battles that brought the Bolsheviks to power (see Chapter 3). This identity was constructed independent of central state leaders and was the basis of their view of themselves as a distinct status group. The regional leaders' perceptions of their formal role were influenced by this elite identity. The center–regional conflict in the 1930s was not just an attempt to uproot patron–client ties, but marked a power struggle over the institutionalization of status and roles in the new state.

Second, Rigby and Gill focused on patronage networks, but these were not the only type of network ties that existed among the regional leaders. David Knoke has identified two types of personal networks: "dominance" networks, defined as hierarchical, mutually dependent relations, and "influence" networks, defined as peerlike relations without mutual obligations.[19] Dominance networks have always existed within the Soviet Russian state, but influence networks have not, or at least not to the extent that they did in the 1930s (see Chapter 5). The regional leaders did not just belong to patron–client-like dominance networks, but also to influence networks, which cut across the formal institutional lines of the state. In the 1930s, central state leaders were more interested in removing particular influence networks from regional administration, than patron–client networks in general.

Third, Gill's argument that personal networks obstructed the process of institution building is rooted in a view that these phenomena were mutually exclusive.[20] Organizational theorists, however, have long noted that informal groups do not necessarily frustrate the capabilities of formal organizations, but in some cases facilitate their realization.[21] Personal networks in the regions at times did work against the interests of the state center, but at other times they helped to extend its capacity to rule (see Chapter 4).

II. PERSONAL NETWORKS IN THE POSTREVOLUTIONARY STATE

In the years immediately following the civil war, a small group of party workers, the Provincial Komitetchiki, rose from obscurity to become the new state's first cohort of regional leaders. The Provincial Komitetchiki were the product of the social and political milieux of regionally based intraparty personal networks. Intraparty personal networks were initially formed in the prerevolutionary underground and later sustained in the postrevolutionary state through a combination of circumstantial, psychological, and instrumental factors.[22]

Personal networks originated as a survival strategy of underground workers during the prerevolutionary period, when the Bolshevik party was an illegal political organization. Party activities were conducted covertly through underground committees, which operated printing presses, distributed propaganda, agitated factory workers, and recruited members.[23] Underground committee workers, or komitetchiki, led a shadowy existence. Underground committees were routinely infiltrated by police informants, who gathered information on party members, their social circles, and their activities. Tsarist police maintained comprehensive files on underground party workers. Valerian Kuibyshev's police file from one year in

Tomsk was over three hundred pages thick. It included lists of his not-so-secret residences and pseudonyms, detailed accounts of his daily activities, and profile sketches of his brother and circle of friends.[24]

The local police sought to disrupt the party's underground operations through the arrest and banishment of leading committee workers. Multiple arrests and internal exile were routine ordeals for the underground workers.[25] In Kuibyshev's case, the Tomsk police, having gathered sufficient evidence, proceeded to arrest the Kuibyshev brothers along with another thirty-four suspected underground workers. Not all party members were willing to commit to the underground lifestyle. The constant threat of discovery and punishment led many party members instead into foreign exile or legal political activity. For those members who chose an underground existence, survival dictated the observance of a strict behavioral code. In his memoirs, Anastas Mikoian, a veteran of the Baku underground, wrote that "underground conditions" required "secrecy, reliability, and the dedication of the people."[26] Underground committees functioned as a kind of secret society, complete with rites of passage and noms de guerre, in order to keep their activities clandestine. Mikoian, for example, related the tale of fellow undergrounder Kamo, who masquerading in the uniform of a tsarist officer entered the local police headquarters to ascertain the identities of the agents provocateurs in the ranks of the local Bolshevik committee.[27]

To evade police infiltration, information exchange and strategy formation were carried out through personal interaction. New party recruits were accepted into committee work only upon the personal recommendation of an established member acting as intermediary. The reputation of the intermediary as a trusted source was a principal concern. In this system of recruitment, trust was a scarce but highly valued personal attribute. Trust, in this case, refers to a system in which an intermediary seeks to assure one actor of the performance reliability of another actor.[28] This kind of trust system has been found by scholars to be an essential component of the internal workings of illegal underground groups, both political and economic.[29] Thus, the Bolshevik underground fostered a conducive environment for personal network ties that revolved around the most trusted and reputable intermediaries. But the obverse side of trust is distrust. Underground conditions also fostered suspicion and fear among committee workers. Distrust would eventually leave an indelible impression on these underground workers. In a later period, distrust contributed to an inability to establish sustained cooperation between the members of different personal networks, even when the benefits were clearly mutual.

From 1918 to 1921, the Bolsheviks faced a series of military challenges across the periphery from tsarist generals, cossack hetmen, and foreign interventionists.[30] Better equipped and better trained armies routed fledgling Soviet governments in the Urals, along the Volga, across Siberia, and in the North Caucasus. At the height of the civil war, restorationist White armies occupied nearly the entire Russian periphery, at one point taking Orel, less than two hundred miles south of Moscow. In the non-Russian regions, the civil war gave rise to both national separatists and national socialists, each laying claim to political authority and driving the Bolsheviks back into the underground. In these circumstances, the prerevolutionary underground ties that existed among Bolsheviks in the periphery provided a core around which more coherent and extensive personal networks were formed along the major battle fronts of the civil war.

The civil war campaigns required the successful fulfillment of a series of military and organizational tasks if the Bolshevik center was to reclaim the periphery. The regime first had to assemble and outfit a regional fighting force and find a competent and loyal military commander. Following several dramatic episodes of commanders switching allegiances, the regime established the position of political commissar, a centrally appointed party official with extraordinary powers to supervise the military command and to ensure an army's fighting capabilities. Kuibyshev's appointment as political commissar to the First Army, fighting in the Middle Volga region, empowered him "to attend with a consulting vote all the discussions of the officer staff" and placed under his direction "all soviet political establishments" in the region.[31]

In the wake of the Red Army's advance, political commissars were responsible for the political incorporation of newly reclaimed territories. Political commissars carried out these tasks through revolutionary–military committees (RMC). The RMCs were the organs that, in effect, imposed martial law in the reoccupied territories. Once the military situation along the Middle Volga front was stabilized, for example, the RMC established under Kuibyshev was issued the following ten tasks: (1) to serve as the unifying center for all underground revolutionary cells in the region, (2) to assume responsibility for governing in the province of Samara, (3) to assume responsibility for the deployment of all party forces in the region, (4) to initiate the creation of a Samaran organization of the Communist party and to try to establish a permanent party collective in Kazan, (5) to enlist new members into the party, (6) to conduct relations with other organizations in the region that are friendly to the Bolsheviks, (7) to organize the rear of the Red Army forces in the region, (8) to act temporarily as a military force when dire situations arise, (9) to organize material assistance for the population of Samara, and (10) to adopt measures in connection with removing the agents of international capitalism from the region.[32]

Political commissariats and RMCs at this time did not exist so much as organizational structures, but as sets of personal relationships. Their political and military tasks were not carried out through a bureaucratic hierarchy, but instead were assigned to trustworthy and reliable personal associates. In this way, the informal social structure of personal network ties provided the principal means of command, coordination and communication in these regional military–political campaigns. The civil war networks overlapped between party cadres and military commanders. Small groups of party organizers and military officers came to depend on one another during the incremental and dangerous process of territorial conquest and consolidation.

The civil war served to solidify personal network ties in two ways. First, the war's major battles, as well as minor skirmishes, fostered a self-image among the participants as war heroes. This heroic service image became a defining component of the identity of the members of the civil war networks. Second, the RMCs along the different civil war battle fronts gave rise to informal groupings of fighter organizers. Not all these groupings disbanded after the war. In particular, some moved into regional administration during the transition to postrevolutionary state building. In this transition, they offered the new state a coherent informal social structure in places where formal political structures were yet to be established.

In the early postrevolutionary period, patterns of patronage and resource allocation in the regions became another factor perpetuating the existence of personal networks.[33] The central state lacked the organizational capabilities to place cadres or to administer funds in the periphery; instead, the center relied on regional party leaders, usually former political commissars and their staffs. While the center formally controlled the powers of appointment, regional leaders exercised enormous influence over cadre selection in their own territories, often recommending particular recruits and sometimes reversing central appointments. In addition, regional leaders and their staffs assumed discretionary power over the distribution of the limited financial resources and material rewards at the local level.

In these circumstances, the patterns of resource allocation in the regions tended to overlap with personal network ties. Regional administration came to be dominated by the same individuals who had served as political commissars during the civil war. Civil war political commissars were recruited to become peacetime territorial administrators. They were charged with the task of creating a political administrative framework to reconnect the regions to the center. As in the civil war, they relied on personal network ties to carry out their assignments. As a consequence of the infrastructural limitations of the center, new regional leaders were entrusted with enormous formal powers to affect life chances in the regions. Employment opportunities, financial assistance and social goods were disbursed along personal network lines.

Personalizing the system of promotion and reward further solidified the personal ties of the members of the regional networks. In the postrevolutionary state, informal networks intersected with formal organizations precisely at those points where resources and rewards were distributed. From this time, clientelistic relations became a fundamental feature of regional administration in the Soviet Russian state.[34]

Center–regional relations in the new state were not conducted along a formal vertical structure connecting two well-defined organizational points. Relations between center and regions were structured along personalistic lines, while organizational roles remained poorly defined and fluid. In the regions, various personal networks competed for access to and control over the new state's organizational distribution points of resources and rewards. This situation was abetted by the efforts of various central leaders to expand their own patronage machines into the regions. For the members of regional personal networks, prospects for advancement became linked to the careers of core network members. Core members who made it to the center could play the role of patron much more effectively. Regionally placed clients benefitted from a patron's proximity to the wellsprings of organizational resources. For this reason, the powers and resources allocated to particular regional organizational positions fluctuated with the political fortunes of centrally located patrons.

In the early postrevolutionary period, numerous personal networks were scattered throughout the regions. Eventually most of these networks were either subsumed or displaced by fewer larger networks. The successful networks in the competition for power and influence in the regions tended to be those that had formed along the major battle fronts in the civil war. Most of the members of the Provincial Komitetchiki belonged to these former civil war networks of fighter organizers. The Provincial Komitetchiki sometimes used the term *druzhina* to describe their circle of wartime companions.[35] Whether they were aware of it or not, the choice of this particular term is noteworthy for its similarity to the *druzhina* of Russia's distant past. Dominic Lieven described the *druzhina* of Muscovite Russia as "the royal military household of comrades-in-arms from which the leading lieutenants of the warrior grand prince came."[36] The Bolshevik *druzhina* of the postrevolutionary period recalled the old Muscovite *dru-*

zhina in at least three areas. First, the Bolshevik *druzhina* were held together by personalistic ties. Powerful patrons existed at the core of these personal networks. Second, the Bolshevik *druzhina* played dual military and political roles. In the civil war, these patrons distinguished themselves in battle against the restorationist forces of the old regime. In peacetime, they aspired to the position of regional lord by monopolizing the distribution of political and economic rewards in the region. Third, the Bolshevik *druzhina* competed for favor and influence in Moscow. The system of allocating power in the new state, during the 1920s and 1930s, very much resembled court politics. Access to organizational resources was conferred on those who were, in effect, in favor at Stalin's court. Regional actors engaged in a constant game of alliance building and alliance shifting with centrally located patrons.

In postrevolutionary regional administration, the Provincial Komitetchiki eventually emerged as the chief beneficiaries of this system of personalized distribution of organizational resources. By such means, they were able to build their own powerful political machines in the regions in the late 1920s and early 1930s. At this point, however, the Provincial Komitetchiki sought to impose a measure of routinization on the relationship between center and regions as a way to consolidate their own political machines. They were ultimately unsuccessful in this attempt and paid with their lives. The system of court politics and personalized center–regional relations, however, continued throughout Stalin's reign.

III. INTRAPARTY CLEAVAGES AND THE POLITICS OF SUCCESSION: THE RISE OF THE PROVINCIAL KOMITETCHIKI

This section explores the social and political conditions, which shaped the Provincial Komitetchiki as a distinct elite cohort within the Soviet Russian state. More specifically, the formation and rise of the Provincial Komitetchiki were influenced by prerevolutionary intraparty cleavage lines and opportunities for advancement created by the politics of leadership succession.

The Provincial Komitetchiki as a group are defined by institutional position, not strictly by social or career patterns. They do not all neatly conform to one particular demographic profile. Yet the individual biographies of the members of this group indicate some general consistencies about their collective past. Indeed, most of the members of the Provincial

Komitetchiki emerged from one of two intraparty cohorts, which originated in the prerevolutionary period. These two cohorts were distinguished by social background and party service.

In a social analysis of the biographies of nearly 250 party activists, W. E. Mosse discovered two successive waves of recruits in the prerevolutionary period, forming two intraparty groups.[37] The first group, which Mosse labeled "Old Bolsheviks," was born between 1868 and 1874; the second group, labeled "New Bolsheviks," was born between 1883 and 1891. Mosse identified three markers that formed a social boundary between the two groups: (1) ethnicity – 70 percent of the Old Bolsheviks were non-Slavic, as compared with 45 percent of the New Bolsheviks; (2) class background – 94 percent of the Old Bolsheviks were middle or upper-middle class, as compared with 58 percent of the New Bolsheviks, while 42 percent of the New Bolsheviks were lower-middle and lower class; (3) education – 70 percent of the Old Bolsheviks received some form of higher education, while 52 percent of the New Bolsheviks had not advanced beyond the secondary level, with over half of this group never advancing beyond the primary level. Mosse concluded that "the differences are so striking that it appears legitimate to speak – with due caution – of separate revolutionary generations."[38]

Party service was also a distinguishing marker among prerevolutionary members. Different service roles reinforced this social cleavage line among prerevolutionary party members. Sheila FitzPatrick has identified two groups based on different service roles: the *intelligenty* and the komitetchiki.[39] The *intelligenty*, or intellectuals, were the first to join the party in the late 1890s. The *intelligenty* established the first underground committees, produced and distributed radical literature, and agitated against the old regime. But in the political reaction following 1905, many of the *intelligenty* migrated abroad, where they remained for extended periods in various European cities. The *intelligenty* abandoned committee work en masse after the failure of the 1905 revolution, leading to a social transformation of the personnel left in the Bolshevik underground. Aleksandr Shliapnikov, a veteran of the prerevolutionary underground, spoke of the "exodus of the intellectuals in 1906 and 1907" in his memoirs.[40] Leopold Haimson provided insight into the withdrawal of the *intelligenty* from active participation in a biographical portrait of Iurii Denike, who prior to 1905 served in the Bolshevik underground in Lugansk. "He felt the need to refurbish his intellectual baggage," Haimson observed, "now that his fundamental assumptions about Russian society had been repudiated by events. He also felt very deeply the sense of revulsion that affected so many of his contemporaries against their earlier life in the underground."[41]

The komitetchiki, or committee men, tended to join at the time of or after the 1905 revolution. The komitetchiki spent little or no time abroad. They became the party's full-time workers in the underground committees between 1905 and 1917. They maintained contacts with the leadership abroad, organized the underground committees, distributed illegal literature, and recruited members. Their activities were conducted under the near constant threat of exposure, arrest, and exile. Their personal experiences during these years were far removed from those of the émigré *intelligenty*. From the komitetchiki perspective, they endured the practical problems of survival in the tsarist police state, while the émigré *intelligenty* engaged in esoteric theoretical debates and counterproductive feuding with fellow social-democrats. Nadezhda Krupskaia, Old Bolshevik and Lenin's wife, observed that "these committee members always rather despised the 'people abroad,' who they considered, just grew fat and organized intrigues."[42]

The party service cleavage line became even more defined by the different roles played by the *intelligenty* and the komitetchiki in the events following the February Revolution. The sudden collapse of the tsarist autocracy stirred the *intelligenty* to return to Russia. During the revolution and civil war, the *intelligenty* tended to gravitate to top leadership positions in the center. By contrast, the komitetchiki tended to participate in the military and political contests that eventually brought Soviet power to the periphery. Collectively, these experiences in the party's march to power fostered a particular and exclusive identity among the komitetchiki, distinguishing them from the *intelligenty* and from later postrevolutionary party cohorts.

In summary, social and service distinctions among the prerevolutionary party membership created intraparty cleavage lines. While individual exceptions abound among the several thousand party workers at this time, a general pattern is discernable of overlapping social and service backgrounds. The *intelligenty* tended to resemble Mosse's Old Bolshevik cohort, while the komitetchiki tended to resemble the New Bolshevik cohort. As a generalization, the social backgrounds of the Provincial Komitetchiki corresponded to the category of New Bolsheviks. Moreover, their service backgrounds, even more so, fit with the category of komitetchiki.

These reinforcing intraparty cleavage lines were politicized during the leadership succession struggle of the 1920s. Succession politics provided the opportunity for the rise to power of the Provincial Komitetchiki. This study does not wish to rehash or reinterpret Stalin's leadership victory, but simply to emphasize the way in which the *intelligenty*–komitetchiki split was a contributing factor to this outcome. At the time of Lenin's death, in

January 1924, Iosif Stalin was considered the least serious challenger in the field of leadership candidates. Yet, in just five years, Stalin emerged victorious from this succession struggle. His triumph would not have been possible without the active support of the komitetchiki.

Stalin alone among the succession contenders identified himself with the komitetchiki. He successfully played on this cleavage line by mobilizing the resentment and hostility that the komitetchiki felt toward the *intelligenty*. The komitetchiki were especially sensitive to a perceived arrogance and condescension of the *intelligenty*. The *intelligenty* leadership disdained the organizational work of the komitetchiki and demeaned their intellectual capabilities. Trotsky's disparaging description of Stalin's pre-revolutionary service aptly captured this attitude: "He remained a 'local worker,' a Caucasian, and a congenital provincial."[43] Molotov later recalled that Stalin's supporters in the intraparty feuds of the 1920s were derisively called "the wild division" by supporters of the United Opposition (Leon Trotsky, Grigorii Zinoviev, and Lev Kamenev).[44]

An illustration of the way in which these mutual antagonisms were expressed in the leadership struggle is provided by the following exchange, which occurred in August 1927 during one of the final stands of the United Opposition. Kamenev was in the midst of a critique of Stalin's central party secretariat, when he was interrupted by Filipp Goloshchekin, a party secretary in Kazakhstan, and Mikhail Shkiriatov, a Stalin appointee to the Central Control Commission.

Goloshchekin: Who wrote this for you? What are you reading?

Kamenev: You are simply an idiot!

Shkiriatov: Is it impossible for us to do without such expressions?
According to you [Kamenev] we are all idiots, only you are intelligent.

Goloshchekin: It is impossible when we only hear from stupid men
[Kamenev].[45]

This tragicomical exchange of petty insults at a high-level party meeting sheds light on the way in which political discourse was infused by the mutual acrimony underlying the *intelligenty*–komitetchiki split. Stalin indeed was rude and crude, as Lenin had earlier noted, and for the komitetchiki that was precisely what made him the preferred choice of party leader over the haughty *intelligenty* contenders.

As part of Stalin's campaign to succeed Lenin, he entered into alliances with the core members of personal networks, which were composed largely of komitetchik members. Stalin used his formal organizational powers to promote the komitetchik members of these networks into positions of power. In the years immediately following the revolution, positions of power in the new state were dominated by the *intelligenty*. By decade's end, however, the political fortunes of the komitetchiki were reversed and they began to occupy positions of power in the new state. In regional administration, no intraparty group was dominant during the first years of the Bolshevik regime. The komitetchiki especially were poorly represented in the leading ranks of regional administration. In 1922, this situation began to change when the new team of Stalin, Molotov, Kuibyshev, and Kaganovich was assembled in Moscow to reorganize regional administrative affairs (see Chapter 4). Regional administration from this time was increasingly dominated by the komitetchiki.

Opportunities for advancement were significantly enhanced by one of the first formal organizational changes undertaken by the new team. In August 1922, the party statutes were revised so that only cadres who had been party members prior to the October revolution were eligible for assignment to regional leadership posts.[46] The earlier party statutes had made no such provision; as a result, nonparty personnel were sometimes entrusted with power in the regions. An extensive turnover of provincial party leaders followed this revision. Less than a year later, in March 1923, Kaganovich's personnel office in the central secretariat already had replaced thirty-seven provincial secretaries and transferred forty-two more.[47] The percentage of komitetchiki in the regional leadership climbed steadily throughout the decade. In 1922, 52 percent of regional party secretaries were members of the komitetchiki from the prerevolutionary underground.[48] Between April 1923 and May 1924, the number of komitetchiki among the regional party secretaries increased from 62.5 percent to 71 percent.[49] And, in December 1927, Central Committee Secretary Stanislav Kosior reported that the komitetchiki composed 78 percent of regional party secretaries.[50]

The Provincial Komitetchiki rose to the rank of regional leader as beneficiaries of the opportunities created by succession politics. The relationship between Stalin and the Provincial Komitetchiki during the succession struggle should be viewed as a mutual exchange of power resources between autonomous actors. Stalin had access to enormous bureaucratic resources, while the Provincial Komitetchiki had access to widespread personalistic resources. Stalin entered into alliances with core members of key regional personal networks. As these core network members gained access to organizational resources, they distributed them along network lines. They gained appointment to regional leadership positions, promotion into collective elite bodies, enhanced territorial adminstrative jurisdictions, and control over patronage. These organizational resources enabled the Provincial Komitetchiki to build their own political machines in the regions.

In exchange, the members of the personal networks employed their personalistic resources to support Stalin's bid to become Lenin's successor. In particular, Valerian Kuibyshev, who had network ties with the Middle Volga region and Central Asia, was promoted into the central leadership in 1922, and Grigorii "Sergo" Ordzhonikidze, who had network ties throughout the North Caucasus and the Transcaucasus, was promoted into the central leadership in 1926. Members of their regional networks were, in turn, promoted into the party central committee, where they voted as a pro-Stalin bloc. By this tactic, Stalin's leadership rivals were systematically removed from central positions of power during the 1920s. The central control commission, which during this period was headed by first Kuibyshev and then Ordzhonikidze, uprooted rival regional political machines and installed fellow network members in their place. In addition, personal network ties in the regions were used to implement central policy resolutions espoused by Stalin.[51]

Stalin's strategy to secure victory in the leadership contest by expanding his political machine into the regions served as the model for subsequent successions in Soviet Russia. Robert Daniels conceptualized this mutually benefical relationship between central contenders and regional leaders as "the circular flow of power."[52] But it is important to stress that the regional leaders in this process were not simply the creation of a central leader. They were, instead, autonomous actors with access to personalistic resources, which central contenders sought to mobilize against their leadership rivals. Regional actors, in turn, obtained control over organizational resources. But while regional leaders identified their institutional interests with Stalin's victory, these interests were not defined by Stalin. As events later demonstrated, Stalin and the Provincial Komitetchiki would clash over the institutional division of power between center and regions. This pattern became a recurring scenario in the Soviet Russian state. Center-regional alliance building during succession periods followed by center-regional conflict was characteristic of the reigns of subsequent leaders Nikita Khrushchev and Mikhail Gorbachev.

IV. THE PROVINCIAL KOMITETCHIKI: A BIOGRAPHICAL SKETCH

This section draws a biographical sketch of the Provincial Komitetchiki. The data for this collective portrait is derived principally from the autobiographical statements and responses to a personal questionnaire that were requested from the Provincial Komitetchiki as part of their membership application to the Society of Old Bolsheviks. This information is supplemented by published memoirs and biographies.[53]

The Provincial Komitetchiki were those members of the komitetchik cohort, who in the late 1920s and early 1930s served as first party secretaries in the rural and major grain-growing regions. At this time, agriculture was administered mainly through the regional party bureaucracy, unlike industry, which was administered through central governmental bureaucracies. The special commissions, created by the center to work out agricultural procurement and collectivization policies, included in their composition these same regional leaders. More than any other, the Provincial Komitetchiki were made responsible for the political and economic integration of the rural and non-Russian regions into the new state. The Provincial Komitetchiki were appointed party leaders of these regions in the late 1920s or early 1930s and remained in their posts until the late 1930s (see Table 2.1).

Geographically, this large agricultural zone forms a crescent that begins in Belorussia and Smolensk, west of the central industrial zone and south of Leningrad, and stretches south-eastward across Ukraine and southern Russia to the Caucasus, then sweeps north again along the Volga river and reaches eastward into western Siberia, southern Urals, and northern Kazakhstan. The administrative–territorial structure of these regions was created in a series of reforms during the 1920s. In the first part of the decade, ethnically defined national republics were created for Ukraine and Belorussia. During the second part of the decade, the numerous Russian *gubernii*, or provinces, across this area were consolidated into several sprawling administrative–territorial units.[54] These new mega-regions included: Western region (Smolensk, Briansk, Kaluga), Central Black Earth region (Orel, Kursk, Tambov, Voronezh, Lipetsk), North Caucasus territory (Stavropol, Kuban, Terek, Dagestan), Lower Volga territory (Saratov, Tsaritsyn, Astrakhan, Kalmykia), Middle Volga region (Samara, Simbirsk, Penza, Tataria, Chuvash, Mari), Urals (Perm, Ekaterinburg, Ufa, Cheliabinsk, Kurgan, Orenburg), and Siberia (Tiumen, Omsk, Novosibirsk). These regions were still overwhelmingly peasant in population.[55] In the 1930s, they became the principal suppliers of grain, vegetables, and cash crops for the rapidly growing urban and industrial regions in the north.

The Provincial Komitetchiki generally shared similar social characteristics (see Table 2.2). They were born between the mid-1880s and mid-1890s. Thus, they arrived as the new state's regional political elite at a relatively young age; most were still in their thirties. The Provincial Komitetchiki generally indicated that they came from lower middle-class or lower-class social origins. They were most often from the poorer north-

Table 2.1. The Provincial Komitetchiki: Served As First Party Secretary, Unless Otherwise Noted

Name	Region	Years
Andreev, Andrei A.	North Caucasus	1927-30
Eikhe, Robert I.	Western Siberia	1929-37
Gamarnik, Ian B.	Belorussia	1928-30
Gikalo, Nikolai I.	Belorussia	1933-37
Goloshchekin, Fillipp I.	Kazakhstan	1925-33
Ivanov, Vladimir B.	Northern	1931-37
	North Caucasus (Second Secretary)	1928-31
Kabakov, Ivan I.	Urals	1929-37
Khataevich, Mendel M.	Dnepropetrovsk	1933-37
	Middle Volga	1928-33
Kosior, Stanislav I.	Ukraine	1928-38
Krinitskii, Aleksandr I.	Lower Volga	1934-37
Kubiak, Nikolai A.	Ivanovo	1931-34
	Russian Commissar of Agriculture	1928-31
Mirzoian, Levon I.	Kazakstan	1933-37
Postyshev, Pavel P.	Ukraine (Second Secretary)	1933-37
Rumiantsev, Ivan P.	Western	1929-37
Sheboldaev, Boris P.	North Caucasus	1930-36
	Lower Volga	1928-30
Vareikis, Iosif M.	Central Black Earth	1928-37

ern rural areas, which were newly experiencing the social dislocations of early industrialization. It was not uncommon among the Provincial Komitetchiki to have been raised in a single-parent household. Few received more than an incomplete secondary education. Prior to joining the party, they appeared to be headed for careers as skilled laborers. After joining the party, however, they tended to eschew outside employment for lives as "professional revolutionaries."

By the early 1930s, they had become the heads of their own households. The typical Provincial Komitetchiki household included a wife, one or two children, and an elderly parent or in-law. Their children tended to be young, six years old or less, indicating that they did not begin to raise families until they were established professionally. Their income from party work was usually listed as the sole means of support for their households. They listed flats in apartment buildings as their place of residence, instead

Table 2.2. Some Characteristics of the Provincial Komitetchiki

Name	Born	Family background	Nationality	Education	Prerevolutionary occupation
Andreev	1895	na	Russian	na	metal worker
Eikhe	1890	landless peasant	Latvian	lower	metal worker
Gamarnik	1894	provincial official	Russian	na	junior officer
Gikalo	1897	na	Georgian	higher	medical orderly
Goloshchekin	1876	na	Jewish	middle	dentist
Ivanov	1893	na	Russian	na	na
Kabakov	1891	unskilled worker	Russian	middle	metal worker
Khataevich	1893	petty traders	Jewish	middle	newspaper vendor
Kosior	1889	peasant	Polish	lower	metal worker
Krinitskii	1894	worker	Russian	na	worker
Kubiak	1882	na	Russian	lower	worker
Mirzoian	1897	peasant	Armenian	na	worker
Postyshev	1888	textile worker	Russian	lower	worker (textile)
Rumiantsev	1886	worker	Russian	lower	worker (shipbuilder)
Sheboldaev	1895	doctor	Russian	na	employee
Vareikis	1894	worker	Lithuanian	lower	worker (craftsman)

of estates and mansions as had the provincial governors of the old regime. These responses suggest that elite status in the postrevolutionary state was not derived from a lavish lifestyle, but rather elite status was associated with the projection of an image of a modest standard of living.

It is more difficult to generalize about the ethnic backgrounds of the Provincial Komitetchiki. Ethnic Russians composed roughly half of the Provincial Komitetchiki. The non-Russians were an ethnically mixed group, including Jewish, Georgian, Armenian, Polish, Lithuanian, and Latvian members. About half indicated that they were multilingual, although this capability was acquired through family life, not by formal education or foreign travel. To the extent to which a pattern can be discerned concerning ethnicity and regional placement, more often than not the Provincial Komitetchiki served in regions where the ethnic identity of the population differed from their own. Although it is necessary to note, the Provincial Komitetchiki did not leave evidence in their formal or informal testimonies, indicating that ethnicity was a defining feature of their social identity; this observation applies to the Russians as well as the non-Russians.

The Provincial Komitetchiki were members of regionally based personal networks. In particular, they belonged to personal networks that had arisen

Table 2.3. Main Regions of Civil War Service

Name	Report
Andreev, Andrei A.	Central Industrial Region
Eikhe, Robert I.	Riga
	Central Industrial Region
Gamarnik, Ian B.	Ukraine
	Southwest
Gikalo, Nikolai I.	Transcaucasus
Goloshchekin, Filipp I.	Urals
	Central Asia
Ivanov, Vladimir B.	Central Industrial Region
Kabakov, Ivan I.	Viatka-Volga
Khataevich, Mendel M.	Middle Volga
	Western Front
Kosior, Stanislav I.	Ukraine
	Siberia
Krinitskii, Aleksandr I.	Central Industrial Region
Kubiak, Nikolai A.	Northern
	Far East
Mirzoian, Levon I.	Transcaucasus
Postyshev, Pavel P.	Far East
Rumiantsev, Ivan P.	Central Industrial Region
	North Caucasus
Sheboldaev, Boris P.	Transcaucasus
Vareikis, Iosif M.	North Caucasus

along the battle fronts of the civil war. Three civil war networks were especially well represented among the Provincial Komitetchiki: first, the southeastern, which began in the Middle Volga and pushed into Kazakhstan and Central Asia; second, the southern, which encompassed the North Caucasus and Transcaucasia; and, third, the southwestern, which secured the Black Sea coast and central-eastern Ukraine (see Table 2.3).

The Provincial Komitetchiki also shared similar patterns of party service see Table 2.4). They tended to join the party either in the wave of recruits between 1905 and 1906, mobilized by the events of the 1905 revolution, or the wave of recruits between 1913 and 1914, stirred by the radicalization of the labor movement after the Lena goldfield strikes in 1912. In the prerevolutionary period, they engaged in "professional revolutionary" work, which indicated service in the underground committees. On the

Table 2.4. Party Service of the Provincial Komitetchiki

Name	Entered Party	Emigration	Repressed	Post-civil war work	Central committee membership	Central administration appointment
Andreev	1915	No	na	Trade union adm.	1920	Yes
Eikhe	1905	Yes	Yes	Regional adm.	1930	No
Gamarnik	1916	No	No	Regional adm. / military	1927	No
Gikolo	1917	No	No	Regional adm.	1934 (candidate)	No
Goloshchekin	1903	No	Yes	Regional adm.	1927	No
Ivanov	1915	No	na	Regional adm.	1934	No
Kabakov	1914	No	Yes	Regional adm.	1925	No
Khataevich	1913	No	Yes	Regional adm.	1930	Yes
Kosior	1907	No	Yes	Regional adm.	1924	Yes
Krinitskii	1915	No	Yes	Regional adm.	1934	Yes
Kubiak	1898	No	Yes	Regional adm.	1923	Yes
Mirzoian	1917	No	No	Regional adm.	1934 (candidate)	No
Postyshev	1904	No	Yes	Regional adm.	1927	Yes
Rumiantsev	1905	No	Yes	Regional adm.	1924	No
Sheboldaev	1914	No	Yes	Regional adm.	1930	Yes
Vareikis	1913	No	Yes	Regional adm.	1930	Yes

questionnaire, not only did the Provincial Komitetchiki respond negatively to one particular question asking if they had spent time in the "emigration," several wrote *"nyet"* in bold capital letters and then underlined it for emphasis.[56] Such was the strength of this identity marker of party service, distinguishing them from the party's *intelligenty* members. While Robert Eikhe, for example, spent several years abroad in the prerevolutionary period, he hastened to note that after arriving in England he soon departed London for the Glasgow coal mines.[57]

The Provincial Komitetchiki generally were not in St. Petersburg in February 1917, nor did they play instrumental roles in the events of the October revolution. They did, however, occupy leading positions in the military–revolutionary committees that consolidated Soviet power in the periphery during the civil war. In the early 1920s, the Provincial Komitetchiki moved into regional administrative work, setting up local networks of party offices. In the first half of the decade, they typically moved as many as four or five times to different regions across the periphery. Between 1922 and 1930, Vareikis, for example, was an administrator in Baku, Kiev, Central Asia, Saratov, and the Central Black Earth; similarly, Krinitskii in this same period was an administrator in Saratov, Omsk,

Donbass, Belorussia, and the Caucasus.[58] New job assignments usually meant an upward promotion. Most of the Provincial Komitetchiki had acquired previous experience, sometimes extensive, in the same regions to which they were eventually appointed to lead in the 1930s.

The career paths of half those listed also included a brief tour of duty in the party's central administrative offices in Moscow. The assignment to the central office was intended to test and groom them as potential regional leaders. In a letter to Molotov in 1925, Stalin considered several regional leaders for promotion to the party's central personnel office. "It is necessary to think about the organizational assignment department," Stalin wrote, "Gei, it seems, is not ready yet. He is young and little known, without much experience; he will not have authority. This is what everybody says, if you ask. Krinitskii is not ready either, truthfully he is less ready than Gei (for the same reason). Is it not time to take Kosior and to direct Gei to Siberia?"[59] In fact, Gei was promoted on this occasion and was later reassigned as a head of Belorussia. Kosior was called up to head the center's organizational assignment department in the center the next year, after which he was reassigned as the head of Ukraine.

By the end of the 1920s, the Provincial Komitetchiki had climbed from local administrative posts to become regional party leaders. It was at this time that most of them were made full members of the party central committee, a formal indicator of their elite status. They became more settled at this time, both professionally and socially, as they assumed their roles as provincial governors. On the questionnaire, they referred to this role as simply a "party worker," an unassuming job description for a position that meant the governor of a region greater in size than most European states. The Provincial Komitetchiki were, in effect, a Soviet reincarnation of the tsarist regime's *nachal'niki gubernii*, or "bosses of the provinces." In the old regime, the governors served as the tsar's viceroys, representing a personal embodiment of the autocracy in the regions.[60] In the new Soviet regime, the Provincial Komitetchiki possessed a similar form of extraordinary and personalized power, representing an embodiment of the authority of the party's central committee.

3

CONSTRUCTING AN ELITE IDENTITY: IMAGES OF SELF, SERVICE, AND STATE

This chapter attempts to reconstruct the elite identity of the Provincial Komitetchiki. It presents common themes about self, service, and state expressed by the Provincial Komitetchiki at the time of their promotion to positions as regional leaders. In the words of Leopold Haimson, I seek to uncover "who they were in order to determine, how they should feel, think, and ultimately to act."[1] The elite identity of the Provincial Komitetchiki expressed the value culture of Russia's new radical socialist regime. The personal traits and experiences emphasized in this identity revealed the sources of elite status in the new state. On the basis of belonging to this intraparty status group, the Provincial Komitetchiki would make a claim on special privileges and powers conferred by the state.

In the postrevolutionary period, the sources of elite status of Russia's old regime had become discredited. Noble inheritance, familial lineage, bureaucratic position, and lavish lifestyle were no longer markers of elite status.[2] Indeed, persons identified with these attributes were sometimes labeled class enemies and risked severe reprisals. The formal administrative structures of the tsarist state were in disarray and its formal elite structure, the table of ranks, was in disrepute. Nor was elite status conferred on the basis of the personal attributes common to other twentieth-century states, such as ethnicity, wealth, and merit.[3]

At this time, the personal networks of civil war fighter organizers, the Bolshevik *druzhina*, emerged to fill this status void. Robert Crummey's description of the old boyar *druzhina* as "a warrior elite who assisted the prince in governing his realm" aptly captured the self-image projected by the Bolshevik *druzhina*.[4] Their claim on elite status was based on their records of service to the party in the underground and the civil war. Unlike Russia's earlier boyar elite, however, the Bolshevik *druzhina* did not eschew state service. As the postrevolutionary state began to take form, they actively sought high-level administrative positions. In the second half of the 1920s and the 1930s, their roles as state actors and their contributions to state building offered an additional claim on elite status. The former civil war *druzhiniki* now sought to identify themselves as economic managers and technical experts, in accordance with the state-led industrial revolution.

This chapter is organized into three sections – self, service, and state – which were essential components to the elite identity of the Provincial Komitetchiki. First, the chapter brings to light the personal traits and early life experiences that were valued by the radical socialist regime. The Provincial Komitetchiki sought to identify themselves as self-made, resourceful, and resilient individuals, who overcame the class barriers of the old regime. Second, the Provincial Komitetchiki touted their war records and battle scars from the civil war. Their perception of themselves as a distinctive status group among the postrevolutionary state elite derived mainly from their service in the civil war. Third, once they moved into positions of formal power in regional administration, the Provincial Komitetchiki sought to project an image of themselves as a state elite, reinforced by the trappings and privileges of state power.

The collective portrait of the Provincial Komitetchiki drawn in this chapter is based largely on the autobiographies and personal questionnaires found in the archive of the Society of Old Bolsheviks.[5] It is important to stress again, however, that the historical veracity of this portrait is not the concern here. Of course, these personal recollections include selective recall, embellishment, and outright fabrication. Indeed, it is for precisely these reasons that these documents are significant. They provide insight into the construction of an elite identity that in turn has meaning in postrevolutionary politics.

I. PREREVOLUTIONARY EXPERIENCES: IMAGES OF SELF

The new regime favored the establishment of a social order that could somehow provide privileges and opportunities to those who could demonstrate their lower-class, and especially working-class, origins.[6] Not surprisingly, the autobiographies of the Provincial Komitetchiki conformed to this official class preference. The most striking feature of the self-image of youth and early life experiences presented in the autobiographies was its resemblance to a more general European working-class literary genre. This particular genre had become somewhat fashionable in certain social circles in early twentieth-century Russia.[7] The autobiographies of the Provincial Komitetchiki suggested its influence in both style and substance. In style, the autobiographies were presented in the form of personal narrative. In substance, the Provincial Komitetchiki placed strong emphasis on their ability to overcome early life adversity, a tendency to be drawn to and to learn from radical workers, and a talent for organization and self-initiative.

Social and economic hardship marked the early life experiences of the Provincial Komitetchiki. They stressed that *vospytanie*, life experience, as opposed to *obrazovanie*, formal education, shaped their basic character. Depictions of childhood frequently presented a scenario of determined family members striving to overcome the material deprivation and social barriers, which characterized life at the bottom of tsarist Russia's social order. In particular, single-parent households, economic obstacles to education and social advancement, and early entry into the workforce were common scenes described by the Provincial Komitetchiki.[8]

The childhood experiences related by Mendel Khataevich and Ivan Kabakov were typical in this regard. Born to a Jewish family in Gomel in Belorussia, Khataevich's father died at the time of his birth, "leaving my mother with a family of four small children and without means of support."[9] Although his childhood was marked by "need and deprivation," his family "strove not to let it show on the outside, to mask the outside as if we were fortunate." As a small child, Khataevich attended a *kheder*, Jewish primary school. But the family's economic situation prevented him from continuing his education. "I passed an examination for a private gymnasium, but for lack of means it was impossible for me to study." Instead, Khataevich, at the age of thirteen, began his working career distributing newspapers. A similar tale was told by Ivan Kabakov, whose mother died before he was two years old.[10] Since his father was a "black worker," constantly on the move in search of work, he was raised by his grandmother. Following primary school, Kabakov was forced to abandon secondary education after a year and a half "for reasons of illness" and "insufficient means." "When I was fifteen," he continued, "I bought a horse and attempted to work in Siberia. After two years, the horse died. In these two years, I succeeded to do another stupid thing by marrying at the age of seventeen and a half."

While their early life experiences were generally difficult, the Provincial Komitetchiki notably refused to accept their fates. Perseverance and self-reliance were characteristic responses. Concerning their blocked access to formal education, for example, the Provincial Komitetchiki acted to educate themselves. Kabakov stressed that he not only acquainted himself with political and historical literature, but "especially loved to read the literature of Russian writers – Nekrasov, Gogol, Pushkin, and Lermontov."[11] Nikolai Kubiak received only a formal primary education, but later "educated myself sitting in jail."[12] As part of the elite identity of the Provincial Komitetchiki, self-education was a highly valued trait, not least for its demonstration of a personal will to overcome adversity. As example, the handwritten autobiographical statement of Maksim Kartvelishvili, the brother of a prominent regional leader, reported that prior to the revolution he worked as an illiterate blacksmith. But in the typed version of this statement, the "illiterate" reference was crossed out.[13] It is not indicated if the reference was removed by Kartvelishvili or someone else. Regardless of whose hand edited the document, the incident sheds light on the values of the group. Having been denied formal education was not a character flaw, but having not taken the initiative to educate oneself was undesirable.

A second early life experience commonly stressed by the Provincial Komitetchiki was a tendency to be drawn to and learn from older politicized workers. These early contacts in the workplace stirred a political awakening that soon led to radical behavior. Most Provincial Komitetchiki first became acquainted with the social-democratic underground by way of such workplace experiences.[14] Before the age of eighteen, Kubiak participated in an uprising in the Briansk metal works factory that "destroyed the workshop."[15] "These circumstances," he wrote, "connected me with a group of active young workers. In 1898, I had already begun to receive illegal literature and to participate in illegal discussions." This kind of experience was an important source of social validation for those whose family backgrounds were not proletarian. Iosif Vareikis, for example, was raised in a Lithuanian village; however, he was exposed to radicalism as a textile worker in the Singer Sewing Machine Company in Podol'sk.[16]

Finally, the portrait of the Provincial Komitetchiki as young men presented ample evidence of self-motivated acts of leadership and organization. These talents were most often displayed to mobilize workers for radical political ends and to direct grassroots party activities. Khataevich, at the age of eighteen, operated a newspaper kiosk, which "gradually became a center where it was possible to find legal and illegal revolutionary literature."[17] Khataevich soon thereafter joined the Bolsheviks, where he "became the leader of an underground circle and a member of a collective of one of our leading organizations." Between 1905 and 1907, Kubiak, in his early twenties, devoted himself to the Bolshevik cause in the Briansk district, where he "organized the underground party press," "organized and led strikes," and "was the boss of a hundred comrades."[18] Moved to action by the war, Vareikis, at the age of twenty, "engaged in illegal agitation against the war," "adopted a leading role in a number of strikes," and "led cultural-education work among the workers."[19] Robert Eikhe, who to avoid arrest fled abroad for several years, stressed that as a coal miner in Scotland he was elected the secretary of a social-democratic circle and organized theoretical discussions among the workers.[20] And, in a display of multiple leadership talents, Stanislav Kosior was the captain of a popular soccer team in the Donbas region. Matches between rival teams served as a convenient forum for Kosior to agitate workers and recruit members for the party.[21]

These early experiences prepared the Provincial Komitetchiki for participation in the Bolshevik underground. Self-initiative, organizational skills and, most importantly, the ability to rise above adversity were necessary personal traits for sustained illegal committee work. Underground life posed a new set of hardships and hazards. With few resources and little guidance, underground workers were responsible for maintenance of an organizational base of operations, dissemination of political literature, and agitation among factory workers. The threat of police infiltration was constant. Discovery usually meant arrest, jail, and exile. To keep an illegal committee operating and to stay one step ahead of the police was a constant challenge.

In the prerevolutionary period, three lifestyles existed for full-time party members: émigré, legal, and illegal. The illegal lifestyle was surely the most trying and the least rewarding. The autobiographies of the Provincial Komitetchiki routinely drew attention to the fact that among party members they were the ones who willingly endured the dangers and deprivations of underground life to advance the party's position among Russia's proletariat. The underground became a self-defining experience for the Provincial Komitetchiki, stressing the notions of sacrifice and service. It distinguished them from the émigrés and legal party workers. Alluding to this special role, Robert Eikhe noted that "it was considered impossible to mix active work in the illegal organizations and a legal life."[22]

A good example of the way in which underground work in the post-1905 period became a defining feature of those who served comes from the memoir account of A. Arosov, an underground companion of Viacheslav Molotov. "The men of the older generation," he wrote, "were turning their backs in disappointment. But in their place came fresh workers in battle order. They were few in number, but by their moral fervor, by their fortitude in the ensuing struggle, they proved to be far stronger than many who had joined the revolution during its romantic period, 1904–5, when its star was rising rather than waning."[23]

In their reminiscences of underground life, the Provincial Komitetchiki placed great emphasis on their ability to endure and to overcome the persecutions of the tsarist police. The amount of time spent in jail or exile as well as the number of times arrested were status symbols for the group.[24] Police persecution served as a rite of passage among the Provincial Komitetchiki. The personal questionnaire for the Society of Old Bolsheviks explicitly asked respondents if they were "repressed" by the tsarist police. "Of course!" wrote Eikhe, who logged two years and eight months in exile.[25] Kubiak boasted that he "was deprived of the right to live in fifty-seven towns" as punishment for organizing labor strikes.[26] Filipp Goloshchekin's record of underground service was even more impressive in this regard, though hardly exceptional: in 1905, worked as a "professional revolutionary" in St. Petersburg; in 1906, arrested and sentenced to two and a half years in jail; in 1907, released from jail, returned to underground work, arrested and sentenced to one and a half years in jail; in 1908, released from jail; in 1909, worked in Riga and Moscow underground committees, arrested and exiled to Narym; in 1910, escaped from exile and returned to work in Moscow underground; in 1912, arrested, exiled to Tobol'sk, escaped from Tobol'sk, returned to St. Petersburg; in 1913, worked in Urals underground, arrested and exiled to Turukhan until February revolution.[27] Alas, Vareikis managed to avoid arrest, jail and exile during his brief tenure in the underground; nonetheless, he still felt compelled to write "only repressed" on his questionnaire.[28]

The hardships of underground life were depicted as character-building experiences, which shaped a self-image for the Provincial Komitetchiki. Having endured the persecutions of tsarist Russia's secret police, the Provincial Komitetchiki developed inner strength and resolve. Speaking in this regard about Sergo Ordzhonikidze, Anastas Mikoian remarked: "Of his fifteen years of underground work, eight were spent in prisons, penal servitude, and exile. The prisons of Tiflis, Sukhum, and Baku, the Schlusselburg fortress, and exiles in Siberia and Yakutsk did not break Sergo's iron constitution, but were the universities that trained him in the struggle and strengthened his ideological convictions."[29]

On the eve of 1917, according to their own depictions, the Provincial Komitetchiki were self-made, men of action, and natural leaders. But the real proving ground for this self-image would be the major events in the Bolshevik struggle to seize and to consolidate power during the period from 1917 to 1921.

II. CIVIL WAR EXPERIENCES: IMAGES OF SERVICE

The revolutionary events between 1917 and 1921 became a fundamental part of the elite identities of the Provincial Komitetchiki. More than any other experience, service to the party during the civil war provided the basis for their claim on elite status. The civil war provided a theater for the Provincial Komitetchiki, who played the role of war heroes. Through the twenties and the early thirties, these images of civil war experiences were reconstructed, mass produced, and celebrated by the official myth-makers of the new Soviet state.

Few of the Provincial Komitetchiki actually participated in the events in Petrograd in 1917. They mostly remained in the provinces. Stanislav Kosior, however, was exceptional among the group in that he experienced the October revolution firsthand. Following the February revolution, Kosior arrived in Petrograd after three years of exile in Irkutsk.[30] In April 1917, Kosior participated in the historic meetings at which Lenin repositioned the Bolsheviks onto a more radical political path. Kosior later recalled these events: "Since a number of us were still young, we listened to Lenin with great intellectual enjoyment. It was the first time that a majority of us were present at such an important party meeting. For us, the April Conference was transformed into the most valuable school. In this school, each day we grew politically and we studied the art of being a Bolshevik"[31] Kosior was assigned to party organizational work in the city's Narva-Petergof district. He engaged in political agitation among the workers of the large industrial enterprises, including Putilov and Treugol'nik. In October 1917, Kosior served in the Petrograd revolutionary–military committee, which staged the Bolshevik uprising. During the civil war, he emerged as a leader of the underground partisan movement that eventually consolidated Soviet power in Ukraine.

For the Provincial Komitetchiki, the various battle fronts of the civil war provided ample opportunity for revolutionary heroics. While it was inevitable that the Bolsheviks would face a military challenge to the October coup, the initiation of hostilities came from an unlikely source. In the late spring of 1918, a Czechoslovak legion, evacuating the German front via the Trans-Siberian Railroad, engaged a Red Army detachment in fighting and seized control of the main railway and telegraph lines connecting European Russia to its vast eastern periphery. A political–military base of operation was quickly established by opponents of the Bolsheviks in the Middle Volga region, less than five hundred miles east of Moscow.

The new regime was ill-prepared for this challenge. Desperate attempts to hold on to the region failed. It would take nearly four months before the Bolsheviks were able to regroup and to recover the strategically vital Middle Volga region.

Among the Provincial Komitetchiki, Mendel Khataevich and Iosif Vareikis earned recognition for valorous service in these early battles along the Volga. Khataevich arrived in Samara in March 1918; soon thereafter, he found himself involved in street fighting against the Czechoslovak forces.[32] He was permanently paralyzed in the right arm as a result of injuries suffered in this skirmish. He later wrote "I was seriously wounded in the chest and the right arm (which presently I cannot move) and was not able to evacuate. I concealed my wounds from my comrades, but, at last, I collapsed in the snow during a counter-search mission. I was horribly tortured and almost did not live. I was directed to jail, where I remained until the return of Soviet power to Samara."[33] Khataevich recovered sufficiently to participate in other civil war episodes, including the Red Army's offensive drive into Poland in 1920.

At the onset of the civil war, Iosif Vareikis served in the Middle Volga region as the chair of the Simbirsk party organization and a member of the local revolutionary–military committee. In the summer of 1918, the rogue military commander Murav'ev and Left Socialist Revolutionaries staged an armed uprising against the Bolsheviks in Simbirsk. In the ensuing conflict, civil war hero Mikhail Tukhachevskii, commanding the First Red Army, was captured and placed under arrest. Vareikis rallied support for the Bolshevik side from the local garrison. He confronted Murav'ev, who was killed resisting arrest, and liberated Tukhachevskii from jail.[34] Later Tukhachevskii wrote, "The creation of the First Army and the suppression of counter-revolution would not have been possible if the Simbirsk party committee had not come to our assistance. Comrade Vareikis, I consider your action and that of the party in defense of Simbirsk as a shining service to the state."[35]

The Bolsheviks engaged in a protracted and hard-fought campaign to secure the regions of the Lower Volga, the North Caucasus, and the Transcaucasus for the new Soviet state. Following the October revolution, a Menshevik government was established in Georgia, while nationalist governments were declared in Armenia and Azerbaijan. A counterrevolutionary White Army, led by Denikin, moved into the region and opened a southern front against the Bolshevik center. Local paramilitary bands of cossacks and mountaineers also took up arms against the Bolsheviks. And, a British naval expeditionary force intervened in the region, occupying strategic transportation and communication centers.

Bolsheviks in the region were physically cut off from the new regime. To survive, they set up a network of underground committees, which endeavored to maintain clandestine lines of communication and supply, to agitate the local populations and to recruit supporters for the Soviet regime. Sergei Kirov, in a speech delivered to sympathizers in the Terek district of the North Caucasus in the winter of 1918, laid out a plan of action in response to the party's fragile position in the region. His words aptly captured the self-image of the Provincial Komitetchiki for withstanding even the most formidable challenges:

> But, of course, no one can help, if we cannot help ourselves. The path for us is not in the north, towards Petrograd. The north can do nothing for us. Between us and the north lies the Quiet Don. At present, counter-revolutionary forces exist all around here. We are not able to establish ties with the Revolutionary Democracy of central Russia. All that we can possibly do is cut out the ground beneath our own counter-revolutionary forces.[36]

Eventually, the Bolsheviks in the region succeeded in overcoming their isolation. In late 1919, Red Army units from the eastern front, with Kuibyshev as political commissar, and the southern front, with Kirov as political commissar, converged on Astrakhan, retaking this strategic city at the mouth of the Volga. On 1 December 1919, Kirov telegrammed Lenin with the news: "The Eleventh Army speeds a dispatch for your revolutionary delight in the case of the complete liquidation of the White Astrakhan cossacks, who, with the bandits of English imperialism, have been lording over the Caspian and the banks of the Volga for over a half year."[37] The Eleventh Red Army, commanded by Tukhachevskii, was at last able to move southward into the Transcaucasus, reclaiming the region for the Soviet regime. Bolshevik workers emerged from the underground to lead local revolutionary–military committees, which consolidated territory for the new regime in the wake of the Red Army's advance.

Veterans of the southern front were later well represented among the Provincial Komitetchiki, including Nikolai Gikalo in Belorussia, Lev Mirzoian in the Urals and Kazakhstan, and Boris Sheboldaev in the Lower Volga and North Caucasus. The civil war experiences of Boris Sheboldaev were typical of those who served in the region. In late 1917, Sheboldaev was part of a small group of soldiers on the Turkish front, who declared allegiance to the new Soviet regime. With the arrival of Turkish and German troops, Sheboldaev was forced to quit his outpost garrison. Sheboldaev fled to Baku, where he entered underground work, maintaining a Bolshevik base of operations in the region.[38] In his memoirs, Anastas Mikoian lauded Sheboldaev's exploits during this time:

During the evacuation of our armed forces from Baku to Astrakhan in
1918, when our ships had been stopped at Zhiloy Island, he and two
comrades had managed to go ashore, seize a fishing boat, and in the face
of great difficulties, make their way to Fort Aleksandrov. From there,
Sheboldaev went to Astrakhan by boat, and was then sent to the Kizlyar
district with the goal of getting through to Dagestan and making contact
there with the local rebels. Displaying exceptional resourcefulness, Sheboldaev managed to carry out his assignment.[39]

Upon his return to Baku, Sheboldaev was arrested and incarcerated by the
nationalist Musavat government. He was liberated during the Red Army's
assault on Azerbaijan and was named head of the revolutionary–military
committee for Dagestan.

The war stories told by the Provincial Komitetchiki reemphasized the
personal traits that were valued in depictions of early life and the underground. The theme of self-sacrifice, for example, was evident in Khataevich's account of his attempt to conceal his wounds from his comrades.
This behavior was consistent with Khataevich's earlier remarks about his
mother's effort to disguise the family's poverty from their neighbors.
Overcoming hardship and obstacles through perseverance and self-reliance
was another recurring theme. Kirov's description of Bolsheviks surrounded
by enemies in the Transcaucasus suggested a desperate situation. But
personal resilience enabled them to surmount the seemingly insurmounta-
ble. And Sheboldaev's "exceptional resourcefulness" secured a line of communication between the stranded Bolsheviks in Transcaucasia and party
leaders on the southern front. Finally, the Provincial Komitetchiki's talents
for organization and leadership were highlighted in their civil war recollections. Along the Far Eastern front, Pavel Postyshev expounded: "after the
abandonment of Khabarovsk by Red forces, I relocated to the nearby
countryside, where I organized the first Tungussk partisan detachment and
led party work until the fall of the warlord Kol'chak and the retreat of the
ataman Kal'mykov."[40]

Civil war experiences were kept alive through a variety of official
sources, which served to reinforce to the participants the significance of
their service. The civil war became an integral part of the folklore of the
new state. A heroic literature was developed from the reminiscences of
civil war combatants.[41] Events and roles were surely reconstructed to suit
both the ideological proclivities of the regime and the personal vanities of
the authors. In the retelling of civil war stories, the Provincial Komitetchiki imbued their accounts with images of revolutionary élan and wartime
comradeship. These images were significant in contributing to the solidi-
fication of group bonds and the construction of a group identity. Shared

battlefield exploits became an enduring feature of the social identities of the members of various civil war Bolshevik *druzhiny*.

The anniversaries of famous battles provided occasions for participants to remind others of their wartime service. Official civil war tributes also served as an opportunity for regional clients to reaffirm their ties to central patrons, whom they had served with during the war. In a personal recollection, marking the eighth anniversary of the outbreak of war in Samara, Buloshev, a local party worker, felt obliged to pause "for a moment to reflect on the personality of Comrade Kuibyshev. Comrade Kuibyshev was always the spirit of the Samara organization, he was its leader, even non-party members listened to him, and the peasants loved him."[42] To celebrate his fiftieth birthday, Ordzhonikidze's civil war exploits in organizing the Bolshevik conquest of the North Caucasus and Azerbaijan were vividly recalled for weeks in the press by his wartime associates.[43]

These examples of the way in which civil war images became incorporated into postrevolutionary social identities were taken from official commemorations. Perhaps, a more telling example is the following passage, which was extracted from private correspondence between two civil war veterans – Arzanian, an agricultural administrator in Baku, and Gaia D. Gai, a military academician in Moscow. Although he subsequently moved into military work, Gai's background was similar to the Provincial Komitetchiki. He became active in the social-democratic underground in the Transcaucasus in his late teens, following his expulsion from the seminary for political radicalism.[44] During the civil war, he organized the famed "iron division" in the Middle Volga region and commanded another division along the southern front. His autobiography proudly noted that during the war he was wounded in the arm and shell-shocked twice. Arzanian wrote:

> Received your letter and photograph from Sergo [Ordzhonikidze]. Your letter reminded me of the old times – our work in Balakhan at the Kavkaz Oil Company, our old arguments with the Dashnaki, and other places. It was good for me to know that you also have not forgotten. You are the same Gai that I knew before. You are the same friend and comrade that I knew before. The Baku proletariat can be proud to have been enlightened by such an ideal comrade as you, who not only could fight with a rifle in hand against enemies, but who could fight on the cultural front in times of peace. Such a person as you, Gai, was very much needed.[45]

Significantly, this passage is from a private letter, written in 1929, not from an official publication. It represents a discourse that reaffirms a perception of self that is rooted in a constructed image of the events of the civil war. The letter from Arzanian to Gai also offers insight into the application of the civil war identity to the post-civil war period. In this particular case, Gai succeeded in demonstrating that he "could fight on the cultural front in times of peace." The Provincial Komitetchiki were called upon to make similar transitions.

III. POSTREVOLUTIONARY EXPERIENCES: IMAGES OF STATE

The need to adapt to the challenges of postrevolutionary state building was experienced by all the civil war political commissars and their staffs. But while these challenges required new roles to be played, the actors brought their old characters to the parts. The Provincial Komitetchiki found new venues to display the talents and traits that had served them so well in the underground and the civil war. In the 1920s, they routed "Trotskyists" from the party and fortified Soviet authority across the periphery. At the beginning of the 1930s, they were once again summoned to battle in the "socialist offensive." Cast in the image of the civil war, the socialist offensive was a state-led campaign of radical economic transformation with no less a goal than the construction of a new socialist order. In less than five years, even this battle was claimed by the Provincial Komitetchiki to have been won.

By the early 1930s, the Provincial Komitetchiki had arrived as Russia's new political elite. According to their own depictions, they achieved this rank by virtue of their personal qualities (images of self) and their wartime contributions (images of service). At this time, the elite identity of the Provincial Komitetchiki underwent further evolution. This change was shaped by their images of the new state and, more specifically, their new role as state actors. The Provincial Komitetchiki now saw themselves as regional governors and economic managers.

As regional governors, the Provincial Komitetchiki sought to reinforce their elite status through the formal trappings of state power. Titles, ranks, privileges, homages, and perquisites were coveted by the Provincial Komitetchiki to validate their elite identity. The hierarchy and status ranking, which had once existed informally within personal networks, was now given formal expression through state officialdom. Four incidents are recounted here, indicating the importance to the Provincial Komitetchiki of formalizing their roles as state actors through appropriate status markers.

The first incident is related by way of a letter from Stalin to Molotov on the proper protocol for issuing an official statement to announce the promotions of Sergo Ordzhonikidze and Anastas Mikoian. In this case, Mikoian was promoted into the center from his post as first secretary of the North Caucasus regional committee. Ordzhonikidze, who at the time was first secretary of the Transcaucasus regional committee, had also been promoted to a central post. Before assuming that position, however, Ordzhonikidze was instructed to move temporarily to the North Caucasus to put together a new regional leadership team. Stalin wrote:

> Sergo was in to see me the other day. He was furious at the formulation of a central committee resolution on his recall. He assessed the formulation of the recall as a punishment or an insult. The phrase that Sergo is to be transferred to Rostov 'in place of Mikoian' implies that Mikoian is higher than Sergo, that Sergo is only fit to be Mikoian's assistant. He understands that the central committee could not wish to insult him or to place him under Mikoian, but he considers that those who receive the letter of the central committee resolution could understand it to mean a put-down against Sergo, and so it is necessary to reformulate it better and more exactly.[46]

Indeed, Molotov issued a follow-up anouncement, which made it clear that Ordzhonikidze's transfer did not indicate that he ranked lower than Mikoian. Ordzhonikidze's perception of status in this incident was directly shaped by informal network relations. Ordzhonikidze and Mikoian both belonged to the Transcaucasian regional network. While Mikoian was indeed a leading member of this network, Ordzhonikidze had acted as his superior in the civil war and in postwar administration. In addition, Ordzhonikidze's new central post, chairman of the party's central control commission, was a more powerful and higher-status position than Mikoian's new assignment, head of the trade ministry. Ordzhonikidze's indignation was roused when the formal announcement of his promotion did not make explicitly clear the preexisting informal status ranking between Mikoian and himself.

A second example of the way in which the formal trappings of state power were used to reinforce an elite identity is culled from the memoirs of Ante Ciliga, a Croatian social-democrat. Ciliga described a meeting with Sergei Kirov in 1929, almost three years after Kirov moved to this high-profile position from the Transcaucasus. The meeting took place in Kirov's office at the Smolney Institute, regional party headquarters and former finishing school for the daughters of the elite in tsarist times. Ciliga noted that "Kirov's office in no way recalled the atmosphere of enthusiasm of the October revolution. Kirov himself, by his manners and methods, reminded me of the cultured high officials of the Austrian administration I had known in Brunn. In the office of Kirov, governor of Leningrad in 1929, one felt the revolution had already been tamed and canalized."[47] Ciliga's observation suggests the direction of evolution in the identity of the Provincial Komitetchiki now that they had become state actors. Kirov was the most prominent provincial governor in the new state and his office, at least through the eyes of Ciliga, expressed this status.

Still another manifestation of the elite identity of the Provincial Komitetchiki was the promulgation of their own regional personality cults. These cults mimicked on a smaller scale the personality cults of central leaders. Most typically, the social and economic achievements of Soviet state building – factories, collective farms, and schools – were named or renamed in honor of the regional leaders. While it is not uncommon for politicians to claim credit for economic development projects, the penchant for naming and renaming in the regions was not always confined to buildings and streets. In Kazakhstan, a massive mountain range runs along the Chinese border, with the tallest peak reaching a height of nearly 7,000 meters. Long known as Khan Tengri, or Tsar of the Spirit, it was renamed "Peak Mirzoian" in honor of Lev Mirzoian, the first secretary of Kazkahstan in the mid-1930s. New maps and textbooks were published to reflect the name change. Later in the decade, under pressure from the center, Mirzoian removed his name from the mountain.[48]

Finally, in the second half of the 1930s, it was proposed by the center that real elections by secret ballot should be held for all regional and local party officials. The Provincial Komitetchiki, not surprisingly, opposed the plan. In his objection to the proposal, Stanislav Kosior, first secretary of Ukraine, provided insight into the perceptions that the Provincial Komitetchiki held of themselves as state actors. Kosior cautioned:

> Elections, of course, will provide a big boost for party democracy, but the question of what offices and who will be elected has colossal organizational consequences. There are special positions, such as the secretary of the party organization and the chairman of the executive committee. If he is deprived of political trust by not being elected to the party committee, it will mean that he will have to be removed from his post. As a result, the importance of the leading party organs will be diminished.[49]

Kosior's comments, of course, were blatantly self-serving, but they also were revealing of the elite identity of the Provincial Komitetchiki by mid-decade. Kosior directly linked the political fate of the regional leaders to the legitimacy of the state itself. As the foremost representatives of the state in the regions, any measure that would undermine their status as individuals would inevitably reverberate back on the state as a whole. Kosior's perception of his role and status as a regional governor, in effect, placed him above popular accountability.

Beginning in 1929, "building socialism" in Soviet Russia came to be defined almost exclusively in terms of economic development. This situation was not the case in the decade following the revolution. In the early 1920s, "building socialism" just as often implied cultural revolution. The regime at that time devoted attention and resources to social causes, such as educating peasants in rural areas and liberating women in Muslim territories. The regime maintained tolerance, if not outright support, for artistic and literary explorations of a futuristic "proletarian" culture. But this situation ended abruptly with the introduction of the five-year plans. From this time, "building socialism" came to mean economic revolution. Soviet Russia's transition to the socialist stage of history was now measured by the indicators of industrial output.

In this campaign, a mixed economy was abandoned for a command–administrative economy, in which economic processes were subsumed into the power structures of the state. The new state seized responsibility for economic development. Affairs of state were increasingly devoted to economic management. The state propagated a cult of production, which influenced the construction of elite identities in the new state and remained a salient feature of state service throughout the Soviet period. In accordance with this official glorification of production, the Provincial Komitetchiki began to identify themselves as economic managers and technical experts.

The Provincial Komitetchiki were leading players in the drive to industrialize Soviet Russia (see Chapter 6). They were made responsible for the transformation of agriculture from individual small-holding production to collective large-scale production so that the state could extract resources directly from the agricultural sector and transfer them to the growing industrial sector. The state's ambitious campaign to expropriate peasant property and to collect the grain harvest incited widespread resistance. In this state–societal conflict, the Provincial Komitetchiki were called upon to revive their former roles as battle leaders. But collectivization also compelled the Provincial Komitetchiki to play a new role, that of economic manager. State-controlled collective farms required innovative forms of administration in order to improve the productivity and efficiency of the agricultural sector. Postyshev's remarks at a party meeting in 1933 reflected this emerging aspect of the elite identity of the Provincial Komitetchiki. "The large-scale collective farm economy," he declared, "needs better management and economic expertise. It is necessary for us to take on the organizational, administrative and developmental leadership of these large-scale economies."[50]

By mid-decade, the industrial sector was growing at an unprecedented rate. And while much of the countryside lay in ruin, the agricultural sector was in fact supplying the state with more grain than ever before. Progress was such that less than halfway through the second five-year plan, the state announced that Soviet Russia had already entered the socialist stage of economic development. The Provincial Komitetchiki trumpeted their contribution to these advances at party meetings throughout the 1930s. Vareikis announced that during the first five-year plan regional leaders "created over 200,000 collective farms in the country."[51] Postyshev noted with much pride his part in the construction of the Kharkhov tractor factory.[52] Sheboldaev, likewise, claimed credit for the work of the Stalingrad tractor factory, "which surpasses even American technology."[53] Kosior boasted that during the first five-year plan they "had taken the lead in economic work," "more than doubled the amount of grain for the state" and "fulfilled the task of building a durable agricultural base for heavy industry."[54] And, Khataevich later recalled that "in these years we achieved a great heroic victory in the struggle to strengthen the collective farm structure and to push further ahead our socialist industry."[55]

In early 1934, the success of the first five-year plan was hailed at a major party gathering, dubbed the "Congress of the Victors." But the victory being celebrated was far greater than simply the most recent economic figures. The congress marked the triumph of Soviet Russia's new state elites: coercive elite (military and police), economic elite (industrial managers), and territorial elite (regional governors). For the Provincial Komitetchiki, the congress represented the crowning moment in their careers and the crystalization of their elite identity.

The elite identity of the Provincial Komitetchiki was a composite of recurring obstacles and triumphs, which began at a personal level and eventually reached worldwide proportions. They overcame childhood poverty, police reaction, world war, civil war, economic depression, and class struggle. They were the faithful toilers of the underground, the soldiers of the revolution, and, finally, the builders of history's first socialist state. They dedicated their lives to the realization of Lenin's revolutionary vision. They believed and so they fought. But more importantly, they won. After a quarter century of political tumult in Russia, from Stolypin to Rasputin, from Kerensky to Trotsky, they were, indeed, "the victors."

But the victory of the Provincial Komitetchiki and the first generation of state elites proved short-lived. By the end of the decade, ruler and elite engaged in an intrastate power struggle in which the postrevolutionary elite was physically destroyed in a reign of terror. The elite identity described in this section helps to explain the dynamics of the ruler–elite conflict of the 1930s. The new state elite included individuals, like the Provincial Komitetchiki, who had participated in the founding events of the new state. Their service in these events made them a distinctive status group within the new state. It distinguished them from the *intelligenty* party members, who abandoned underground work and emigrated to the West after the failure of the 1905 revolution, as well as from the post-civil war party members, who were too young or too late to fight in the civil war. Most importantly, their service records conferred upon them an elite status independent of the actions or opinions of central state leaders. They believed that they had earned this elite status and did not owe anyone else for it, particularly Stalin. For this reason, elite identity became an informal power resource for the Provincial Komitetchiki in the center–regional conflict of the 1930s. This identity provided a source of status that even Stalin was unable to manipulate. His frustration in this regard was made explicit on numerous occasions in the 1930s, when he railed against those regional leaders "who presume that they cannot be touched because of *their past services*. These overly conceited grand princes (*vel'mozhi*) think that they are irreplaceable and that they can violate the decisions of the leading organs with impunity."[56]

PART II

INFORMAL SOURCES OF POWER IN THE POSTREVOLUTIONARY STATE

4

EXTENDING THE REACH OF THE STATE: PERSONAL NETWORKS AND TERRITORIAL ADMINISTRATION

How did the new Bolshevik state, in less than a decade, develop its capacity for territorial administration and extend its reach across its expansive regions? Extending the reach of the new Bolshevik state beyond the central industrial region to the rural and multiethnic periphery presented a daunting task. The revolutions of 1917 had severed the formal bureaucratic lines which long connected center to periphery in the old regime. Although the Red Army reclaimed most of the territory of the former tsarist empire, the institutions of regional administration could not simply be reoccupied, but had to be rebuilt. The new state was constrained in this effort by an acute shortage of trained personnel, broken lines of communication and transportation, and the uncooperativeness and at times outright hostility of the local populations.

The study contends that personal network ties played a more significant role in the state-building process than has previously been recognized by Western scholars. The argument does not assert that formal organization and coercion were not important to the process of postrevolutionary state building, but rather that these factors alone do not explain the outcome. The intersection of informal and formal structures enabled the weak post-revolutionary state to develop a capacity for territorial administration.

This chapter shows how personal network ties intersected with formal organizational structures in a way that significantly strengthened the new state's poorly developed infrastructural powers. Three aspects of this process are explored in this chapter: (1) the movement into the central leadership of core members of regionally based personal networks, (2) the intersection of informal and formal structures within the new state's terri-

torial–administrative framework, and (3) the utilization of personal network ties to extend the territorial administrative reach of the state through
a case study of the Transcaucasian regional network.

I. CENTRAL LEADERSHIP, PERSONAL NETWORKS, AND REGIONAL ADMINISTRATION

In the new Bolshevik state, the intitial patterns of power allocation employed by central leaders facilitated the adaptation of personal networks
for administrative tasks. During the four and a half years that Vladimir
Lenin headed the state, he displayed a consistent leadership style. Lenin
loathed the drawn-out discussions and procedural formalities that characterized committee rule and collective bodies. Instead, decision making was
confined to small inner circles of five or so members. Formal power was
delegated on a personalistic basis. Lenin entrusted the affairs of the new
Soviet state to several trusted and like-minded individuals.[1] In the area of
regional administration, Lenin at first came to rely almost exclusively on
Iakov Mikhailovich Sverdlov.

In the weeks following the February revolution, Iakov Sverdlov arrived
in Petrograd from political exile in Siberia. In August 1917, he formed an
administrative office attached to the party's central committee to establish
lines of communication and command between the Bolshevik leadership
in Petrograd and the local committees, now emerging from the shadows of
the underground. Sverdlov worked out of a two-room office on the second
floor of Kshesinskaia mansion. The office was the primitive forerunner of
what would become the most powerful bureaucracy in the Soviet state, the
central party apparat. Sverdlov occupied this space despite the strong
objections of Madame Kshesinskaia, a former ballerina and well-connected
St. Petersburg socialite, who entreated in vain to have the "vast mob"
removed from her house.[2] Personal ties were a feature of central party
administration from the very beginning. Sverdlov's five-person staff included: Klavdiia Novgorodtseva, his wife; Nedezhda Krupskaia, Lenin's
wife; and, the wife and sister-in-law of another Old Bolshevik, Mezhinskii.
Only Elena Stasova was not related to any other party leaders.[3] This office
initiated the first steps to connect the party's central leadership with the
regional committees. It conducted a membership census, devised a system
of correspondence (*perepiski*) between center and locality, and disseminated
instructions and publications.[4]

Lenin charged Sverdlov with the enormous responsibility of designing and staffing the new state's bureaucratic apparatus. Sverdlov enthusiastically undertook the task of creating an administrative structure for the new state. In an effort to restore the center's ties to the western borderlands, he organized the First Conference of Communist Organizations of the Occupied Regions, which became the basis for the June 1919 military alliance between the Soviet governments of Russia, Ukraine, Belorussia, Latvia, and Lithuania. This act was an important first step toward the reintegration of the non-Russian periphery into the new state. Sverdlov chaired the commission that drafted the first Soviet constitution, oversaw the creation of the first state control agency and initiated the opening of the first school for training administrative cadres (later renamed Sverdlov University).[5] He organized a special "at large" department (*inogorodnii otdel*) for the assignment of party cadres to regional administrative posts. Sverdlov remarked that "for the establishment of ties with the localities, which were unusually weak at first, we commanded to the localities several thousand men and emissaries; in the center, this work was organized by the at-large department."[6]

But the new state lacked the human, technical and financial resources to construct a "bureaucratic" system of infrastructural power. In response, Sverdlov unhesitatingly utilized personal network ties to facilitate the development of the new state's capacities of rule. Sverdlov was the core member of an extensive personal network of underground committee workers, many of whom he met as a political exile in the Urals and Siberia. Sverdlov readily tapped these informal lines to carry out the affairs of the new state. He promoted a group of associates from the Urals into positions of administrative power in the center and assigned personal acquaintances from his years in exile to positions of regional leadership.[7] By all accounts, Sverdlov possessed an encyclopedic knowledge of the prerevolutionary community of underground Bolsheviks. According to Bolshevik historian Emilian Iaroslavskii, Sverdlov's "head became the personnel records department, his memory contained the dossiers of thousands of underground workers."[8] His official Soviet biographers claimed that "the word of Sverdlov was sufficient recommendation" for the placement of any individual cadre.[9] According to Trotsky, even Lenin conceded to Sverdlov's judgement on personnel matters.[10]

In early March 1919, upon returning to Moscow from a series of meetings with local party leaders in preparation for an upcoming congress, Sverdlov fell ill with Spanish influenza. A week later, at age thirty-three, he was dead. Among his contemporaries, Sverdlov was considered no less than the organizational genius of the revolution. Stalin eulogized him as the man who "painlessly solved the organizational task of building a new Russia."[11] "Sverdlov was truly irreplaceable," Trotsky recalled:

> Confident, courageous, firm, resourceful, he was the finest type of Bolshevik. Lenin came to know and appreciate Sverdlov fully in those troubled months. How many times was it that Vladimir Ilyich would telephone Sverdlov to suggest one or another urgent measures, and in most cases would receive the reply, 'Already!' This meant that the measure has already been undertaken. We often joked about it saying 'With Sverdlov, it is no doubt – already!'[12]

And Lenin, speaking shortly after Sverdlov's death, lamented: "I am unable to replace him even in one-hundredth part, for in this [organizational] work we were obliged and absolutely justified to rely entirely on Comrade Sverdlov."[13]

Replacing Sverdlov indeed proved to be a most difficult task. Lenin first opted for Nikolai Nikolaevich Krestinskii, naming him secretary of the party's central committee. Krestinskii was a graduate of St. Petersburg law faculty and served for a short time as legal counsel to the tiny Bolshevik faction in the duma. During the war, Krestinskii spent time as a political exile in the Urals region, where he became acquainted with Sverdlov. In 1917, he worked briefly in the party's Ekaterinburg organization until Sverdlov promoted him into the central financial administration.[14] Krestinskii was soon joined in the central secretariat by two assistant secretaries, Evgenii Preobrazhenskii and Leonid Serebriakov. In less than a year, the work once organized by Sverdlov alone was divided among five departments. The party's central administrative staff, meanwhile, expanded from thirty workers at the time of Sverdlov's death, in February 1919, to one hundred and fifty workers, in March 1920, and to six hundred and two workers, in March 1921.[15]

Unlike Sverdlov, Krestinskii had little direct contact with the party's underground workers, the komitetchiki, who at this time were moving into regional administration. Krestinskii identified himself with the *intelligenty* cohort within the Bolshevik party.[16] In his memoirs, Aleksandr Shliapnikov remembered Krestinskii as part of a small group of intellectuals engaged in legal work, whose world was far removed from that of the prerevolutionary underground.[17] Under Krestinskii, the center's relations with regional leaders became strained almost immediately.

While Sverdlov had responded to the challenge of extending central authority by exploiting personal networks, Krestinskii instead attempted to rid regional administration of personal networks. He sought to build a "bureaucratic" system of infrastructural power in the new state. Krestinskii vowed to abolish the existing system of nepotism and corruption, and in its place to establish a system of merit-based service. He criticized regional leaders for their lack of formal education or knowledge of Marxist theory. He appointed regional leaders on the basis of experience and training, not personal connections. Indeed, under Krestinskii, nonparty members were sometimes appointed to regional administrative positions. He initiated the practice of interregional personnel transfers to break up local cliques, created a central office to hear complaints about local abuses of power and privilege, and established the first control commission to monitor the compliance of local officials. Krestinskii envisioned a rational–legal bureaucratic order for the new Soviet Russian state, based on the latest advances in scientific management.[18]

Krestinskii's office, however, sorely lacked the resources needed to build such a state infrastructure. In practice, his anticorruption campaign proved an ineffective means of extending the center's administrative reach. These policies simply antagonized regional officials, who remained firmly entrenched in local political machines. Krestinskii's political downfall came after less than two years on the job. At a party congress, in early 1921, he was roundly criticized for his handling of regional administrative affairs, leading one speaker to mourn that "the place left vacant by Sverdlov was still not filled."[19] To make matters worse, Krestinskii had lost Lenin's confidence as a result of his benign tolerance of an internal party faction that had been openly critical of Lenin's command–administrative methods. Krestinskii could not even muster the minimal support necessary to remain a member of the central committee, falling short by almost eighty votes.[20] Following the congress, he was transferred to foreign affairs and diplomatic exile in Germany.

In the spring of 1921, Viacheslav Mikhailovich Molotov was promoted from the ranks of regional administration to succeed Krestinskii as secretary of the central committee. Molotov was a core member of a personal network based in the Viatka-Volga region. During the civil war, he worked in Nizhnyi Novgorod and in the Donbas region of Ukraine.[21] Although his prerevolutionary experiences included higher education and legal party work, Molotov identified with the underworld of the party's komitetchik cohort. On his questionnaire for the Society of Bolsheviks, he claimed "professional revolutionary" for his prerevolutionary service, instead of *intelligenty*.[22] In his new post, he displayed much greater sympathy toward regional officials than had Krestinskii. Molotov promised to extend the reach of the new state by improving the administrative performance of the center, instead of attacking the regional leaders. He proposed to update the personnel files of regional officials, to routinize the process of information gathering from the regions, and to devise a more effective means for disseminating central instructions to the regions. Meanwhile, the anticorruption campaign was quietly brought to a halt and the complaints office was closed. The practice of transferring local officials for disciplinary reasons continued under Molotov, although the criterion for reassignment became factional politics, rather than professional ethics.[23]

Before the year was over, a special commission, headed by the respected Old Bolshevik Viktor Nogin, was formed to evaluate the center's supervision of the regions. The investigation revealed that the party's central administrative offices were badly mismanaged. Within the organizational department, for example, no effort was made to coordinate the work of an overstaffed informational office, which collected data on local conditions, with an understaffed instructional department, which maintained liaisons with local party organizations. "Moving from one office to the other," Nogin described, "is like entering another realm, encountering a completely different approach to affairs."[24] Personnel files of regional leaders were often incomplete and in some cases nonexistent. Nogin expressed dismay that these "veritable unknowns" had turned the party's central administrative office into their own personal fiefdom.[25]

The findings of the Nogin Commission caused a small scandal for Molotov. Lenin responded typically in several terse and critical letters. "The power of the central committee is huge," he reminded Molotov, yet "in these important posts sit idiots and pedants. The affairs of communism are spoiled by dull-witted bureaucratism."[26] In the wake of the Nogin Commission's report, two central committee secretaries, two department heads and one assistant department head were sacked. Molotov was not removed, but demoted to a less responsible post. In his place, Lenin turned to a trusted and long-time member of his inner circle, Iosif Vissarionovich Stalin.

In May 1922, Stalin was offically named general secretary of the party's central committee. Stalin distinguished himself early as one of Lenin's chief troubleshooters. At the time of his appointment, Stalin's credentials as an authority on administration in the new Soviet state were unsurpassed. He was included in nearly all of the small planning and decision-making groups organized by Lenin.[27] More significantly, he was well experienced in regional administrative affairs. His resume included: the party's resident nationalities expert, member of Sverdlov's constitutional commission, and chair of the Viatka Commission, which investigated the collapse of Soviet power in the Urals during the civil war. As Robert Tucker has rightly noted, Stalin at this time saw himself as "the successor to Sverdlov."[28]

With his appointment to the party's central secretariat, his early personal ambition was fulfilled.

Lenin's selection of Stalin indicated that his understanding of administration in the new Soviet state had not changed significantly over four and a half years. Lenin's displeasure with Molotov in 1922, for example, was not for the increasing concentration of formal powers in the central secretariat, but rather for a leadership style that underutilized these powers. Lenin generally favored the trend toward greater centralization in political and economic relations with the regions. Lenin passed this responsibility to Stalin with full knowledge that the central party apparat was already becoming a political force and that Stalin would not shrink from employing its powers. As T. H. Rigby expressed: "The ability to 'exert pressure' was what Lenin prized so highly in Stalin."[29]

When Stalin's appointment was criticized, Lenin responded that postrevolutionary circumstances dictated the choice and that "a better candidate than Comrade Stalin could not be named."[30] Lenin understood the problems of building administrative structures in the new state in terms of the personal character and capabilities of organizational leaders. He consistently advocated centralized political and economic administrative forms as a way to insulate state power from the petit bourgeois and "anarchist" forces which, he believed, pervaded postrevolutionary Russian society.[31] Even Lenin's final writings, which were highly critical of Stalin, do not suggest a fundamental revision of this view; rather, they dwell on Stalin's personal shortcomings.

Joining Stalin and Molotov in the central secretariat at this time was another veteran of the Bolshevik prerevolutionary underground, Valerian Vladimirovich Kuibyshev. In 1917, Kuibyshev was a leading figure in the establishment of Soviet power in Samara. During the civil war, he served as political commissar to Red Army forces that reclaimed the Middle and Lower Volga and Central Asia.[33] On Lenin's recommendation, Kuibyshev was promoted to economic administration in Moscow, including a position in the new high-profile Main Department for the Electrification of Russia.[34] After serving one year in the party's central secretariat, Kuibyshev was reassigned to head the enlarged and restructured central control apparat. Under Kuibyshev, the control apparat became one of the principal organizational forces in the centralization of regional administration in the mid-1920s.

In June 1922, Lazar Moseevich Kaganovich was appointed to head the central committee's organizational–instructional department, overseeing regional affairs.[35] Kaganovich worked in the Ukrainian underground and

in Nizhnyi Novgorod and Central Asia during the civil war. Kaganovich
was considered an energetic and capable local leader and an early advocate
of the centralization of regional administration.[36] He was personally singled out by Lenin as an up-and-coming future party leader.[37] Boris Bazhanov, who assisted Kaganovich in the central apparat, described him as
"lively and intelligent, always comprehending things quickly."[38] Molotov
remembered him as "a tremendous organizer, but coarse. He was a Stalinist
two hundred percent."[39] In his memoirs, Nikita Khrushchev begrudgingly
complemented his former political patron and later rival: "Kaganovich was
a man who got things done. If the central committee put an axe in his
hands, he would chop up a storm; unfortunately he often chopped down
the healthy trees with the rotten ones. But the chips really flew, you
couldn't take that away from him."[40]

The assembling of this new team around Stalin in 1922 marked the
end of the search for central leadership over regional administration that
had begun with Sverdlov's untimely death. This team was instrumental in
shaping the subsequent development of center–regional relations in the
new Soviet state. They quickly moved to consolidate organizational resources in the center in the party secretariat and the control bureaucracy.
They continued the practice, begun by Sverdlov, of utilizing personal network ties as the means by which the center supervised regional administration. Each member of the team had personal ties with different regional networks. Stalin was connected to a southern regional network,
based in the Transcaucasus. While Stalin had not spent any significant
length of time working in the regions since his years in the Georgian underground, he was a close friend of Grigorii Kostantinovich ("Sergo") Ordzhonikidze, who was the core member of the Transcaucasian network.
Ordzhonikidze eventually joined the central leadership in 1926, securing
the center's ties to the Transcaucasus. Molotov was connected to the
Viatka-Volga regional network from the underground and civil war period, which included the strategic industrial center of Nizhnyi Novgorod.
Kaganovich's network ties were mainly in Ukraine, where he worked in
the underground and later in postrevolutionary regional administration.
He was also connected to the Central Asian region. Kuibyshev was the
core member of personal networks in the Middle Volga and Central Asian
regions. An informal division of labor existed among the members of this
team by which they were made responsible for administrative affairs in
the regions to which they were personally connected.[41]

II. INTERSECTION OF INFORMAL AND FORMAL STRUCTURES: DEVELOPING A CAPACITY FOR TERRITORIAL ADMINISTRATION

Regionally based personal networks provided the center with an informal social mechanism by which the new state was able to administer the periphery. As the civil war came to an end, the Bolshevik *druzhina* began to move into regional administrative work. These wartime network members tended to find work in the local party committees. During the 1920s, personal networks became embedded in the territorial party apparatus. But simply the movement of personal networks into local political organs did not facilitate the extension of central administrative capacities to the periphery. Indeed, in the early 1920s, personal networks often acted as a constraint against the center's attempts to administer particular regions. In these regions, the structure of network ties indicated limited reach and core members remained located in the region. Efforts to uproot these inwardly structured networks frequently led to protracted power struggles.[42] The new state's capacity for territorial administration, however, was gradually enhanced as regional network ties were restructured outwardly. By the end of the decade, regional network ties exhibited more extensive cross-regional reach and the relocation of core members to the center.

This process occurred in two successive stages: at the regional level, where personal network ties were stretched horizontally; and, at the central level, where personal network ties were stretched vertically. In the first stage, new "regional" administrative bodies were created, linking the center and the provinces. These new regional units consolidated smaller administrative–territorial units into a horizontally structured whole. The leaders of these administrative units were the core members of personal networks based in the region. They employed their network ties to carry out the tasks of political consolidation in the reconquered peripheral territories.[43] The second stage involved the promotion of core network members from the regions into the center. In this way, network ties were extended vertically, providing the state center with an informal social structure to help extend its reach to the regions.

To begin, the "regionalization" of the state's administrative framework marked the first step in the process of developing a state capacity for territorial administration. The revolutions of 1917 and the civil war caused the collapse of the institutions that had long connected center and regions in the old regime. These events gave rise to a spontaneous wave of localist movements, seeking greater autonomy or in some cases independence from the new Bolshevik center. Centrifugal forces spread across the periphery from the non-Russian borderlands, to remote regions of Siberia, and even to the heartland provinces of European Russia.[44] This resurgent localism led to the parcelization of the preexisting regional administrative structure. Between 1917 and 1921, the number of provinces (*guberniia*) increased from 64 to 93, the number of districts (*uezd*) from 567 to 701, and the number of counties (*volost*) from 10,622 to 15,064.[45]

The new state was incapable of containing the process of territorial–administrative restructuring "from below." This rampant localism aptly demonstrated the underdeveloped administrative capacities of the new state. Even the Bolshevik party as yet could not provide a formal organizational structure to help impose some administrative order on the regions. A survey of forty local party committees conducted in October 1920 found, to the chagrin of central leaders, that no two had the same internal organizational scheme.[46] Further, local party committees were in many places dominated by personal cliques, which displayed "local chauvinism" by actively resisting incorporation into a new centralized administrative command chain.[47] Merle Fainsod observed that "the effectiveness of Communist controls decreased in direct relationship to the distance from the great urban areas."[48]

In response, central leaders devised a strategy of "regionalization" of the administrative structure of the new state. Regionalization meant the creation of a new administrative tier between the center and the traditional Russian provinces. The regional administrative structure incorporated groups of provinces on the basis of common economic, geographic and ethnic criteria. The party first adopted a regional structure as a strategy to organize the emerging underground committees in the peripheral territories during the civil war. After the war, the regional scheme was further extended and applied to the government's ministerial bureacracy as well. This regional territorial–administrative structure was used from the early 1920s to the mid-1930s, when the state finally returned to a revised version of the traditional tsarist territorial–administrative framework.

In the spring of 1920, regional (*oblastnyi*) bureaus were officially introduced for Siberia, the Transcaucasus and the Urals. Within a year, regional bureaus also were established for the Far East, the Northwest, Turkestan (Central Asia), the Southeast (North Caucasus), and Kirgizia (Kazakhstan). They were administered by the party's central organs and described as the "fully-empowered representative of the central committee" in these regions. Regional bureaus were authorized to coordinate the political and economic activities of the individual provinces within their jurisdictions, to pass on information and central directives and to intervene directly into local political affairs when local officials strayed too far from central guidelines. Where local party organizations did not yet exist, regional bureaus were responsible for their creation.[49]

The leadership of the regional bureaus was entrusted to many of the same party leaders, who served as political commissars in the civil war.[50] Securing access to the organizational resources of the regional bureaus enabled these particular regional leaders to displace or absorb rival local personal networks. The members of their civil war *druzhina* were strategically placed into key local positions throughout the region. These personal networks were used to distribute scarce resources, to exchange information and to coordinate activities. In this way, civil war *druzhina* provided the informal social structure around which regional political machines were constructed.

The regional bureaus developed a "patrimonial" system of infrastructural power. The bureaus, for example, conducted face-to-face meetings with local leaders. Personal interaction became the principal means by which the bureaus attempted to bring central authority to the periphery. At first, local secretaries were required periodically to attend meetings of the regional bureau to report on local affairs and answer questions. As their staffs expanded, instructors were routinely dispatched by the bureaus to attend provincial meetings. For example, between March 1921 and December 1922, the Southeast bureau heard twenty-five reports from Stavropol party officials, 18 reports each from Terek and Kubano-Chernomorsk, 11 reports from the Don, and 10 reports from the Mountain region. Meanwhile, between April and August in 1921, Siberian bureau instructors participated in 17 provincial meetings; and, between October 1921 and July 1922, Northwest bureau instructors participated in 15 provincial meetings.[51]

The regional bureaus also became involved with a variety of other tasks. The Far East bureau, for example, engaged in military matters to a much greater extent and for a much longer period than other bureaus. Although the military occupation of Western Siberia and the Far East by former tsarist officers had collapsed in the winter of 1919, pockets of resistance remained until the mid-1920s.[52] In addition to political administrative consolidation, the bureaus worked toward the economic integration of the regions into the new state. The Far East bureau nationalized large, privately owned industrial enterprises.[53] The Transcaucasus bureau assumed direct control over railroads and foreign trade.[54] And, the Central Asian bureau introduced a unified currency system and organized a series of land and water reforms.[55]

The regionalization strategy was employed in the first major territorial–

administrative reform of the new state. The Bolsheviks inherited a territorial–administrative framework that had not changed significantly since
Catherine's reign in the late eighteenth century. Regionalization was seen
not just as a political instrument, but as a necessary precondition for
economic development. A proposal to restructure the territorial–administrative framework of the state was presented to the central leadership by a
special commission in March 1921.[56] The proposal favored the abandonment of the tsarist territorial–administrative scheme (*guberniia*, *uezd*, and
volost) in favor of a new set of administrative units (*oblast* or *krai*, *okrug*,
and *raion*). The new units were fewer in number and larger in size. The
new scheme would reflect the predominant economic activity in a region,
the consolidation of local population around an industrial center, the
existence of working lines of communication and transportation, and the
ethnic composition of the local population.[57]

The implementation of the plan, however, was delayed by the protests
of local leaders.[58] A modified version of the plan went into effect on an
experimental basis in the spring of 1923. The Urals region was chosen as
a test site because of its complementary economic sectors and ethnic
homogeneity.[59] The reform consolidated four existing provinces (*guberniia*)
into a single regional unit (*oblast*). Below the *oblast*, fifteen new medium-
sized administrative units were created (*okrug*). Each *okrug* was supposed to
reflect an individual economic specialty, so that as a whole they would
compose an interdependent self-sustaining regional economy. Below the
okrug, new local administrative units (*raion*) were formed by consolidating
the existing local units (*volost*).[60] By 1925, 205 *raiony* existed in the Urals,
where once had been 984 *volosty*. The North Caucasus was the next region
to be organized as a regional administrative entity in 1925. By the end of
the decade, this territorial–administrative scheme was applied across the
entire Russian periphery outside the central industrial region, where the
historical provinces remained intact.

In the non-Russian periphery, a modified regionalization scheme was
applied to fit within the national–federal administrative framework. Non-
Russian regions were incorporated into a federal structure with the promulgation of the 1922 Union Treaty and the 1924 Soviet Constitution.[61]
The administrative units of the federal structure were defined by ethnic
boundaries, consolidating non-Russian peoples into discrete territorial enclaves. Several tiers of national political–administrative units (union republic, autonomous republic, autonomous *oblast*, and autonomous *okrug*) were
formed largely on the basis of population size, geographic location and
cultural identity. Some union republics, including Ukraine and Belorussia,
adopted internal administrative structures similar to the Russian *oblasty*

during the 1920s. To this extent, these national republican administrative units served as the rough equivalent to the new regional administrative units. Despite the federal structure, individual national republics in the Transcaucasus and Central Asia remained subordinated to overarching transregional administrative organs until the second half of the 1930s.

Not surprisingly, regionalization was met by hostility and resistance from local political machines. The process was disparaged by one local leader as "good for nothing."[62] Numerous disputes between the new regional authorities and existing local cliques arose during the implementation phase. Local resistance in the Far East, for example, became so blatant and routine that Moscow issued a special directive stating that "the Far East bureau of the RKP(b) is the single highest party center in the Far East, and therefore the separate actions of individual party organizations in the Far East is completely intolerable."[63] In September 1921, the central committee published a general statement reaffirming the subordination of all lower-level administrative organs to the regional bureaus.[64]

Those personal networks that gained control of the new regional administrative organs were placed in a strategically superior position. They secured a monopolistic control over the distribution of centrally allocated organizational and material resources for the region. These resource-advantaged networks were able to dislodge or subsume their regional rivals. In the late 1920s, they uprooted the "NEP coalitions" from local administration in the major agricultural regions in anticipation of collectivization.[65]

The second phase in the intersection of informal and formal structures was the promotion into the state center of the core members of regionally based personal networks. An examination of the individuals occupying the central leadership posts from the civil war period through the first half of the thirties indicates the upward movement of regional network members.[66] Between 1919 and 1925, twenty-six individuals held central leadership positions of which only five were regional leaders. Between 1927 and 1934, however, twenty-three individuals occupied central leadership positions of which fourteen were regional leaders.

As core network members moved to the center in the mid- to late twenties, they named fellow network members to their regional leadership posts. These newly appointed regional leaders subsequently assumed responsibility for overseeing the lower levels of the administrative apparatus. This process of upward promotion did not severe network ties; instead, these ties took on a vertical dimension within the formal administrative structures of the state. Table 4.1 lists the first party secretaries, in 1929 and in 1934, of the major administrative-territorial regions beyond the

Table 4.1. Leadership in Rural Russian and Non-Russian
Regions, 1929, 1934

| | First Party Secretary | |
Region	1929	1934
1. Western	Rumiantsev	Rumiantsev
2. Central Black Earth	Vareikis	Vareikis
3. Lower Volga	Sheboldaev	Krinitskii
4. Middle Volga	Khataevich	Shubrikov
5. Urals	Kabakov	Kabakov
6. Siberia	Eikhe	Eikhe
7. Far East	na	Kartvelishvili
8. Ukraine	Kosior	Kosior
9. Belorussia	Gamarnik	Gikalo
10. Crimea	Kostanian	Semenov
11. North Caucasus	Andreev	Sheboldaev
12. Transcaucasus	Orakhelashvili	Beria
13. Kazakhstan	Goloshchekin	Mirzoian
14. Uzbekistan	Ikramov	Ikramov

central industrial region. Table 4.2 then presents a matrix indicating the
informal ties, which linked the 1929 and the 1934 regional leadership
groups to the central leadership.[67]

During this period, an increase occurred in the cross-regional reach of
informal network ties across formal territorial administrative lines. When
informal network ties are taken into account, it suggests that the regional
leadership was not beset by constant change, but instead experienced
relative stability. The leadership changes in Table 4.1, for example, reveal
that turnover was far more common in the non-Russian regions than in
the Russian regions. But even in the non-Russian regions continuity existed in the informal connections to the center. Nikolai Gikalo in Belorussia and Lev Mirzoian in Kazakhstan were both members of the Transcaucasian network and had personal ties with Ordzhonikidze and Kirov.[68]
Meanwhile, other regional leaders were simply transferred horizontally,
which did not severe their informal network ties to central actors. Mendel
Khataevich (who does not appear on the 1934 list) moved from the Middle
Volga to the Dnepropetrovsk province in Ukraine; Boris Sheboldaev moved
from the Lower Volga to the neighboring North Caucasus region.

Table 4.2. Network Ties between Central Leadership and Regional
Leadership, 1929 and 1934

	Andreev	Chubar	Kaganovich	Kalinin	Kirov	Kosior	Kuibyshev	Mikoian	Molotov	Ordzhonikidze	Petrovskii	Rudzutak	Stalin	Syrtsov[a]	Voroshilov	Totals
Andreev[a]	X	0	1	0	1	0	0	0	1	0	0	0	0	0	0	3
Beria[b]	0	0	0	0	1	0	0	1	0	1	0	0	0	X	0	3
Eikhe	0	0	0	0	0	1	1	0	0	0	0	1	0	0	0	3
Gamarnik[a]	0	1	1	0	0	1	0	0	0	0	1	0	0	0	0	4
Gikalo[b]	0	0	0	0	1	0	0	1	0	1	0	0	0	X	0	3
Goloshchekin[a]	0	0	0	0	0	0	1	0	0	0	0	X	0	0	0	1
Ikramov	0	0	1	0	0	0	1	0	0	0	0	1	0	0	0	3
Kabakov	0	0	1	0	0	0	1	0	1	0	0	0	0	0	0	3
Kartvelishvili[b]	0	1	1	0	1	1	0	1	0	1	1	0	1	X	1	9
Khataevich[a]	0	0	0	0	0	0	1	0	0	0	0	0	0	0	0	1
Kosior	0	1	1	0	0	X	0	0	0	1	1	0	0	0	1	5
Kostanian[a]	0	0	0	0	1	0	0	1	0	1	0	0	0	0	0	3
Krinitskii[b]	0	0	0	1	0	0	0	0	0	0	0	0	0	X	0	1
Mirzoian[b]	0	0	0	0	1	0	0	1	0	1	0	0	0	X	0	3
Orakhelashvili[a]	0	0	0	0	1	0	0	1	0	1	0	0	1	1	1	6
Rumiantsev	0	0	0	0	1	0	0	0	1	1	0	0	0	0	0	3
Semenov[c]	0	0	0	0	0	0	0	0	0	0	0	0	0	X	0	0
Sheboldaev	0	0	0	0	1	0	0	1	0	1	0	1	0	1	1	6
Shubrikov[c]	0	0	0	0	0	0	1	0	0	0	0	0	0	0	0	1
Vareikis	0	0	1	0	1	1	1	0	0	1	0	1	0	0	1	7
Totals	0	3	7	1	10	4	7	7	3	10	3	4	2	2	5	

[a] *Held position in 1929 only.*
[b] *Held position in 1934 only.*
[c] *Held position in 1934 only; incomplete information on early career.*

The rise to power in the regions of dominant personal networks, whose ties extended across the territorial and organizational boundaries of the region and whose core network members moved into the center, created a web of informal relations which provided an underlying mechanism for the development of the new state's capacities for territorial administration and revenue extraction. The next section demonstrates this process in action through a case study of the Transcaucasian regional network.

III. PERSONAL NETWORKS AND TERRITORIAL ADMINISTRATION: THE TRANSCAUCASIAN NETWORK

This section presents the findings of an investigation of the Transcaucasian regional network based mainly on archival sources previously unavailable to Western scholars.[69] Using personal correspondences, biographical data, and official personnel files, the study attempts to piece together the informal ties of the Transcaucasian regional network and to discern the ways in which these ties were employed to enhance the state's capacity for territorial administration.

The Transcaucasus region provides a good example of the process by which personal networks intersected with the new regional administrative structures. In the prerevolutionary period, the Bolshevik party was not at all well established in the Transcaucasus (Georgia, Armenia, Azerbaijan, North Caucasus) with the exception of Baku, the capital of Azerbaijan and center of the oil industry.[70] The Transcaucasian regional network was most strongly shaped by civil war experiences as new members enlisted, personal ties were strengthened and hierarchical relationship patterns were defined. At this time, formal organizational structures simply did not exist for the Transcaucasian Bolsheviks. When the Red Army eventually made its way into the region, Bolsheviks emerged from the underground to join the military campaigns. Military–revolutionary committees (MRCs) were formed to consolidate the army's territorial gains. The Bolshevik underground network provided personnel and structure for these committees.

Sergo Ordzhonikidze and Sergei Kirov were appointed as leaders of the Transcaucasian MRCs.[71] Correspondence found in the personal archives of Ordzhonikidze and Kirov demonstrate the utilization of network ties to establish a regional base for the new state. As regional leader, Ordzhonikidze quickly developed a system of information gathering built on preexisting network ties. He relied almost exclusively on network ties (Kirov, Kvirikeli, Gikalo) to track the progress of territorial consolidation in the mountainous and ethnically fractious North Caucasus.[72] In the campaign to incorporate independent Georgia by force into the new Soviet state, Ordzhonikidze relied on network ties (Eliava, Orakhelashvili) to coordinate the military and political aspects of the takeover and, later, to staff the formal positions of power in Soviet Georgia.[73] Similarly, in early 1920, Kirov and Mikoian relied exclusively on personal network ties to open supply and communication lines between the North Caucasus and advancing Red Army forces.[74] In June 1919, when Kirov had to report to Lenin and Stalin on the progress of establishing Soviet power in Armenia, he based his assessment almost exclusively on a letter he had recently received from Mikoian.[75]

In 1920, a "regional bureau" was created for the Transcaucasus. The regional bureau became the main institutional link between the Transcaucasus and the state center in the decade following the civil war. The creation of the regional bureau marked the intersection of informal and formal structures in the Transcaucasus. This nascent formal organization for territorial administration was constructed upon the preexisting informal ties of Ordzhonikidze's Transcaucasian network. Members of the network came to dominate the formal positions of power in the regional bureau. Ordzhonikidze and Kirov were appointed to the top leadership of the bureau. In 1921, a separate regional bureau was formed for the North Caucasus region, headed by Anastas Mikoian, another core member of the Transcaucasian network. Much as they had done in the underground and in the civil war military campaigns, these leaders employed their informal network ties to perform the task of territorial administration.

The establishment of a Transcaucasian administrative tier provided Ordzhonikidze and Kirov with an opportunity to extend the influence of their civil war network. Ordzhonikidze aggressively sought to appoint his own network clients to positions of power throughout the region, which in turn provoked a bitter intraregional network competition. Rival network groups resisted the creation of the new regional administrative unit. In particular, a Georgian network, which centered around Budu Mdivani and Filip Makharadze, strongly protested incorporation into the new regional organ and instead sought to maintain direct relations to the center. The conflict became particularly ugly when at a meeting between the two warring networks a representative of the Georgian group referred to Ordzhonikidze as "Stalin's ass." Never one to conceal his true emotions, the hot-tempered Ordzhonikidze responded by promptly thumping the man.[76] Despite incurring the wrath of Lenin for his actions, Ordzhonikidze recognized that control over the new Transcaucasian regional body was a patronage prize worth fighting for. The victory of Ordzhonikidze's and Kirov's network was finally consolidated in the spring of 1923, at the first Transcaucasian regional congress. The meeting provided an official occasion to expel 116 Mensheviks from the party, most of whom were members of the rival Georgian network.[77]

As informal network ties fused with formal state structures, core network members gained greater access to the financial resources and valued goods distributed from the center. Regional party leaders and their staffs were besieged with requests for financial assistance, food, housing, employment, and education. These scarce resources were distributed in a way that rewarded and reinforced network ties. Ordzhonikidze's office was able to secure admittance to a higher technical school in Moscow for the son of Gegechkora, a former colleague in the Georgian underground.[78] In a private letter to Ordzhonikidze, Kirov described an overwhelming demand for financial resources coming from local party organizations. As a consequence of the chronic shortage of revenues, Kirov chose to dispense funds to Gikalo, with whom he shared a personal tie, while other local organizations, at least on this occasion, had to go without.[79]

In the second half of the 1920s, core members of the Transcaucasian network began to move out of the region to the state center or to other regions. In 1926, Ordzhonikidze, Kirov, and Mikoian were promoted into the party's central executive organ, the politburo, as candidate members. In addition, they moved into new formal positions with access to vast organizational resources: Ordzhonikidze to the central control apparatus, Kirov to the Leningrad party organization, and Mikoian to the commissariat of internal and external trade.

Network members with whom they shared strong ties, in turn, were promoted in their place into leadership posts within the region. Ordzhonikidze's replacement as head of the Transcaucasian party organization was Mamia Orakhelashvili, with whom he had formed an informal tie in the civil war and early political–administrative work.[80] He was described in *Pravda* as Ordzhonikidze's "close friend" and "wartime counselor."[81] Orakhelashvili also shared a personal tie with Kirov, with whom he had worked closely in the North Caucasus during the consolidation of Soviet power.[82] In addition, Amaiak Nazaretian, with whom Ordzhonikidze and Kirov shared a personal tie, was also named to the regional party leadership.[83] Orakhelashvili and Nazaretian were eventually removed from the Transcaucasian leadership only to be replaced by another client of Ordzhonikidze, Beso Lominadze. In Azerbaijan, Levon Mirzoian and Nikolai Gikalo, who shared personal ties to Kirov, were promoted to leadership positions.[84] In this way, the Transcaucasian network developed a vertical dimension as informal ties were stretched from the region to the center.

By the late 1920s and early 1930s, the Transcaucasian network had developed an extensive reach across the regional and formal organizational structures of the postrevolutionary state. The regional leaders at this time who were also members of the Transcaucasian network included: Boris Sheboldaev in the Lower Volga and the North Caucasus, Levon Mirzoian in the Urals region and Kazakhstan, Iosif Vareikis in the Central Black Earth region, and Nikolai Gikalo in Belorussia.

Significantly, as core network members moved into new formal positions outside the region, they continued to engage their informal ties as they had always done. Personal network ties provided members with an informal social structure along which information was exchanged, valued resources were obtained and activities were coordinated. Ordzhonikidze provided insight into how central patrons used this informal structure to ensure the continued compliance of their regionally based clients in a letter rebuking Lominadze for publicly voicing disagreement with central policy. "You know exactly what I am driving at," Ordzhonikidze reminded Lominadze, "a cat knows who feeds him."[85] The archival findings showed that personal network ties were used in such ways to facilitate the development of a capacity for territorial administration at a time when the state's formal administrative mechanisms were still not reliable beyond the central industrial region.

A basic aspect of territorial administration, for example, is information exchange. Yet, as late as 1930, the state center by its own admission was incapable of knowing whether local organizations were even aware of its decisions, let alone fulfilling them.[86] More than one-third of the North Caucasus region at this time remained without telephone and telegraph connections.[87] In the Transcaucasus, network ties served as a principal means by which the center was able to disseminate information about policy priorities to the region as well as to gather information about regional affairs. Personal correspondence found in Ordzhonikidze's archive showed that after his promotion to the center he regularly monitored events in the region through his informal ties to Orakhelashvili and Nazaretian.[88] These letters typically included information about personal affairs, a steady stream of gossip from the region, and, more significantly, mutual consultations on policy matters. By such informal means, Ordzhonikidze directed the reorganization of economic administration in Georgia in anticipation of the five-year plan.[89] Through other network ties, Ordzhonikidze monitored political developments in Georgia, Azerbaijan, and Armenia for the center during the late twenties and early thirties. His informal supervision of the regional leadership continued into the early thirties, even though he was by that time employed in the central industrial bureaucracy with no formal responsibility for regional political affairs.[90]

Kirov, likewise, relied on informal ties to network members in Azerbaijan, Mirzoian and Khanbudagov, to gather information about regional affairs and to emphasize the center's policy priorities. In 1928, over two years after he had departed the region, Kirov still employed a personal network tie to Kartvelishvili in Georgia in order to insist that local officials immediately undertake the establishment of production trusts in the economy.[92] And, in 1931, Kirov instructed Central Black Earth regional party leader Iosif Vareikis, with whom he shared a strong network tie, on the implementation of a program to resettle peasants uprooted by the collectivization campaign.[93]

Another aspect of territorial administration is personnel policy and the resolution of local disputes. From the mid-1920s to the early 1930s, Transcaucasian regional politics was riven by intraorganizational feuds and power struggles. Again, despite their formal departures, Ordzhonikidze and Kirov continued to direct personnel policy and to broker power conflicts in the region. Kirov involved himself in personnel politics on numerous occasions. In 1926, for example, six months after his transfer to Leningrad, he intervened to resolve an internal dispute between the party organization and the control bureaucracy in Azerbaijan; in 1928, he overturned the decision of the Transcaucasian regional bureau to reassign Khanjian outside Georgia; in 1929, he directly appointed a new party leader, Gurzof Osipov, to the local organization in Astrakhan.[94] Similarly, Ordzhonikidze received a steady barrage of personal correspondence from various actors who sought to secure his favor in the seemingly endless leadership struggles and interethnic conflicts that marked Transcaucasian politics at this time.[95]

The interventions of core network members into regional administrative affairs were especially common in the first years of the state's radical campaign for economic restructuring. The plan for rapid industrialization called for a comprehensive reorganization of the rural economy, consolidating small peasant holdings into large collective farms. In this way, the state sought to develop a system in which revenue, in the form of agricultural products, would be extracted directly from the agrarian sector and reallocated to the industrial sectors of the economy. The state's initial plunge into collectivization, however, generated widespread social unrest and economic crises. This situation was exacerbated by the underdeveloped organizational capabilities of regional administrators. While bogus information routinely passed from villages to regional leaders to central planners, central economic plans often failed to reach their intended destinations along the territorial-administrative command chain.

Collectivization proved especially difficult to realize in the predominantly rural Transcaucasus, where private, small holdings had long characterized the structure of agriculture. Moreover, as the region was not a major grain-producing area, some Transcaucasian leaders favored a moderate implementation schedule. Ordzhonikidze and Kirov were forced to intervene frequently into local affairs during the first two years of the campaign to ensure regional compliance with the center's more radical implementation schedules.[96] One notable example involving Kirov came to be known as "the Azerbaijan affair." By the autumn of 1930, Azerbaijan had fallen so far behind in its implementation of collectivization policies that the state center ordered an investigation of the regional leadership. Although Kirov had not formally worked in the republic for almost four years, he was charged with the task of sorting out the political blame, recommending solutions to the center, and reasserting the center's implementation priorities in the republic.[97]

It is significant to note that Kirov continued to use informal ties to individuals from the Transcaucasian network even after they were transferred to posts outside the region to define policy priorities and to guide the implementation process.[98] Levon Mirzoian, for example, was named party head of Kazakhstan in late 1932. He was assigned the task of developing a grain production sector and integrating it with the central economy in this geographically remote and undeveloped region. While Kirov had never previously been involved in Kazakhstan administrative affairs, he quickly developed regular informal communications with Mirzoian. Kirov instructed Mirzoian on the internal organization of collective farms, grain production quotas and bread allocations.[99] Kirov further lobbied the head of the central railroad administration on Mirzoian's behalf for the construction of a new railroad line connecting Kazakhstan to Soviet Russia's central industrial region.[100] In this way, the cross-regional reach of the Transcaucasian network ties enhanced the center's capacity to administer the periphery.

As the state campaign for economic restructuring unfolded, central planners showed themselves incapable of efficiently reallocating resources across regions. The campaign was at once threatened by chronic and widespread shortages of material resources.[101] Again, archival sources show that personal network ties were employed to supplement the shortcomings of the state's new formal administrative–command structures. Kirov was especially adept at using network ties to bypass the central planners in

obtaining badly needed material and human resources. When food shortages occurred in the early thirties, Kirov was able to secure extra supplies
by making direct appeals to Boris Sheboldaev in the North Caucasus for
bread, Iosif Vareikis in the Central Black Earth region for vegetables and
Ivan Rumiantsev in the Western region for potatoes.[102] Although these
individuals were now party leaders in various Russian agricultural regions,
they shared ties to Kirov through the Transcaucasian regional network.[103]
During the 1932 grain crisis, Kirov used his personal ties to Ordzhonikidze and Mikoian in the center to obtain "vodka and spirits" for Leningrad's factory workers for the new year holiday.[104] In 1933, Kirov used his
network tie to Nikolai Gikalo, who had recently been appointed party
head of Belorussia, to request a transfer of available workers from Belorussia
for Leningrad's growing industrial labor force.[105]

By providing a means for information exchange, resource allocation and
coordinated action, the Transcaucasian personal network served as an informal power resource facilitating the development of a capacity for territorial
administration in the new Soviet Russian state. In so doing, the findings
suggest an answer to the larger question at the outset of the chapter: How
did the "infrastructurally" weak Soviet Russian state carry out such an
extensive economic reform in the early thirties? While coercion and social
forces were both part of this process, neither explains sufficiently how the
new state implemented and managed these policies across Soviet Russia's
vast periphery. In this regard, the intersection of informal network ties and
formal organizational structures offers an alternative to existing explanations of how the new Soviet Russian state successfully strengthened its
"infrastructural" powers.

5

THE CONSTRAINTS OF POWER: PERSONAL NETWORKS AND CENTRAL RULERSHIP

The Bolsheviks came to power with great ambitions. Across a vast territory and underdeveloped economy, they aspired to build the world's first socialist state. In the early 1930s, they put their plans into action in a state-led campaign of rapid industrial development. In this effort, the state succeeded in building a command–administrative structure through which it ruled the regions and managed the economy for more than half a century. But as was demonstrated in the last chapter, the command–administrative system did not operate on strictly "bureaucratic" principles. The means of administering the new state relied to a large extent on personalistic structures. The state, in fact, rested on a "patrimonial" system of "infrastructural" power. For central state leaders, the patrimonial system of infrastructural power directly impinged upon their exclusive claim on the "despotic" powers of the state.

The intersection of informal and formal structures served to strengthen infrastructural power, but at the same time it formed constraints on despotic power in the new state. An examination of the formal chain of command in the new state would show that, in principle, bureaucratic and coercive powers were clearly concentrated in the state center. But the flow of power was distorted by the intersection of informal personal networks with formal organizational structures. As a result, the interactions between central and regional leaders were constrained by this intersection of informal and formal sources of power. Central state leaders may have had access to bureaucratic and coercive power resources, but they never used them during the period when these underlying constraints were in place. By such means, the Provincial Komitetchiki sought to share in the despotic powers of the state.

This chapter examines three aspects of the intersection of informal personal network ties and formal bureaucratic lines of command, which constrained the despotic powers of central leaders: (1) The location of core network members in the center who at times acted as central patrons and protectors, (2) the cross-organizational reach of network ties, which at times muted the center's formal checking and coercive mechanisms, and (3) the strategic place of the Provincial Komitetchiki in the policy implementation process, which enabled them to build personal political machines in the regions.

I. PERSONAL NETWORKS, CENTRAL PATRONS, AND THE MODERATE BLOC

The intersection of informal and formal structures in the new state was especially notable in the composition of central state bodies. The upward promotion of core network members stretched network ties vertically from the regions to the state center. As demonstrated in the previous chapter, the verticalization of network ties provided an informal social structure that was employed by the center to extend its administrative reach to the periphery. But this informal structure worked in both directions. While it was used by central leaders to facilitate the policy implementation process in the regions, it was also used by regional leaders to gain access to the policy-making process in the center. Core network members located in the center served as informal conduits for the expression of regional interests. The Provincial Komitetchiki, in particular, routinely communicated a variety of requests as well as opinions to their central patrons.

By the early 1930s, the composition of central party and governmental organs was dominated by former underground committee workers and regional administrators. The influence of the Provincial Komitetchiki was especially strong in the party's politburo and central committee. Shortly after the revolution, the politburo emerged as the top decision-making organ in the new state. Between 1919 and 1924, not one full, or voting, member or one candidate, or consultative, member was from either the party's komitetchiki or regional administration.[1] By the second half of the decade, this situation was changing. A party congress, in December 1927, marked the beginning of the departure of the *intelligenty* from the central leadership, signaled by the ousting of Lev Trotsky, Grigorii Zinoviev, and Lev Kamenev from the politburo. They were replaced as full members by

Valerian Kuibyshev and Ian Rudzutak, former core members of the Middle Volga and Central Asian regional networks. All eight candidate members of the politburo, in 1927, were either engaged in or formerly engaged in regional administration. In June 1930, two regional leaders, Sergei Kirov in Leningrad and Stanislav Kosior in Ukraine, were elected full members of the politburo.[2]

Over this same period, the composition of the party's central committee also reflected the political ascent of the regional leadership. While the actual decision-making powers of the central committee declined during this time in relation to the party's smaller executive bodies, membership was still considered a formal indication of elite status. Further, the central committee provided a forum for policy debate into the early 1930s. In 1919, only two of nineteen full, or voting, members of the central committee formally held positions as regional leaders: Grigorii Zinoviev in Leningrad and Khristian Rakovskii in Ukraine. Both were from the party's *intelligenty* cohort. In 1922, two additional provincial leaders were named full members of the central committee: Ordzhonikidze in Transcaucasia and Ian Rudzutak in Central Asia. The regional party leadership steadily increased its representation in the central committee from this time. In 1924, nine of fifty full members were provincial party secretaries. In 1930, the figure rose to sixteen provincial party secretaries among the seventy full members. And, by 1934, twenty-two of seventy-one full members were provincial party leaders. Of the 139 total central committee members in 1934, including candidate members, forty-four were provincial party leaders, nearly one-third of the overall membership. An additional fifteen members of the overall central committee membership in 1934 were leaders of provincial governmental administrative organs.[3]

An intricate web of informal network ties connected central and regional actors at this time. This web provided an underlying support structure for what became known as the "moderate bloc" in Soviet leadership politics in the early 1930s. The moderate bloc consisted of a group of politburo members who periodically stood apart from Stalin to argue for less radical economic targets and to protect individual cadres in disfavor at Stalin's court.[4] The politburo members included in the so-called moderate bloc were the core members of the Transcaucasian and Middle Volga regional networks: Sergo Ordzhonikidze, Sergei Kirov and Valerian Kuibyshev.[5] These three central actors had the most extensive informal ties to the regional leadership (see Table 4.2).

These individuals were committed to the state's overall development plans and worked tirelessly to fulfill them. It would be inaccurate to depict these leaders as economic moderates, since they ardently supported the radical restructuring of the economy. In practice, however, they sometimes openly supported less radical implementation schedules. The moderate bloc members were personally connected to most of the Provincial Komitetchiki, who kept them informed on the state of affairs in their regions. Investigation into the personal correspondences of the moderate bloc politburo members showed that the Provincial Komitetchiki regularly used their informal ties to lobby their central patrons for relief from the burdens of fulfilling the center's radical economic plans. While the moderate bloc members did not automatically accommodate the requests of the Provincial Komitetchiki, they exhibited greater sensitivity to their concerns than did other politburo members at this time. By speaking out in favor of less radical economic plans when they did, Ordzhonikidze, Kirov, and Kuibyshev, directly or indirectly, were supporting the position of the Provincial Komitetchiki.

Transcaucasian network members besieged Ordzhonikidze with informal requests to ease the implementation schedule for collectivization.[6] While it is not evident that Ordzhonikidze directly responded to their pleas, the pace of implementation of collectivization in the Transcaucasus lagged considerably behind other regions. Several Transcaucasian regional leaders with close personal ties to Ordzhonikidze were later removed for opposing its widespread application to the region. For the second five year plan, the center's proposed target figures for industrial growth provoked an intense debate among the state's political and economic elites. Ordzhonikidze emerged as the main advocate of a less radical plan than the one initially endorsed by Molotov and Kuibyshev. The less radical target figures were supported by many regional leaders, including those with personal network ties to Ordzhonikidze.[7] Ordzhonikidze's position prevailed on this occasion and the modified growth figures were incorporated into the second five-year plan.[8]

Like Ordzhonikidze, Kirov was at the forefront of the state's campaign for rapid industrialization. To describe him as a moderate therefore is misleading. But again, like Ordzhonikidze, Kirov at times favored less radical industrial target figures than other central leaders.[9] After the disastrous 1932 harvest, moreover, Kirov began to speak out in favor of less radical target figures for the state's extraction of agricultural resources. He publicly criticized the continuation of the procurement "squeeze" on the peasantry, which, he warned, threatened to undermine the productivity of the agricultural sector.[10] This issue was of utmost importance to the Provincial Komitetchiki with whom Kirov shared personal network ties (see Chapter 6). Furthermore, in 1934, Kirov supported the Provincial Komitetchiki against the center on the issue of dismantling the political departments of machine-tractor stations, which had recently been created as a rival organization to the party committees in rural areas.[11] Kirov delivered a particularly harsh indictment of the performance of political departments in agricultural administration in Kazakhstan.[12] Central leaders shortly thereafter gave in to the regional leaders on this issue (see Chapter 7).

Of the members of the moderate bloc, Valerian Kuibyshev appeared to be less responsive to the petitions of former network members than were Ordzhonikidze and Kirov. Iosif Vareikis, for example, lobbied to have his region's grain procurement quota reduced as a result of bad weather.[13] Kuibyshev, however, refused to support Vareikis in this case, insisting that the procurement quota must be met "in order to feed the workers."[14] But while Vareikis was not successful in this particular attempt, Kuibyshev only recently had chaired a special committee that in fact lowered the center's grain procurement plans for several regional leaders, including Vareikis and Khataevich, both former members of Kuibyshev's Middle Volga network.[15] Hiroaki Kuromiya found evidence that Kuibyshev acted to moderate aspects of the state's initial industrialization plans by intervening to reduce several growth target figures in his examination of the first five-year plan.[16]

Besides economic issues, Ordzhonikidze and Kirov acted as central patrons by protecting their clients in the regions, when they fell into disfavor with the center. In the early and mid-1930s, Ordzhonikidze and Kirov intervened routinely to defend former members of the Transcaucasian regional network, especially Amaiak Nazaretian and Mamaia Orakhelishvili, who incurred the center's wrath for among other things their lack of enthusiasm for collectivization.[17] On another occasion, Ordzhonikidze refused to turn over to Stalin an incendiary letter written by Lominadze, explaining that he "gave his word" to Lominadze. In frustration, Stalin complained that Ordzhonikidze acted "like a feudal lord, even like a prince" in matters concerning his network clients.[18] Later in the decade, Ordzhonikidze emerged as the chief protector of the industrial managerial elite, the Red Directors, against more radical central leaders.[19] This situation, however, did not last. By the beginnning of 1937, Ordzhonikidze on his own now in the politburo could not prevent the arrest of his closest assistants or even his own brother.

In the early 1930s, Kirov protested the application of extreme sanctions against party colleagues, who campaigned against the use of coercion to implement collectivization. One such group even circulated a platform that openly espoused the removal of Stalin from the central leadership.[20] In a speech before the Leningrad party organization, Kirov insisted that the participants in this opposition had not engaged in any counter-revolutionary activity and, as a result, should receive no more severe a punishment than censure or expulsion from the party.[21] By contrast, Lazar Kaganovich, in an address before the Moscow party organization, argued that given the intensification of the class struggle these cases should be treated as a criminal matter and the most severe sanctions applied. Kaganovich seemed to attack Kirov's more moderate position, when he warned that some party leaders "had evolved a definite theory of a milder, more liberal attitude, which only increased the danger of losing the struggle."[22]

The notion of a moderate bloc implies that its members acted in concert, but this was not the case. Kuibyshev and Ordzhonikidze, in particular, were the core members of opposing regional networks. They followed identical promotion paths from regional administration to the central control bureaucracy and finally into industrial management. In Stalin's court, they acted more often as rival patrons than as policy partners. They vied for influence over economic policy and patronage over the new industrial administrative elite.[23] The relationship between Kuibyshev and Kirov, however, was much more cooperative. During the civil war, Kirov and Kuibyshev worked together in the revolutionary–military committee that organized the strategically critical capture of Astrakhan, opening a corridor through which the Red Army finally entered the Transcaucasus.[24] Kuibyshev later publicly endorsed Kirov's promotion to the head of the Leningrad party organization as well as into the central leadership.[25] More importantly, perhaps, Kirov's formal position, unlike Ordzhonikidze's, never placed him into direct competition with Kuibyshev. An examination of personal correspondences indicated that Kirov and Kuibyshev maintained a good working relationship, at times requesting assistance from one another and regularly exchanging information about policy matters.[26]

The relationship between Ordzhonikidze and Kirov was especially close. They were the core members of the Transcaucasian regional network. Together they commanded the reconquest of the Transcaucasus for the new Soviet Russian state. In the Red Army's assault on then independent Georgia, for example, Kirov dispatched the following message: "Pray Sergo that we accomplish everything and do not lose now. But we haven't a minute to waste. From Zaromak to the border, we will march all day and night. We will keep pushing the line until we have taken Tiflis."[27] A strong and lasting friendship between Ordzhonikidze and Kirov was forged in these civil war battles. After the war, they continued to work closely together for another five years as regional leaders in the Transcaucasus. Following their promotions to more powerful positions in Moscow and Leningrad, they still maintained close personal ties. They vacationed together, Kirov always stayed at Ordzhonikidze's apartment when visiting Moscow, and they kept signed photographs of each other in their offices.[28]

If not a moderate bloc, then Ordzhonikidze and Kirov composed at times a moderate pair in the politburo. Personal correspondence, from the late 1920s and early 1930s, showed that they frequently coordinated positions on personnel and policy issues.[29] Anastas Mikoian reported in his memoirs that Kirov had confided to him that he and Ordzhonikidze were, in fact, playing a moderating role in the central policy-making process.[30] For the Provincial Komitetchiki, the presence of Ordzhonikidze and Kirov on the politburo gave them indirect access to the state's highest policy-making body and an informal check on the formal powers of the center.

II. COERCION, CONTROL, AND THE CROSS-ORGANIZATIONAL REACH OF PERSONAL NETWORKS

Another way in which informal and formal structures intersected in the new state was the cross-organizational reach of personal network ties. The formal structure of the new state was arranged according to parallel vertically organized bureaucracies. The Soviet state adopted this organizational scheme from its tsarist predecessor. It was a system whose shape reflected, on the one hand, the desire to concentrate decision-making powers in the state center and, on the other hand, the demands of administering a multiethnic and rural territory that stretched across eleven time zones. For the state center, this parallel scheme was intended to provide access to alternative channels of information and communication from below and to serve as a checking and enforcement mechanism on lower-level state officials.[31]

According to this scheme, regional officials in the party organizations, the economic ministries and the military administration, in principle, were subordinated to their bureaucratic supervisors in the center. In addition, a separate vertically structured control bureaucracy was created to audit the activities of regional party and economic officials and report their findings directly to Moscow. Despite this scheme, regional actors, in practice, did not always function as simply the representatives of central bureaucracies. Instead, regional officials became enmeshed in informal horizontally structured relationships, which enabled them to cooperate apart from the center. Personal network ties cut across these formal bureaucratic lines and, in so doing, became a constraint on the center's system of checking and control.

The Provincial Komitetchiki belonged to two types of network ties at this time. First, they were the patrons to teams of clients in "dominance" network ties. These networks existed across the formal structures of the state, clustered around the state's distribution points for valued resources. The "dominance" network ties of the Provincial Komitetchiki were particularly effective in disabling the formal checking powers of the center's control bureaucracy. Second, the Provincial Komitetchiki were part of "influence" network ties. These networks were not resource driven, but instead consisted of informal peer relations along which information was exchanged and opinions were formed. These ties originated in the underground committees and along the civil war battle fronts. The Provincial Komitetchiki, in particular, shared "influence" ties with the new state's military elite that checked the state's coercive capacities.

To begin, the formal structure of power in the new state was distorted by the cross-organizational reach of network ties into the control bureaucracy. The initial decision to resort to a bureaucratic instrument for ensuring the accountability of lower-level officials was typical of Lenin's resistance to popular mechanisms of checking and control. In 1923, the party and governmental control agencies were merged into a single overarching bureaucracy with enhanced responsibilities and powers, the Central Control Commission and Worker-Peasant Inspectorate. A corps of regional control officials was created at the same time. Regional control officials were supposed to monitor the behavior of local political figures, to verify the implementation of central policy directives and to report violations to the central board of control commissioners in Moscow.[32]

This powerful control bureaucracy became the organizational prize, first, of the Middle Volga regional network and, later, of the Transcaucasian regional network. Valerian Kuibyshev headed the control bureaucracy from 1923 to 1926, when he was replaced in that position by Grigorii Ordzhonikidze, who headed the organization until 1930.[33] In each case, clients of these patrons soon followed them into the control bureaucracy. Joining Kuibyshev in the control bureaucracy, for example, were his former assistants in the Samara RMC, Nikolai Shvernik and K. A. Popov.[34] In the 1920s, the control bureaucracy was used as a political weapon in intraparty factional power struggles. The Middle Volga and Transcaucasian regional networks were positioned advantageously in these contests through their access to the organizational resources of the control bureaucracy.

The penetration of the control bureaucracy by regionally based personal networks, however, had an adverse effect on the state center. By decade's end, the control bureaucracy was rendered ineffective as a checking mechanism over regional and local political leaders. The Provincial Komitetchiki were not constrained by the control bureaucracy. Control officials were either coopted by the regional leaders or simply too intimidated to carry out their responsibilities. In his richly detailed study of the control bureaucracy, Paul Cocks concluded that the "vertical lines of communication and interdependence were never as strong as the horizontal chains of dependence which bound the control commissions to the party committees."[35] The ability of the Provincial Komitetchiki to constrain the control bureaucracy was revealed in a resolution, issued in 1930, which demanded that "the Central Control Commission must remove those who do not fulfill Party and governmental directives with all exactingness and honesty, regardless of prestige, position, or past services."[36]

The center's frustration with the ineffectiveness of the control bureaucracy continued throughout the 1930s, leading to still more venting and several major reorganizations. The lack of accountability of the control bureaucracy was even greater below the regional level. Local control officials were routinely rebuked for protecting local leaders accused of obstructing the fulfillment of the center's agricultural policies. The head of the central control commission, Ian Rudzutak, referred to "a conspiracy of silence" among local control officials.[38] Further, in the early 1930s, the center authorized a mass screening of the party membership in order to obtain a more accurate profile of the rank and file and to weed out those with undesirable political backgrounds. To the dismay of central leaders, more than one half of the members expelled at this time were reportedly reinstated by district control officials, citing insufficient evidence.[39]

Cross-organizational network ties also existed between the Provincial Komitetchiki and the military elite. The intersection of informal and formal structures in the new state's civil–military relationship occurred by three means: (1) the internal organizational scheme of military administration, (2) the central administration of the military, and (3) the "influence" ties of the civil war *druzhina*. First, the internal organizational scheme of the military served to promote informal ties between regional leaders and military commanders. After the civil war, a territorially based scheme that was adopted by the military roughly overlapped with the regional administrative–territorial structure. A system of personal interaction was established between regional party leaders and district military commanders. District commanders almost always were provided seats on the executive bureaus of regional party committees; likewise, regional party first secretaries were formally included in district military councils. While this system of interlocking directorates was an example of the center's strategy of parallel bureaucratic control, in practice, regional leaders and military commanders very rarely interfered in each others' affairs.[39]

Second, the central administrative leadership of the military was pene-

trated by the personal networks that also included several leading representatives of the Provincial Komitetchiki. In particular, members of the
Middle Volga–Central Asian and the Ukrainian networks moved into
central military administration in the mid-1920s. In 1924, a politburo
faction conspired to prevent Trotsky from making a bid to succeed Lenin
as leader. As a result, Trotsky was forced to resign as war commissar and,
in effect, give up his power base in the central administration of the
military. Leading members of the RMC of the Fourth Red Army, which
led the reconquest of Central Asia, were among the main beneficiaries of
the ensuing personnel maneuverings. The commission charged with the
reorganization of military administration, for example, selected Mikhail
Frunze, the commanding officer of the Fourth Red Army, as Trotsky's
replacement as war commissar.[40] The commission was headed by S. I.
Gusev and also included Valerian Kuibyshev, who served alongside Frunze
as political commissars in the RMC of the Fourth Red Army.[41] The
commission additionally included two of Kuibyshev's network ties from
the Samaran underground, Andrei Bubnov and Nikolai Shvernik.[42] Bubnov
at this time was promoted into the central military administration and was
appointed to candidate membership in the party's central committee, replacing Vladimir Antonov-Ovseenko, who was personally connected to
Trotsky. In the civil war, Bubnov served in the RMCs in Ukraine and the
North Caucasus.[43]

Third, the civil war *druzhina* provided the context from which later
emerged a web of "influence" ties between regional leaders and the military's high officer corps. As former members of the revolutionary–military
committees, the leading members of the Provincial Komitetchiki had
worked closely with Red Army officers along the battle fronts. The matrix
in Tables 5.1 and 5.2 is meant to indicate the extensiveness of network
ties between the military elite and the regional leadership in the early
thirties. The table includes, as of June 1934, the commissar of defense
(Voroshilov), three deputy commissars (Gamarnik, Tukhachevskii, Egorov)
and eleven district commanders.[44]

Indeed, members of the Provincial Komitetchiki fought side by side
with the military commanders during the civil war. Iosif Vareikis, for
example, physically rescued Tukhachevskii after he had been captured and
held prisoner by anti-Bolshevik forces in Simbirsk in the summer of
1918.[45] As military commander of the Eleventh Red Army, Levandovskii
worked closely with the core members of the Transcaucasian regional
network in the campaigns to reclaim the Transcaucasus and North Caucasus for the Bolshevik regime. He was given the nickname "Intrepid" by

Table 5.1. Positions Held in January 1937

Name	Position	Name	Position
Voroshilov	Commissar of Defense	Belov	Moscow Military District
Gamarnik	Head of MPA	Dybenko	Volga Military District
Tukhachevskii	First Deputy Commissar of Defense	Kashirin	North Caucasus Military District
Egorov	Chief of the General Staff	Galit	Siberian Military District
Uborevich	Belorussia Military District	Velikanov	Central Asian Military District
Griaznov	Transbaikal Military District	Garkavy	Urals Military District
Levandovskii	Transcaucasus Military District	Dubovoi	Kharkov Military District
Iakir	Ukraine Military District	Bliukher	Far East Military District

Table 5.2. Civil War Ties with Military Elite

	Voroshilov	Tukhachevskii	Gamarnik	Egorov	Uborevich	Griaznov	Levandovskii	Iakir	Belov	Dybenko	Kashirin	Galit	Velikanov	Garkavy	Dubovoi	Bliukher	Totals
Andreev	1	0	0	0	0	0	0	0	0	0	0	0	0	0	0	0	1
Eikhe	0	0	0	0	0	0	0	0	0	0	1	0	0	1	0	0	2
Gamarnik	1	0	X	0	0	0	0	1	0	1	0	0	0	0	0	1	4
Gikalo	0	1	0	0	1	0	1	0	0	0	0	0	1	0	0	0	4
Goloshchekin	0	1	0	0	0	0	0	0	1	0	1	0	1	1	0	1	6
Ivanov	0	0	0	0	0	0	0	0	0	0	0	0	0	0	0	0	0
Kabakov	0	0	0	0	0	0	0	0	0	0	0	0	0	0	0	0	0
Khataevich	0	1	0	0	0	0	0	0	0	1	0	0	1	0	0	0	3
Kosior	1	0	1	1	0	0	0	1	0	0	0	0	0	0	1	0	5
Krinitskii	0	0	0	0	0	0	0	0	0	0	0	0	0	0	0	0	0
Kubiak	0	0	0	0	1	0	0	0	0	0	0	0	0	0	0	1	2
Mirzoian	0	1	0	0	1	0	1	0	0	0	0	0	1	0	0	0	4
Postyshev	0	0	0	0	1	0	0	0	0	0	0	0	0	0	0	1	2
Rumiantsev	0	0	0	0	0	0	0	0	0	0	0	0	0	0	0	0	0
Sheboldaev	0	1	0	0	1	0	1	0	0	1	1	0	1	0	0	0	6
Vareikis	1	1	0	0	0	0	0	0	0	1	0	0	1	0	0	0	4
Totals	4	6	1	1	5	0	3	2	1	4	3	0	6	2	1	4	

Ordzhonikidze.[46] These "influence" ties did not give the Provincial Komitetchiki access to coercive resources, instead, they served as a check on the
new state's coercive forces.

A particularly good example of the way in which the cross-
organizational reach of network ties constrained the state center occurred
in Ukraine in the early 1930s. At that time, the Ukrainian countryside
was in crisis, experiencing drought, grain shortages, and widespread famine. Despite the exceptionally harsh conditions, Moscow blamed the regional leadership's lack of political vigilance for the crisis and refused to
lower the region's grain procurement quotas for the central economic
plan.[47] Kosior appealed, publicly and privately, to the center for relief from
the "unrealistic" grain quotas.[48] In this confrontation, Vlas Chubar, the
head of the Ukrainian government, sharply criticized the center's ill-
conceived plans. More significantly, the regional heads of the control
bureaucracy and the military district also joined in the defense of the
regional leadership and the counterattack on the center.

Although Volodymyr Zatonskii was the formal representative in
Ukraine of the central control bureaucracy, he defended Kosior and the
regional party leadership against the center's charges and echoed their
argument that the center's extraction policies were excessive.[49] The central
control commission was forced to issue a strong reprimand to the Ukrainian control apparat, singling out officials in Kiev, Kharkov, Dnepropetrovsk, and Odessa for their failure to inform Moscow of "the real situation
in Ukraine."[50] Meanwhile, Iona Iakir, the commander of the Ukrainian
military district, openly objected to the use of the armed forces to implement collectivization. In personal letters to Stalin, Iakir and Fedor Raskol-
nikov, Admiral of the Black Sea fleet, supported the position of the
regional leadership in the dispute over grain procurement quotas.[51]

It is noteworthy that behind their formal positions these officials were
also connected by a web of personal network ties. Zatonskii was a veteran
of the civil war in Ukraine. He worked alongside Kosior organizing the
Bolshevik underground during the German occupation.[52] He remained in
administrative work in Ukraine after the civil war and was appointed head
of the control bureaucracy in 1927. Iakir was a leading military commander in Ukraine during the civil war. He continued to serve in Ukraine
after the war and was named head of the military district in 1925. Like
Zatonskii, he had strong network ties with the Ukrainian regional leadership.[53] The military's political–administrative department, which was supposed to ensure the political reliability of officers, was also penetrated by
network ties. The head of this bureaucracy in Moscow, Ian Gamarnik, and

the head of its Ukrainian office, Mikhail Amelin, both served on the same civil war battle front in southern Ukraine as Iakir and Zatonskii.[54]

The circumstances of this episode in center–regional relations could easily be interpreted as a clash of bureaucratic interests. And, at one level, it certainly was just that. Below the level of formal bureaucratic positions, however, a web of informal network ties existed among the participants. The incident illustrates well how the center's formal instruments of control and coercion could be blunted by the cross-organizational reach of informal network ties.

III. PERSONAL NETWORKS AND STRATEGIC LOCATION IN THE POLICY IMPLEMENTATION PROCESS

The intersection of formal and informal structures was further reinforced by two related features of the policy implementation process. First, the new state's weakly developed infrastructural capacities made central leaders dependent on particular regional leaders who were strategically located in the implementation process. These regional leaders were often issued mandates as "fully empowered representatives of the central committee." Rather than being given a prescribed set of bureaucratic routines, these officials were given carte blanche to implement central policy. Second, the lack of a formal infrastructural framework for policy implementation contributed to a system of policy implementation that utilized the informal social structure of regionally based personal networks. Moreover, these personal networks became centered around the same regional officials, who were designated as the center's representatives. In order to carry out their assignments for the center, they built "implementation teams." These teams were most often composed of individuals who were known to be reliable workers and personally loyal to a particular regional leader. For the Provincial Komitetchiki, their strategic location in the policy implementation process and their reliance on implementation teams enabled them to build formidable political machines in the regions. These political machines became entrenched within the formal structures of regional administration and became another informal constraint on the formal powers of the center.

Beginning in 1929, the state embarked upon a program of radical economic reform that included the rapid development of heavy industry and the collectivization of agriculture. But the state's institutional capacity to carry out this program of economic transformation was poorly developed. Trained personnel were in chronic short supply, material and technological resources were scarce, and organizational routines were as yet not established. Given these weaknesses, central leaders resorted to the campaign methods of the civil war to implement its radical reform program. Veteran party cadres with a reputation for "getting things done" became an indispensible resource to the center. In military campaign style, they were mobilized "to storm the grain front" or "to hold the line on steel production."

The overall labor shortage of state builders forced central leaders to make concessions to regional officials. This constraint on central state actors was evident in a personal letter from Stalin to Molotov, written in September 1929. The letter discussed the case of Lev Mirzoian, a party leader in Baku and member of the Transcaucasian regional network. Mirzoian, at this time, had just been involved on the losing side in an internal party squabble in the Transcaucasus, which aroused the displeasure of at least some central leaders. Nonetheless, Stalin was adamant against losing the services of a proven party cadre; he wrote:

> You know that I'm not a supporter of 'tolerance' regarding comrades who have committed grievous errors from the perspective of the party's interests. I must say, however, that it is not in the party's interests to *finish off* Mirzoian. I think it wouldn't be a bad thing to appoint Mirzoian secretary to the Perm (Ural) Regional Committee and give him an urgent combat assignment: *to move the oil business forward* in the Urals. He knows the oil business well.[55] (emphasis in original)

Central state leaders were especially dependent on the Provincial Komitetchiki for the implementation of collectivization and the economic transformation of the agricultural sector. At this time, the central agricultural bureaucracy lacked the necessary organizational depth, technical expertise, and political clout to assume command of the implementation of collectivization policies.[56] Compared to industry, the administration of agriculture remained far less centralized in the 1920s. Moreover, several leading officials in the agricultural bureaucracy were only recently on public record as opponents of collectivization.[57] Thus, as the campaign unfolded, the central agricultural bureaucracy "was simply bypassed, rendered powerless in the creation and implementation of rural policy."[58] Instead, central leaders looked to the Provincial Komitetchiki. In January 1930, regional party committees were formally charged "to guarantee the organization of collectived agricultural production and to fulfill completely the plan to expand the total area sown."[59]

It is also notable that several individuals promoted into the central leadership for agricultural administration at this time included former regional actors with personal network ties to the Provincial Komitetchiki. For example, Anastas Mikoian, the head of the domestic trade bureaucracy, played a prominent role in the state's system of extracting and redistributing agricultural resources. As a core member of the Transcaucasian regional network, Mikoian had personal network ties to Sergei Kirov, Boris Sheboldaev, and other provincial leaders. Similarly, the head of the new central agricultural bureaucracy, Iakov A. Iakovlev, had personal network ties to Stanislav Kosior and the Ukrainian regional network.[60] Out of either sympathy or necessity, Iakovlev formed a cooperative working relationship with leaders in the major agricultural regions and, at times, supported their position in policy disputes.[61] The Russian republic's agricultural bureaucracy was headed by Nikolai Kubiak, a regional leader throughout the 1920s and a member of the Far East regional network.[62]

The campaign style of implementation of economic reform fostered conditions that supported personal political machines. The organizational and technical weakness of the state in the rural areas meant that regional and local relations still relied heavily on personal interactions. Regional leaders assembled implementation teams to travel throughout the territory and to supervise the implementation process. They established special schools and programs, where cadres received crash courses in the political administration and economic management of the collective farms.[63] In Ukraine, Kosior organized a special corps of cadres to direct local officials in the collectivization campaign in the spring of 1930. This group of seventy-three workers supervised an area that in square miles was roughly the size of France.[64]

Regional party leaders tended to recruit familiar and trusted cadres for their own administrative staffs. In Leningrad, Sergei Kirov waged a continuous battle with the party's central personnel department to obtain cadres with whom he had worked in the past and to prevent the reassignment of members of his administrative staff.[65] Kosior explained that the practice of "co-opting" cadres was driven by the demands of policy implementation. "In Kiev," he pointed out, "fifty workers were recently co-opted, of which ten to fifteen were absolutely necessary. They are our people and part of a household connected by personal relations to the leadership. Co-optation is employed as a means by which we can build an arrangement for our people."[66] The center frequently relented to the personnel demands of regional leaders out of a concern for policy implementation. Even Stalin admonished Molotov for "looting" proven cadres from strategically important economic regions.[67]

When regional leaders were reassigned, they routinely brought their former coworkers with them. Thus, a party leader in Uzbekistan, Lepa, was appointed to head the Tataria party organization in 1933. Within a short period, former colleagues of Lepa in Uzbekistan occupied the following positions in the Tataria party apparat: head of the cadres department, head of the industrial–transportation department, head of the schools and science department, assistant head of the propaganda department, assistant head of the trade department, and, secretary of the Kazan city party organization.[68] The former party chief of Tataria, Razumov, meanwhile, was reassigned to head the party's East Siberian regional organization. Soon after, the following positions in East Siberia were held by recent transfers from Tataria: head of the industrial–transportation department, head of the agricultural department, instructor of the regional party organization, secretary of Irkutsk city party organization, secretary of the Zalarinsk district party organization, secretary of the Usol'sk district party organization, and the director of a large industrial enterprise (named for Kuibyshev). In addition, while the new procurator for East Siberia was not from Tataria, he, in fact, had previously worked with Razumov in Orel.[69]

In this way, personal networks were allowed to take root within the formal structures of regional and local administration under the guise of implementation teams. But these personal networks also worked as a constraint on the formal powers of the state center by acting as informal mutual protection groups, the so-called family circles. Fainsod's description of the "family circles" operating across the middle and lower levels of Soviet officialdom has remained the standard: "Party as well as governmental functionaries are tempted to seek a degree of independence from control by organizing mutual-protection associations in which they agree informally to refrain from mutual criticism and to cover up for each others' mistakes and deficiencies."[70] In the late 1930s, Stalin indicated the center's frustration with the insular protectiveness of these personal networks in words that echoed Fainsod's. "Most often," he declared,

> so-called acquaintances and personal friends are selected regardless of their suitablity from a political or practical stand point. It is not difficult to understand that such family circles allow no place for criticism of shortcomings in performance. Such family circles create a favorable environment for raising toadies. In selecting cadres for their personal devotion, these comrades evidently want to create conditions which make them independent from the locality as well as from the center.[71]

By the end of the 1920s, the formal lines of power in the new state indicated a highly centralized bureaucratic structure. Bureaucratic and coercive power resources were concentrated in the central administrative organs of the party and the government. The formal command chart of the state, however, did not reveal the pervasiveness of informal personal network ties. These ties extensively criss-crossed and ultimately distorted the formal lines of power in the new state. For central state leaders, they became a constraint on their exclusive claim on the state's "despotic" powers. For regional leaders, personal ties provided an informal means of access to the state's rule-making process. Moreover, the intersection of informal and formal structures enabled regional leaders to solidify their own personal political machines. These informal power resources accorded the Provincial Komitetchiki an area of autonomy from central state leaders. This situation eventually brought central and regional leaders into conflict. The center–regional conflict and the attempts by both sides to redefine the constraints of power in their relationship are the focus of the next two chapters.

PART III

INTRASTATE CONFLICT AND THE CONSTRAINTS OF POWER REDEFINED

6

CENTER AND REGIONS IN CONFLICT I: COLLECTIVIZATION AND THE CRISIS OF REGIONAL LEADERSHIP

The conflict between center and regions that unfolded in the 1930s represented a clash of interests between two distinct power centers within the state. On one side, a group of central actors was intent on concentrating the despotic powers of the state in the center, in general, and in the person of Stalin, in particular. They sought to transform the infrastructural powers of the state along bureaucratic rather than patrimonial lines. Central actors defined their interests in a monopolistic claim on national security policy and national economic development. On the other side, a group of regional leaders sought to share in the despotic powers of the state. They sought to eliminate arbitrariness in the state's rule-making process. They wanted to maintain the patrimonial system of infrastructural power. The interests of this group were shaped by more narrowly defined corporate interests and a distinct status image. The center–regional conflict, in effect, was a battle over the institutionalization of power and status in the new state. The center preferred a "bureaucratic absolutist" regime type for the state, while the Provincial Komitetchiki preferred a "protocorporatist" regime type.

No issue did more to expose the strains in the center–regional relationship in the first half of the 1930s than the collectivization of agriculture. By the end of the 1920s, a consensus formed within the political elite that agricultural collectivization was a necessary component of any plan for national economic development. Collectivization was viewed as a panacea for the stifled growth of industrialization. The Provincial Komitetchiki were charged with the responsibility for the implementation of collectivization. Although in principle the Provincial Komitetchiki strongly supported collectivization and in practice ruthlessly strove to bring it to realization, they almost immediately found themselves in conflict with central leaders over the implementation process. As the conflict intensified through the early 1930s, the Provincial Komitetchiki were increasingly able to assert their own interests into the policy process and to force modifications of the center's plans.

Although the Provincial Komitetchiki were formally subordinated to the center through an array of formal power structures, they did not act in the course of collectivization as unwitting henchmen or bureaucratic supplicants. Instead, the Provincial Komitetchiki displayed a greater degree of autonomy and "corporate consciousness" than has previously been recognized by Western analysts. The ability of the Provincial Komitetchiki to engage the center in this conflict derived from the constraints of power in the postrevolutionary state. The cross-organizational reach of informal network ties and the protection afforded by central patrons, in effect, constrained the center's formal power resources. Elite identity further emboldened the Provincial Komitetchiki to stake out a more prominent position in the policy process than central leaders envisioned.

This chapter presents a case study of the intrastate conflict that arose between center and regions in the first half of the decade. It explores three aspects of this defining episode in the evolution of center–regional relations in the new state: (1) a discussion of the role of the Provincial Komitetchiki in working out the collectivization policies, (2) an overview of the crisis of regional leadership that the collectivization campaigns caused to the Provincial Komitetchiki, and (3) the positions staked out by central and regional leaders in the conflict over the implementation of collectivization.

I. THE PROVINCIAL KOMITETCHIKI AND AGRICULTURAL COLLECTIVIZATION

In response to a wave of peasant unrest at the end of the civil war, the Bolsheviks initiated a New Economic Policy (NEP). The NEP was founded on an uneasy coexistence between a radical socialist regime and a small property-holding peasantry.[1] The NEP was supposed to reconcile the divergent interests of proletariat and peasant through a regulated market relationship involving the exchange of food and agricultural products from the countryside for consumer and manufactured goods from the urban areas. The state played both an economic role, as tax collector and grain purchaser, and a political role, as guardian of the still weak working class. In the second half of the 1920s, a sudden downturn occurred in the amount of grain that peasant producers made available to the state through market purchases. By the end of November 1927, state grain collections were more than 50 percent lower than they had been at the same time the previous year.[2]

The grain shortages prompted a bitter debate within the party over economic policy.[3] Fundamental questions about the ideological character and socioeconomic commitments of the postrevolutionary state lay at the core of this debate. Any attempt by the state to alter the NEP terms of trade threatened the relative social peace of the mid-1920s. Yet the short-fall in the amount of grain that peasants made available to the state adversely affected the already meager consumption levels of the urban proletariat and the lagging growth rates of industrial development.[4] In this charged atmosphere, the private, small property-holding structure of agriculture, characteristic of the NEP, quickly came to be seen as the major obstacle to the regime's goal of large-scale industrialization. In December 1927, a decision was made to move forward with a plan for agricultural collectivization.[5] It was not until the second half of 1929, however, that state actors were ready to put this plan into effect.

Collectivization became the solution by which state actors would release the economy from its NEP shackles. In postrevolutionary Soviet Russia, agricultural products were the principal form of revenue available to the state for extraction. During the NEP, the state acquired agricultural products through a tax-in-kind and market purchases. Collectivization was meant to restructure agriculture so that the state could directly extract revenue from the agricultural sector and reallocate it to the industrial sector.[6] By consolidating individual peasant households into large-scale, mechanized units of production, collectivization was supposed to improve economic efficiency, free labor resources and increase output levels. Agricultural products would be used to feed the growing labor force in urban and industrializing areas. In addition, the anticipated grain surpluses would be sold on international commodity markets raising investment capital so that industrial technology could be purchased from abroad. Finally, collectivization would undermine the petty capitalist behavioral tendencies exhibited by the peasantry. The 1927 grain shortage was blamed on the speculative nature of the peasants and their inherent class-based hostility to radical socialism.

Draped in rhetoric that recalled the civil war, the state's program for radical economic restructuring, the "socialist offensive," elicited enthusiastic endorsements from the Provincial Komitetchiki. As the state's leading representatives in the rural and non-Russian regions, the Provincial Komitetchiki were formally charged with responsibility for collectivizing Soviet

Russia's huge agricultural sector.[7] Central state actors believed that the success of this ambitious attempt at economic modernization ultimately hinged on the outcome of the collectivization campaigns in the countryside. As Valerian Kuibyshev succinctly stated, "we cannot industrialize with a feudal peasantry."[8] Collectivization required regional leaders to oversee the complete transformation of social and economic relationships in the peasant villages, to fulfill extremely high agricultural production targets for state procurement, and to wage class war against the kulaks, or wealthy peaants.[9]

Throughout the second half of 1929, central and regional actors convened to work out the details of agricultural collectivization. While these discussions were conducted in a general atmosphere of consensus, differences of opinion were discernable on particular aspects of the implementation process. Significantly, these seemingly minor differences at the time anticipated the impending conflict between central and regional leaders. The issues included the pace and scope of implementation, the levels of procurement quotas, and the application of class war tactics.

In late August 1929, the Khoper district in the grain-rich Lower Volga region resolved to collectivize agricultural production completely within five years. Boris Sheboldaev, the Lower Volga's regional leader at that time, declared that "the wave of the collective farm movement has risen so rapidly that the figures defy life itself."[10] Buoyed by these optimistic reports of a mass movement of peasants joining collective farms, central state leaders endorsed a rapid and comprehensive implementation schedule. In November 1929, Central Committee Secretary Viacheslav Molotov argued that the moment was ripe for "the collectivization of millions of peasant households in the nearest months, weeks and days."[11] He insisted that it would be possible to collectivize entire regions by the end of the summer, that is, in less than ten months. Stalin speculated that if the collective farm movement could be accelerated, then within three years Soviet Russia would become "one of the world's largest grain producers, if not the largest."[12]

The Provincial Komitetchiki responded with an ambitious, but less radical, implementation schedule. Sheboldaev, in the Lower Volga region, advocated a schedule of one and a half to two years, explaining that local officials were not yet capable of handling a more rapid pace.[13] In the North Caucasus, Andreev supported a similar time frame. Notably, Andreev had only the previous month described collectivization as a "long-term policy" that would not be completed for at least five years.[14] And, Kosior, in Ukraine, cautioned central leaders that, upon closer investigation, the optimistic reports on the collective farm movement that the center had

been receiving were grossly exaggerated. "We had complete collectivization in ten villages," he related, "but then it was discovered that it was
entirely hollow, the people in these villages not only did not participate in
the collective farms, but did not even know they existed."[15]

The influx of peasants into collective farms that was supposedly occur-
ring in the second half of 1929 was depicted by central leaders as a
voluntary and spontaneous movement. Coercion was said to have been
employed only against the wealthy peasants, or kulaks, who stood accused
of attempting to disrupt the movement. The more radical implementation
schedules were justified on the basis of this depiction of the process. The
Provincial Komitetchiki, however, expressed disagreement with this depiction. They reported that coercive tactics and administrative methods had
been routinely employed to induce peasants to enter the collective farms.
They cited cases of local officials withholding grain seed, issuing fines and
threatening deportation in order to force peasants to join the collective
farms.[16]

A second issue was the target levels of the center's grain procurement
plans. Manifestations of the dispute over grain procurement appeared as
early as 1929, as indicated in the following exchange of letters between
Stalin and Andreev in the North Caucasus.[17] Stalin's letter conveyed the
sense of urgency and impending doom that by this time characterized
nearly all central pronouncements on collectivization. "The present pace of
grain procurement in the North Caucasus is simply ruining us and it is
necessary to undertake measures to increase grain procurements. Be mind-
ful that we have very little time remaining." Andreev responded by listing
a number of actions, including coercive, taken by local officials to fulfill
the center's procurement demands. Nonetheless, he concluded that "despite all this, we have to say that it will be impossible to fulfill the plan.
We have been *over assessed by the plan*." (emphasis added)

Finally, central and regional leaders debated the introduction of class
warfare as part of the campaign to restructure agriculture. Wealthy peasants and traditional village leaders were labeled kulaks by the regime and
targeted for repression. A state-sanctioned campaign "to liquidate the
kulaks as a class" was proposed as a tactical means for overturning the
traditional political and socioeconomic structures in rural and non-Russian
localities.[18] The campaign against the kulaks was depicted by central state
leaders as a life-or-death struggle. The success of collectivization, it was
argued, required the complete elimination of Soviet Russia's remaining
class nemesis, the kulak. Stalin and Molotov strongly advocated a resolute
campaign against "the capitalist elements in the countryside, who are
inciting all the forces of the old world against socialism's advance."[19]

The Provincial Komitetchiki shared these anticapitalist sentiments and favored the application of class war tactics to the countryside.[20] They endorsed the campaign against the kulaks in rhetoric that recalled civil war days. Robert Eikhe, in the West Siberian region, for example, called for "a strong strike against the kulak."[21] In Kazakhstan, Filipp Goloshchekin spoke enthusiastically about the "intensified new forms of class struggle" against the *bai*, the traditional leader in native Kazakh communities. "The *bai*," he claimed, "felt the process of collectivization and felt that the hour to fight was upon him. At present, he is employing acute forms of struggle against the poor peasants, against Soviet power and against the Communist party."[22]

Disagreement, however, arose among regional leaders over the punishment to be applied to the kulaks, ranging from loss of property to arrest and exile. A further complication arose over the criteria to be used to distinguish wealthy peasants from middle peasants in the villages.[23] One of the narrower definitions suggested using personal livestock holdings as the main indicator of kulak status. Khataevich, however, strongly criticized this solution. He reported that such an indicator was already in use in the Middle Volga region and had caused a dangerously sharp drop in overall livestock holdings, as peasants destroyed their livestock so as not to be identified as kulaks. He argued that another means of classifying kulaks should be "adopted immediately," without going through "all kinds of Moscow red tape."[24] More generally, Khataevich warned that the arbitrary application of class war tactics in the countryside would disrupt the production process. In expressing reservations toward class warfare, Khataevich was alone among the Provincial Komitetchiki at this time. Within several years, however, other regional leaders would come to share Khataevich's concerns.

Despite the general commitment to collectivization, the details of the campaign were as yet undetermined in late 1929. "I think that we are still unprepared for this movement," Sheboldaev observed at this time. He proposed the formation of a "special permanently working commission" to resolve "the principal questions of socialist transformation in the countryside and the daily leadership of the collective farm movement."[25] In this way, the Provincial Komitetchiki would routinely participate in the formal process of defining goals, strategies, and tactics. Instead, in early December, an ad hoc committee, including regional leaders from the major grain-growing areas, was formed to work out the details of implementation. The commission was headed by the newly chosen head of the All-Union Commissariat for Agriculture, Iakov Iakovlev. Regional representatives on the committee included: Andrei Andreev and Vilen Ivanov from the North Caucasus, Boris Sheboldaev and M. Khlopiankin from the Lower Volga, Mendel Khataevich from the Middle Volga, Iosif Vareikis from the Central Black Earth, Stanislav Kosior from Ukraine, and Filipp Goloshchekin from Kazakhstan. The committee also included fifteen members from various central organs.

After two weeks of intensive work, the committee issued its recommendations.[26] Concerning implementation schedules, the committee allowed the major grain-producing regions to complete collectivization in two to three years and the grain-consuming regions to complete the transition in three to four years. Although the caveat was added that implementation schedules generally should reflect the level of preparedness of the peasantry in a given locality. Local party organizations were warned not to force the pace through coercion or administrative methods in areas where the peasantry was not prepared. The committee, furthermore, refused to endorse the widespread application of class war tactics against the kulaks. Rather, the committee called for a differentiated approach, wherein some kulaks would be allowed to remain in their localities and even join the collective farms.

While the committee's recommendations represented an extremely ambitious approach to collectivization, they were not sufficiently radical to satisfy all central state actors. Stalin, in particular, spoke out against the committee's implementation schedules. He urged the major grain-growing regions to complete the transition to collectivized agriculture in one to two years.[27] Stalin further called for an escalation of class warfare against the kulaks. The relationship between the state and the wealthy peasants, he railed, had become a "life-or-death struggle." As the "sworn enemies of the collective farms," he insisted that under no circumstances should kulaks be allowed to remain in the villages or to participate in the collective farms.[28] On 5 January 1930, an official directive, reflecting the more radical implementation strategy, was issued by the center and the campaign for agricultural collectivization was underway.[29]

At this point, the campaign seemed to develop a dynamic of its own, frantically lurching ahead in a flurry of pronouncements and decrees issued from all corners of Soviet officialdom. The Provincial Komitetchiki contributed to this campaign frenzy as much as anybody else, if not more so. Following the January resolution, regional leaders closed ranks and fell in line behind the central leadership. Andreev informed the North Caucasus party organization that the entire region would be collectivized by the end of the year and the main grain-producing districts by the end of the spring.[30] He exhorted local officials not to adopt "half measures, but to create real collective farms with socialized livestock, family lands and means of production."[31] Sheboldaev promised that all poor and middle peasants in the Lower Volga region would join collective farms by the end of the year.[32] Vareikis, meanwhile, claimed that the Central Black Earth region would be completely collectivized in just six months. Vareikis, in addition, declared an "all-out offensive against the capitalist strata in the countryside."[33]

The hurried pace of the campaign quickly spread beyond Russia's main grain-producing regions. Ivan Kabakov, in the Urals, resolved to collectivize 80 percent of the peasant households by the end of 1930 and to complete the transition in the region in less than two years, that is, nearly two years ahead of schedule.[34] The non-Russian regions, likewise, plunged ahead with their own collectivization campaigns. In January, Belorussian leader Ian Gamarnik issued orders to move up the date of completion by two years. In February, Belorussian leaders went still further, vowing to collectivize 75 to 80 percent of all peasant households by the end of the spring and the entire republic by the end of the year.[35] By the end of January, the Transcaucasian and Central Asian regions were also caught up in the collectivization race. In Kazakhstan, Filipp Goloshchekin initiated a particularly brutal campaign to settle forcibly that region's sizable nomadic population as part of the collectivization process.[36]

Whatever reservations that may have been expressed earlier, the Provincial Komitetchiki now actively spurred on the radicalization of the campaign. The central leadership had issued a challenge and the Provincial Komitetchiki responded characteristically with self-initiative, resourcefulness, leadership and zeal. Once again, they donned their battle regalia "to storm the grain front," "to smash the kulak," and "to forge proletarians out of peasants." An interregional competition ensued in which the Provincial Komitetchiki promised to bring more and more lands under collective production. No regional leader wanted to be outdone in this contest. Stanislav Kosior later recalled, in a sober reassessment of the intitial campaign delirium, that he felt compelled by "the force of revolutionary enthusiasm" to set no limits on the campaign.[37]

The helter-skelter pace of the collectivization campaign, however, precipitated a multilevel crisis for regional leaders. In response, the Provincial Komitetchiki sought to secure greater control over the implementation process and to limit the ability of central leaders to dictate policies arbitrarily to the regions. As a result, central and regional leaders soon found themselves embroiled in conflict.

II. COLLECTIVIZATION AND THE CRISIS OF REGIONAL LEADERSHIP

The collectivization campaign was abruptly called to a halt in early March 1930. The signal for the reversal was a *Pravda* editorial by Stalin that acknowledged that the campaign was out of control. Despite the advances, Stalin wrote that "some comrades have become dizzy with success and for the moment have lost sobriety of mind and clarity of vision."[38] The editorial reestablished the less radical implementation schedules for the nongrain producing regions and denounced the use of coercion to hasten the movement. In the weeks that followed, a spate of published decrees and secret orders from the center to the regions confirmed that a more moderate course had become official policy.[39] For the moment, the storming rhetoric of the previous months was tempered and attention was redirected to the spring sowing season, which was in jeopardy as a result of the disruption of traditional cultivation routines.

For the Provincial Komitetchiki, this pause provided an opportunity for a reevaluation of the collectivization campaign in their regions. The figures on the growth of the collective farm movement that regional leaders were receiving from the localities were astounding, but so too were the reports of bureaucratic excesses and the use of force. Even before the publication of Stalin's editorial, regional leaders were becoming increasingly aware of the unintended consequences of the forced pace of the campaign. In February, Vareikis sent a letter to central leaders, stating that the campaign had produced a tangle of new problems, which local officials attend to "at their own fear and risk."[40] At the same time, Khataevich lobbied central leaders to readjust the priorities of the campaign to reflect qualitative, as opposed to quantitative, measures of success.[41] And, Sergei Syrtsov, head of the Russian republican government and a strong supporter of collectivization, now openly criticized the "administrative ecstasy" and "conveyorbelt of repressions" that characterized the implementation process.[42]

The initial collectivization foray was halted in early March 1930 for a period of reassessment. The ensuing public discussions degenerated almost immediately into mutual recriminations over who was to blame for leading the campaign awry.[43] To make matters worse, local officials began to report a mass exodus of peasants from the collective farms throughout the countryside. In early summer, however, tensions were eased by the optimistic reports of a bumper crop in the field. The 1930 grain harvest, in fact, turned out to be the largest, 77.1 million tons, since the prewar period. From this total, the state extracted 22.1 million tons of grain, almost 6 million tons more than the year previous and roughly 11.5 million tons more than two years previous.[44] In response to these reports, a series of central directives were issued during the second half of 1930, restoring the more radical implementation schedules.[45] But subsequent grain harvests showed that the state's heavy-handed extraction methods could not be sustained; instead, these methods exhausted the productive capacities of the countryside. By 1932, an agricultural disaster had arrived: Major grain-growing regions were ravaged by famine, urban areas suffered severe bread shortages, industrialization target figures were reluctantly reduced, and internal party opposition groups began to surface.

Throughout the early 1930s, the center's unrelenting pressure to implement collectivization and to fulfill grain-delivery quotas engendered a crisis for regional leaders on three interconnected levels: administrative capacities, political stability, and agricultural production.

To begin, the collectivization campaign overwhelmed the limited administrative capacities of regional leaders. As the principal intermediary link between the state center and the rural periphery, the Provincial Komitetchiki were entrusted with responsibility to oversee the realization of collectivization. But they were constrained in this task by the lack of organizational, technical, and human resources needed to coordinate and to supervise the campaign. In reality, regional leaders did not so much direct the collectivization campaign, as they did react to it. They instructed, pressured, bullied, and begged lower-level officials to fulfill the production targets issued by Moscow. They were constrained by weak administrative capacities, including unreliable means of information exchange, chronic shortages of personnel, and underdeveloped functional specialization.

The regional administrative–territorial unit was notable for its extensive geographical reach. Regions typically encompassed the area of as many as seven or eight traditional provinces of the former tsarist regime. While regional leaders represented the main administrative link between center and periphery, in practice they operated much closer to the center than to the village. In the administrative–territorial chain of command, regional leaders were three levels removed from the point of agricultural production.[46] Moreover, an underdeveloped communication and transportation infrastructure placed the peasant villages even further beyond the reach of regional leaders. In the North Caucasus, more than one-third of the district level party organizations had no direct telephone or telegraph connection to the regional capital in Rostov.[47] Eikhe, in Western Siberia, and Goloshchekin, in Kazakhstan, complained that the lack of telephones, telegraphs, and roads undermined the policy implementation process.[48] It was for such reasons that personal network ties were so crucial to the implementation process.

The most important items of information were handled through personal contacts between regional and lower-level units. Regional party organizations were staffed with instructors, who routinely conducted information and inspection tours of lower-level organizations. These staffs represented the teams of the regional leaders. But these staffs were woefully undermanned and experienced frequent personnel turnover, which frustrated efforts to develop a reliable system of information exchange.[49] These personnel shortages were exacerbated by the decision of the central leadership to reduce the staff size of regional administration at the beginning of 1930.[50] This decision was intended to streamline the command–administrative structure, to redeploy personnel closer to the point of production and to reduce the costs of regional administration. Over the strong objections of the Provincial Komitetchiki, the overall size of the regional party apparat was trimmed by nearly 30 percent between January and July 1930.[51]

Regional administration was further constrained by its undeveloped functional specialization. At the beginning of the 1930s, the regional organizations were structured according to the "universal" scheme, in which no clear delineation of function existed among the various departments.[52] At this time, central party leader Lazar Kaganovich was made responsible for reorganizing the party apparat. The "universal" scheme soon gave way to the "functional" scheme, so as to facilitate personnel recruitment and resource mobilization in conjunction with the campaigns for radical economic reform.[53] But the functional scheme proved ill-suited for the increasingly complex economic assignments. Kaganovich illustrated the shortcomings of the functional scheme with cases like the dairy district besieged with orders for rabbit-breeding and the flax-growing district charged with fulfilling the potato supply plan.[54]

Throughout the early 1930s, the Provincial Komitetchiki insisted on the need to maintain, at least, a department for peasant affairs to assist in the implementation of collectivization.[55] The first step toward an internal organizational scheme based on economic specialization was made in February 1931, with the establishment of special territorial–production sectors, which defined districts by common economic activities.[56] Finally, in 1934, the "production-branch" scheme, which was based on economic sectoral lines, was formally adopted as regional administration's internal structure.[57]

Underdeveloped administrative capacities hampered the efforts of regional leaders to stay in front of the collectivization campaign. The information that regional leaders received from lower-level officials was often bogus and misrepresented the actual state of affairs in the villages. Especially during the first months of the campaign, regional leaders announced the formation of thousands of collective farms, which, in fact, existed only on paper. The regional leaders' difficulties in obtaining reliable information on the progress of the collectivization campaigns became a constant source of tension between center and regions during the early thirties.[58]

A second aspect of the crisis of regional leadership was the threat to political stability arising from an insurgent peasantry. Class war tactics were applied indiscriminately. The arbitrary application of coercion and the forced dispossession of personal property incited a backlash of peasant resistance, ranging from mass demonstrations to random acts of violence to organized armed uprisings.[59] The Bolshevik regime was again challenged by wide-scale peasant opposition as it had been at the end of the civil war. This surge of violent peasant resistance, R. W. Davies argued, was the main reason for the center's call for a temporary halt in the collectivization campaign in early March 1930. Davies, in particular, cited a report from the Lower Volga region to Moscow, written in February 1930, which claimed that "anti-collective farm agitation has never been on so broad a scale as now."[60]

A rash of "terrorist acts," as they were officially labeled, were perpetrated by peasants during the early thirties in reaction to collectivization. The governmental head of the Udmurt autonomous province in the Urals region, Berezner, elaborated on the various forms of peasant resistance. In the first half of 1931, he reported nearly five hundred cases of "kulak terror," including 266 cases of physical assaults, 98 cases of destroyed machinery, 45 cases of arson, 28 cases of trampling over sown fields, 26 cases of poisoned livestock, and 35 cases of minor acts of sabotage. Such incidences were widespread. Between January and May 1930, over fifteen hundred "terrorist acts" were reported in connection with the collectivization campaign in Ukraine; meanwhile, over three hundred cases were reported in the countryside around Moscow in the same period.[62] In the Central Black Earth region, Vareikis informed Moscow that thirty-eight peasant uprisings occurred between late December 1929 and mid-February 1930.[63]

Village-level collective farm organizers were exposed to the greatest personal risk.[64] In the center, Kuibyshev routinely received letters detailing the murders of collective farm leaders.[65] But, some higher-ranking party officials were also felled by peasant violence. The North Caucasus region was especially fraught with danger for party leaders. An instructor of the regional party organization as well as the party leader of Ingushetia were killed in early 1930.[66] Andreev, regional leader of the North Caucasus, somberly reported the murder of the first secretary of the Terek district party organization.[67]

Regional leaders lacked the coercive capabilities to suppress peasant resistance. Central state leaders responded by mobilizing the state's coercive organs, the secret police and the Red Army, to assist in the collectivization campaigns. The secret police were made responsible for carrying out the policy of class warfare against the kulaks.[68] In the North Caucasus, in the early spring of 1930, police officials devised a plan for identifying, expropriating and evicting tens of thousands of kulaks in the region.[69] The center also directed the Red Army to organize collective farms, to extract grain, and to battle class enemies in the villages. The Red Army's deployment in the countryside posed new problems for the center, however, as peasant recruits sympathized with villagers and as commanding officers objected to the use of their troops for domestic purposes.[70] While regional leaders generally cooperated with the coercive organs, this relationship was not a normal state of affairs. The presence of these coercive organs in the regions provoked interbureaucratic rivalries and jurisdictional disputes.[71]

Agricultural production constituted the third aspect of the crisis of regional leadership in the early thirties. The primary responsibility of the Provincial Komitetchiki in the "socialist offensive" was to ensure the delivery of agricultural products to the state for reallocation to the industrial sectors of the economy and for export to world grain markets. By 1932, regional leaders were increasingly unable simultaneously to meet the state's extraction quotas and to sustain the viability of the rural economy.

The bounty of the 1930 harvest proved short-lived. The 1931 grain harvest fell short of the year previous by more than 7.5 million tons. Despite the overall decline in grain available for extraction, the state was still able to collect 22.8 million tons, a small increase from the 1930 harvest.[72] For 1932, central leaders boldly announced an extraction target of 29.5 million tons of grain, nearly 7 million tons more than the previous year's take. But by early summer it was clear that the 1932 harvest would fall far short of official expectations. The crop in the field was significantly smaller than the two previous seasons. A comparison of the figures for grain deliveries actually received by the state as of July 1932 with the figures from the year before indicated the dramatic downturn in grain available for extraction (see Table 6.1). The contribution of the major grain-producing regions was especially meager; Ukraine and the Central Black Earth region were roughly 60 percent behind the previous year's pace, while the Lower Volga and the Middle Volga regions were more than 80 percent behind. At the beginning of September, state grain procurements were still running almost 50 percent behind the year previous.[73]

Ironically, the sharp decline was caused by the initial successes of the collectivization campaign. Despite the early confusion, the 1930 harvest yielded a bumper crop and a windfall of grain for state stores. These results

Table 6.1. Comparison of Grain Collections
(in million poods) 1931, 1932

Region	July-1931	July-1932
Western	1.7	0.6
Urals	5.3	5.5
Middle Volga	6.8	1.0
Central Black Earth	4.4	1.7
Lower Volga	4.2	0.7
North Caucasus	1.2	1.2
Kazakhstan	3.4	1.4
Western Siberia	6.8	3.0
Ukraine	14.8	5.6
Belorussia	1.7	0.9

Source: RTsKhIDNI, f. 79,op. 1,d. 381, 1.7

muted public criticism of the conduct of the campaign and emboldened central leaders to renew the more radical implementation schedules. But the process of extraction by administrative fiat and coercion had the unintended effect of undermining the productive capacities of the agricultural sector. While total agricultural output declined in the first half of the 1930s, especially in grain crops, the state's procurement quotas continued to increase.[74]

For a combination of reasons, the anticipated boom in agricultural output following the 1930 harvest was not forthcoming. First, harvest yields in 1931 were adversely affected by weather conditions. Particularly damaging in this regard was the dry summer and rainy autumn experienced in the Lower Volga, the Middle Volga, Kazakhstan, Western Siberia, and the Urals. Central leaders responded to the decline in output in these regions by raising the procurement quotas in Ukraine and the North Caucasus.[75] By raising procurement quotas in disregard of the overall smaller harvest, state extractions cut deeply into grain reserves and seed stocks necessary for the 1932 planting season.[76]

Second, central resolutions ordering the collectivization of personal livestock holdings, as Khataevich had earlier warned, prompted peasants to destroy their livestock, rather than turn it over to the state. The massive slaughter of livestock, in turn, had a devastating impact on the agricultural sector, including an overall decline of animal products, a loss of drafting power for the planting season, and a shortage of fertilizer to regenerate nutritionally depleted soils.[77] Third, the outflow of labor from the country-side, through voluntary migration as well as forced expulsion, severely hindered sowing and harvesting campaigns. The conversion of agricultural production from a manual, labor-extensive process to a mechanized, labor-intensive process never occurred as originally planned.[78] The result was a significant net loss in agricultural manpower. The cumulative effect of these developments was a harsh winter of famine, 1932–1933.[79] The forced transition to collectivized agriculture was especially painful in Ukraine, the North Caucasus, and the Lower Volga region, where the structure of agriculture had long been characterized by single household land-owning patterns.[80]

The crisis in agricultural production forced regional leaders into a quandary over the conflicting demands of the center's extraction quotas and the region's economic survival. Throughout the early 1930s, the Provincial Komitetchiki lobbied central leaders for relief from the excessive procurement targets. In this regard, the Provincial Komitetchiki were not acting as representatives of the peasantry or any particular ethnic group. Instead, they were acting out an interest to maintain the vitality of their regional economies and the survival of their political machines.

The crisis of regional leadership led the Provincial Komitetchiki to oppose the center on issues related to agricultural resource extraction. They were not motivated by differences over the collectivization policy in principle, but rather by the desire to alleviate the crisis of regional leadership that collectivization had unleashed. In this regard, the crisis of regional leadership fostered a more acute awareness of their particular corporate interests within the institutional framework of the new state. It defined more clearly the competing interests of central and regional actors. The ensuing conflict between center and regions was much greater than a dispute over procurement policies, but instead represented a struggle over the institutionalzation of power in the new state.

III. COLLECTIVIZATION AND THE CONFLICT BETWEEN CENTER AND REGIONS

In the early 1930s, collectivization provoked a conflict between two distinct power centers in the new state. For the central leadership in general and Stalin in particular the conflict demonstrated a desire to establish an exclusive claim on decision making in matters of national security policy and national economic development. In this regard, agricultural collectivization was viewed as an essential component of the center's survival strategy for the postrevolutionary state. The efforts of regional leaders to assert themselves into the collectivization policy process was resented by central leaders as an encroachment on their perceived state role. The resistance of regional leaders to various aspects of the collectivization policy, moreover, was viewed by central leaders as ultimately harmful to the interests of the new state.

The Provincial Komitetchiki, meanwhile, shared the center's vision of an industrialized and armed Soviet Russia. They agreed with the policy to transform agriculture from a private, small-holding structure to a state-directed, collective structure. They differed, however, on the organization of power through which that vision would be realized. More specifically, the Provincial Komitetchiki sought to be included in the collectivization policy-making process. They believed that they deserved to participate because of their present positions as regional governors as well as their past service as the party's elite corps of fighter organizers. The Provincial Komitetchiki surmised that if the state's regional leaders were not allowed to determine the best means for carrying out their entrusted responsibilities, then the state's larger policy goals would remain unfulfilled. From their perspective, the success of the campaign demanded their participation at all levels of the policy process.

For central state actors, national security and economic development goals depended on the success of agricultural collectivization. Stalin emphasized this connection: "Is it possible for Soviet socialism to be constructed on two different foundations – a large-scale, concentrated socialist industry and a disunited, backward small-commodity peasantry? No, it is not possible. At some point, this would have to end in the complete collapse of our national economy."[81] The Provincial Komitetchiki, likewise, agreed that command–administrative methods were preferable to regulated market relations as the means by which agricultural resources were reallocated for industrial development. But the crisis of regional leadership forced them to be concerned with the more immediate issue of survival of their political machines.

The conflict between central and regional leaders was played out over a series of practical issues related to the policy implementation process, particularly grain procurements. How much grain could the agricultural sector afford to give up annually to industrial development? Who controlled the extraction process? What was the most effective method of extraction? In the end, the central leadership's insatiable appetite for grain simply overwhelmed the capabilities of the Provincial Komitetchiki.

In the political discourse of the 1930s, the grain issue was debated through two catchphrases: "Bolshevik tempos" and "realistic plans." Central leaders employed the catchphrase "Bolshevik tempos" to describe their radical implementation schedules and high procurement quotas. It meant that willpower alone could fulfill the center's directives. This voluntarist aspect of the campaign was expressed in the popular saying of the period that "no fortresses existed that Bolsheviks could not storm." Thus, unfulfilled directives implied insufficient revolutionary enthusiasm. The Provincial Komitetchiki insisted that only "realistic plans" could be fulfilled. This catchphrase indicated that grain procurement shortages were the result of the ill-conceived policies of the center, not the political character of regional leaders. They pressed the center to adopt realistic plans so that the agricultural sector could support industrial development without simultaneously destroying itself.

The disastrous 1932 harvest forced the conflict into the open. The Provincial Komitetchiki bore the burden of finding a way out of this disaster. While the Provincial Komitetchiki pleaded with central leaders to lower their extraction demands; central leaders chided the Provincial Komitetchiki to heighten their revolutionary enthusiasm. In Ukraine, Kosior called the center's procurement quotas "unrealistic" and the collectivization implementation schedule "too strenuous."[82] Representing the center in this dispute, Molotov disparagingly remarked that "the Ukrainian Bolsheviks failed to cope with their assignments" and that their requests for relief were an "anti-Bolshevik" attempt to shirk responsibility.[83] In the North Caucasus, the 1932 crop was roughly 40 percent smaller than the year previous, although the center's procurement quota was only barely reduced. Sheboldaev insisted to central leaders that the plan was impossible to fulfill under such conditions. But he was told that the real cause of grain shortages in the region was "kulak resistance," which must be combatted, not accommodated.[84] The Central Black Earth region also incurred the center's wrath for failing to meet its procurement quotas in the summer of 1932. Vareikis answered the center's charges, asserting that "we unconditionally fulfilled as much of the plan as was possible."[85]

During the first half of 1932, the Provincial Komitetchiki succeeded to persuade central leaders to lower somewhat the target figures for the 1932 procurement plan. Kuibyshev headed a special committee in the center that reduced the original plan by roughly 20 percent.[86] In May 1932, Kuibyshev wrote in a draft resolution that "I consider it necessary to be firm with the regions about the need to fulfill the procurement plan," but it is also necessary "to adopt a realistic course of action."[87] Eventually, the state's extraction demands were reduced to 18.1 million tons of grain, almost a third smaller than the original procurement plan.[88] By midsummer, central leaders refused to compromise further on their extraction demands. At this point, the conflict between center and regions intensified.

In July 1932, central leaders reaffirmed their commitment to a hardline in a spate of new directives, instructing regional leaders "to fulfill the established plan for grain procurements at whatever cost."[89] In August, a set of severe penalties were passed into law to discourage peasants and collective farm workers from withholding even the smallest amounts of grain from the state.[90] The autumn grain harvest and the state's unrelenting procurement campaign were conducted under extraordinarily adverse conditions. In November, the center declared an emergency situation and mobilized special collection brigades for the major grain-growing regions. Martial law, in effect, was imposed on Ukraine, the North Caucasus and the Lower Volga. Central plenipotentiaries were charged with extraordinary powers to direct small armies of grain collectors and to combat class enemies in these regions.[91] Soviet historian E. Oskolkov described the ensuing events as "a literal orgy of repression."[92] In December, entire populations of "blacklisted" villages in the North Caucasus were rounded up by the police and deported to Soviet Russia's desolate northern territories.[93] By the end of 1932, the state's extraction campaigns left behind countless villages without enough grain for spring sowing, livestock forage, or even minimal levels of human subsistence.

Central and regional leaders clashed over the answers to questions concerning the collectivization crisis: Who was to blame? What went wrong with the campaign? What were the appropriate solutions? Central and regional leaders formed opposing views on these issues, which reflected their different roles and conflicting interests as competing state actors.

Who was to blame for the crisis? On this question, at least some consensus existed between central and regional leaders. Both sides heaped most of the blame on local officials. Throughout the period, turnover rates among local officials were extremely high, but especially so following the disastrous 1932 harvest. Stalin harshly criticized local-level officials for their misplaced zeal in an early assessment of the campaign.[94] The Provincial Komitetchiki constantly faulted lower-level officials for disorder in the countryside and unfulfilled procurement plans. Kosior stressed that "we did not push our local organizations down the path of forced collectivization, rather, local workers did not pay attention to the real conditions in their districts"[95] Sheboldaev explained that "a major problem is local communists who do not fulfill plans and are just bad workers. We consider them to be ballast."[96] During the 1932 crisis, local officials were lucky just to be considered bad workers and not class enemies. Postyshev revealed the fate of these less fortunate local workers: "it is necessary to say directly that in a number of cases we shot them."[97]

Central and regional leaders, at first, appeared somewhat relunctant to blame each other directly. In 1930, for example, Stalin wrote of "a real danger of the Party's revolutionary measures being turned into empty bureaucratic decrees by individual representatives in one corner or another of our boundless country. I have in view not only local workers, but also individual provincial officials, and even individual Central Committee members."[98] But after the 1932 crisis, central leaders increasingly assailed the Provincial Komitetchiki for lacking sufficient "revolutionary vigilance" and behaving as "pen-pushing bureaucrats, far removed from the real-life problems of the collective farms."[99] Throughout this period, the Provincial Komitetchiki generally avoided public criticism of central leaders; instead, they directed their attacks at central plans. Vareikis cautioned against "revolutionary impatience."[100] Sheboldaev argued that any mistakes made by regional leaders during the collectivization campaign were a result of the excessive demands of the procurement plan.[101] In the Western region, however, Ivan Rumiantsev was quite specific in his allocation of the blame: Local leaders were 50 percent responsible for errors made in the implementation phase and central leaders were 40 percent responsible for mistakes made in the decision-making phase.

What went wrong with the campaign? Central leaders refused to acknowledge that their excessive extraction demands were the cause for the 1932 agricultural crisis. Stalin insisted that the center's hardline stance during the autumn harvest had in fact deterred would-be foreign aggressors from launching a surprise attack on the country.[103] The agricultural crisis, he maintained, was the result of "the resistance of the last remnants of the dying classes" to socialism's advance. Grain procurement, Kaganovich contended, had become "a concrete form of class struggle."[104] As part of this struggle, socialism's class enemies in the countryside, the kulaks, sought to prevent the collectivization of the rural economy, to deny grain for state extraction, and, ultimately, to destroy the Bolsheviks.

The Provincial Komitetchiki did not directly dispute the center's position that class enemies had undermined the 1932 harvest. In their accounts, however, they painted a different picture of events. Indeed, a common theme among the Provincial Komitetchiki was that the 1932 crisis was really not so bad. While it was true that the center's procurement's goals were not met for that season, overall progress in the transformation of the agricultural sector was the more noteworthy issue.[105] "Despite the difficulties at present," Kosior expounded, "it seems to me that compared to the situation we had at the outset of the five-year plan, we have indisputably expanded and strengthened agriculture in Ukraine."[106] It was not the kulaks, they argued, as much as it was the weather that caused the drop off in grain procurements in 1932. Vareikis reported that in the Central Black Earth region the class struggle was "not so acute," but "the lack of rain made things difficult."[107] Kosior stressed that a limit existed to what "even Bolsheviks could accomplish in the very severe climatic conditions of the previous summer."[108]

What was the solution to the crisis? The center's response to the crisis was made clear in a secret directive issued to regional leaders in December 1932. It explained that the kulaks had infiltrated the collective farms and had co-opted local officials in a concerted attempt to disrupt the distribution of bread to the rest of the country.[109] Accordingly, the center declared that any further reduction in the procurement plan signified a concession to "the most spiteful enemies of the party." Thus, the center's solution was to maintain procurement targets and "to continue a resolute Bolshevik offensive against this rabid opposition." This response entailed the continued use of coercion as a means to extract agricultural resources. Kaganovich, for one, demonstrated his "revolutionary vigilance" by presiding over several well-publicized executions in the North Caucasus of collective farm officials, accused of withholding grain from the state.[110] "Disarm these people!" Stalin demanded.[111]

The Provincial Komitetchiki, by contrast, proposed four alternative solutions. First, they charged that the center's grain-procurement plans were set arbitrarily and did not take into account the particular conditions of the regions.[112] Sheboldaev reasoned that lowering procurement quotas "in the short term was more beneficial in the long term." He explained that taking grain from the stores set aside for the next planting season in order to fulfill the present procurement targets led to a widespread perception in the villages of a "conflict of interest between the collective farm and the state." He continued: "We often hear people say how can you leave us without seeds? It is necessary first to create a seed fund and then to fulfill the obligations to the state. Otherwise, class enemies will take advantage of this attitude."[113]

Second, the Provincial Komitetchiki called for the strengthening of regional administrative capacities. They readily acknowledged the dismal performance of many lower-level organizations. To rectify this situation, they sought to secure an increase in organizational–technical resources and greater control over personnel policy at the lower levels. In response to the 1932 crisis, central leaders had forced a complete turnover of lower-level party officialdom. Since regional supervision of the lower levels was dependent on personal contacts, these mass dismissals further weakened regional administrative capacities. The Provincial Komitetchiki also resented the center's frequent "raiding" of competent personnel from regional administrative ranks, leaving a chronic shortage of expertly trained workers.[114]

Third, the Provincial Komitetchiki lobbied the center for greater economic investment into the agricultural sector. They especially demanded the long-promised increase in the mechanization level of the agricultural production process. Khataevich, responding to criticism that some lands in the Middle Volga region had been left uncultivated, curtly noted that "anyone who thinks that the land on the right bank can just all of a sudden be turned over must also know that it is immediately necessary to convert from wooden plows to tractors."[115] Robert Eikhe bemoaned the low levels of mechanization in Western Siberia. His comments also revealed the sometimes bitter interregional competition for scarce centrally allocated resources. "Presently, the central apparat directs all its attention to the south," he complained, "and such mighty grain regions as Western Siberia do not receive sufficient assistance."[116]

Finally, the Provincial Komitetchiki sought a devolution of control over regional economic activities and resources. They believed that as regional governors and economic managers they knew better how to direct regional economic affairs. They strongly urged the center to decentralize administrative control over trade and investment resources. The centralized system of allocation, Khataevich criticized, "is not working correctly. It is too centralized and does not take into account local conditions. The countryside sometimes goes several months without receiving goods and we are not receiving our funds."[117] The Provincial Komitetchiki insisted that the solution to the present procurement problems was to focus more attention on economic management. Vareikis explained that "the transition from individual-based peasant economy to a collective economy demands new forms and methods of agricultural administration. It is necessary to develop correctly the management of the collective farm economy and the utilization of labor in the agricultural sector."[118]

These opposing solutions to the 1932 crisis – economic management versus class struggle – became the focal point of the center–regional collectivization conflict. Postyshev argued the case for the Provincial Komitetchiki: "At present, we have to administer the affairs of huge economies and not hide behind the back of the kulak, which is not as broad as it once was. We will shriek that kulaks, wreckers, officers, and such are ruining the harvest or sabotaging the grain procurements, but it will not change the situation. And then where will we be?"[119] The implication of this argument was that class war tactics had reached their effective limits in the economic transformation of the countryside. This position was not left unchallenged by the center. Stalin responded that "some comrades have interpreted the thesis of the creation of a classless society as a justification of laziness and complacency. Needless to say, such people cannot have anything in common with our Party."[120]

During 1933 and 1934, several solutions proposed by the Provincial Komitetchiki were incorporated into official policy. These policy modifications did not seek to undo collectivization, rather they aimed to improve the management of the agricultural sector. Historian B. A. Abramov noted that "at the beginning of 1933, collectivization entered a new period of organizational–economic strengthening of the collective farms."[121] This less radical agricultural policy incorporated several demands of the Provincial Komitetchiki. First, the forced-pace implementation schedule for collectivizing the entire countryside was revised. While the main agricultural regions were for the most part collectivized by this time, the process was not completed across the rest of the countryside until the second half of the decade. Second, a new contract system was introduced to determine the state's annual procurement targets. Accordingly, state procurements would take the form of a compulsory tax on the villages, based on a fixed percentage of the actual area sown. The contract system was intended to impose regularity on the center's "unpredictable and capriciously changing" extraction demands.[122] Beyond this predetermined amount, collective farm officials were allowed to decide for themselves how to dispose of the surplus. Third, a central resolution promised to increase the import of production supplies and consumer goods to the countryside.[123] Finally, the center scaled back the use of class war tactics as an instrument of the implementation process. In early 1933, the class struggle in the countryside was officially declared to have been resolved in favor of the forces of socialism.[124]

The revised agricultural policy was designed to bring routine, predictability, and realism to the agricultural policy process. By moderating the more extreme implementation schedules and extraction demands, the revised policy was meant to alleviate the crisis of regional leadership brought on by collectivization. Vareikis reported that industrial output targets were also revised downward at this time, from 21 to 22 percent a year to 13 to 14 percent a year, despite the objections of Stalin.[125] In practice, however, relations between central and regional leaders remained conflictual. The concessions apparently won by the Provincial Komitetchiki in early 1933 were not immediately realized. The harsh grain procurement campaigns of the autumn continued in some regions through early 1933.

Central leaders worked to manipulate the new contract system of grain procurement through what Postyshev called "a mechanical approach to the distribution of sowing quotas."[126] During 1933 and 1934, relations between central and regional leaders were characterized by stalemate.

What was the significance of the center–regional conflict over collectivization? To begin, it is necessary to stress that the conflict was not over collectivization in principle. The Provincial Komitetchiki supported the collectivization of agriculture and worked relentlessly to fulfill the center's policies. They favored the use of command–administrative methods as a means of rapid economic development. They supported a strong interventionary state in the rural economy, which enhanced their own power resources. Indeed, the Provincial Komitetchiki were instrumental in building this system by which the Soviet Russian state was able to extract agricultural resources directly and routinely from the countryside.

Nor did the Provincial Komitetchiki clash with central leaders out of some sense of identity with societal forces. They did not see themselves as the political representatives of peasant or ethnic–national interests. Before the crisis of regional leadership, they enthusiastically supported the application of class warfare against the kulaks. The Provincial Komitetchiki were hardly in a position to express the sentiments of ethnic natives in their regions: Kosior in Ukraine was a Pole, Khataevich in Russian and Ukrainian regions was a Belorussian Jew, Vareikis in a Russian region was a Lithuanian, Eikhe in a Russian region was Latvian, Mirzoian in Kazakhstan was Armenian, and Gikalo in Belorussia was Georgian. They were not even especially protective of their own lower-level officials. Regional leaders unloaded on local officials a barrage of unreasonable demands, arbitrary complaints and severe punishments.

The objections of the Provincial Komitetchiki lay in the way in which the center attempted to implement collectivization and to fulfill procurement plans. Their protests were in response to the crisis of regional leadership and to the efforts of the center to shut them out of the policy process. As their civil war records testified, the Provincial Komitetchiki were not adverse to storming fortresses and routing class enemies. But they had undergone change in the ten years since the civil war. The Provincial Komitetchiki were now provincial governors, economic managers, and state builders. The solutions that they put forward would have the effect of institutionalizing their perceived role, status and identity in the new state. Thus, the conflict between center and regions represented an intrastate power struggle.

The solutions proposed by the Provincial Komitetchiki had several objectives. Foremost, they wanted relief from the crisis of regional leadership and the consolidation of their political machines. They sought to achieve these ends by formally including themselves into the decision-making process for agricultural administration. They sought to routinize the policy process in place of the arbitrariness that so often characterized central directives. They wanted greater control over regional personnel and regional economic resources. They wanted the center to defer to them on matters that affected their regions. The challenge of the Provincial Komitetchiki was directed at the institutionalization of power and status in the postrevolutionary state. They wanted their elite status as regional governors and economic managers to be recognized by the center. In this regard, they offered a protocorporatist alternative to Stalin's bureaucratic absolutism. The Provincial Komitetchiki, however, did not articulate an alternative to the command–administrative state. They never offered an alternative vision for state–societal relations. At best, they represented, in the words of historian V. P. Danilov, a kind of "Stalinism with a human face."[127]

The conflict between center and regions, in the first half of the 1930s, was shaped by the constraints of power in the new state. Both sides generally worked to achieve their goals within the parameters of established power constraints. At this time, central leaders employed their organizational and coercive power resources in the conflict with discretion and moderation. Although central leaders were increasingly frustrated by this arrangement, their efforts to dislodge regional leaders from their strategic location in the implementation process and to uproot regional political machines were restrained in this period. The Provincial Komitetchiki, meanwhile, used their strategic position in the policy process and their informal power resources to assert their interests. The Provincial Komitetchiki used their personal network ties to lobby the center for more-moderate policies. The protection provided by central patrons emboldened the Provincial Komitetchiki to challenge central policy positions. The revised agricultural policy of 1933 and 1934 indicated the capabilities of regional leaders to wrest concessions from the center.

7

CENTER AND REGIONS IN CONFLICT II: THE FALL OF THE PROVINCIAL KOMITETCHIKI

The center–regional conflict of the 1930s was shaped by the constraints of power formed by the intersection of formal organizational and informal social structures within the postrevolutionary state. Despite the accumulation of formal powers in the state center, the Provincial Komitetchiki were nonetheless able to assert their own interests into the policy process during the early 1930s. Central leaders did not directly challenge the informal power resources of the Provincial Komitetchiki at this time. Instead, they resorted to a series of organizational reforms that ultimately failed to dislodge the Provincial Komitetchiki from the policy process. The years 1933 and 1934 were characterized by stalemate in the center–regional power struggle. During the mid-1930s, each side attempted to redefine the constraints of power to its own advantage. The Provincial Komitetchiki were unsuccessful in this attempt. Central leaders, however, devised a strategy that moved beyond the established parameters of constraint in the relationship. Through coercive resource mobilization and coalition building, the center engaged in a direct and systematic assault on the informal power resources of the regional leadership. As a result, central actors successfully restructured the relationship between center and regions in the new state. The power constraints in the center–regional relationship were not static, but dynamic. By the end of the 1930s, central actors, in general, and Stalin, in particular, were able to realize more fully their claim on the "despotic" powers of the state.

This chapter demonstrates how the constraints of power shaped the interactions between central and regional actors and the process by which these constraints were redefined. The chapter focuses on three aspects of this process: (1) the limits of central actors to dislodge the Provincial Komitetchiki as a result of the constraints of power in the early 1930s; (2) the unsuccessful attempt of regional leaders to redefine the constraints of power and the successful effort of central leaders to redefine the constraints in the relationship in the mid-1930s; and (3) the center's reign of terror unleashed on the Provincial Komitetchiki in the late 1930s.

I. THE CONSTRAINTS OF POWER AND THE LIMITS OF CENTRAL RESPONSES

In the early 1930s, central state actors did not yet resort to coercion in relations with the Provincial Komitetchiki. At this time, central leaders attempted to take advantage of their preponderant formal organizational strength to impose policy solutions on the regions. Between 1930 and 1934, central actors developed a series of measures to achieve this end: (1) manipulating the personnel mechanism, (2) circumventing the regional leaders in the policy implementation process, (3) reorganizing the control bureaucracy, and (4) conducting normative campaigns. These tactics did not directly challenge the constraints of power and ultimately proved ineffective. The position, role, and status of the Provincial Komitetchiki in the new state remained secure during these years.

To begin, central leaders actively manipulated the personnel mechanism in an attempt to induce greater productivity and compliance from regional and local administrators. The Communist party's nomenklatura system was founded in the early 1920s. The powers of appointment to almost all elite positions in the new state were concentrated in the central offices of the party bureaucracy, headed by Stalin, Molotov, and Kaganovich. They defined the state's cadres policies and directly supervised the appointment process. The center's formal control over personnel selection was indeed vast, encompassing the many sectors of political and economic activity. Kaganovich boasted, for example, that the center's main personnel office authorized nearly 11,000 appointments between 1928 and 1930 alone.[1] On two occasions in the early 1930s, central leaders mobilized these powers to stir waves of personnel change within regional and local administration. The first wave of personnel changes occurred in mid-1930 in the aftermath of the first collectivization campaigns; the second wave of changes was conducted during the grain procurement crisis in late 1932 and early 1933.

In the 1930 wave, three categories of personnel changes were carried out by central leaders. The first category of removals involved overzealous officials who were made into scapegoats for the excesses and confusion of the initial collectivization drive. These officials were accused of imprudently pushing the implementation process beyond the limits defined in official policy. But these removals were more symbolic than punitive. The accused officials did not suffer serious career setbacks; instead, they were transferred to comparable administrative positions in other regions. Most notable in this category was Karl Bauman, who was sent from Moscow to Central Asia.[2] Personnel changes in the Transcaucasus in the spring of 1930 also were meant to indicate a less extreme approach to collectivization. The regional officials removed at this time were simply redeployed to new assignments outside the Transcaucasus; they included A. Krinitskii, M. Khakiani, A. Kostanian, and N. Gikalo.[3]

The second category of removals included regional leaders who publicly withdrew their support for collectivization in the wake of the disastrous first campaign. These officials exhibited little restraint in their criticisms of the center's campaign to implement collectivization by force during the spring of 1930. V. V. "Beso" Lominadze, head of the Transcaucasian regional party organization briefly in 1930, and S. I. Syrtsov, head of the Russian republican government, were prominent in this regard. Lominadze argued that the peasantry was not yet ready for a rapid transition to socialist forms of economic organization. He observed that the party had adopted "a lordly, feudal attitude toward the needs of the workers and the peasants" in its haste to realize this transition.[4] Lominadze and Syrtsov were soon after expelled from the party's central committee for their "oppositionist" behavior.

The third category of removals represented routine promotions or transfers. These regional leaders were not subjected to criticism or rebuke by the center. These changes particularly affected officials who had previously worked outside of regional administration. For example, Ian Gamarnik, head of the Belorussian party organization, and Andrei Andreev, head of the North Caucasus party organization, were appointed to regional leadership posts in 1928. Their prior experiences were in the military and the trade unions, respectively. In 1930, Gamarnik moved up to head the central military–political administration and Andreev was appointed to the leadership of the central control administration.[5] To replace Andreev, Boris Sheboldaev was transferred horizontally from the Lower Volga region to the North Caucasus region, where he had first begun his career in regional administration in the early 1920s.[6]

The 1932 wave of personnel changes came in direct response to the disastrous grain harvests, famines, and procurement crises. The major grain-producing regions and the non-Russian regions were the principal targets of the center's personnel changes. Local-level administration in Ukraine, the North Caucasus and the Lower Volga underwent comprehensive personnel turnover in late 1932 and early 1933. In Ukraine, newly appointed party leader Pavel Postyshev oversaw the removal from district-level administration of 237 party secretaries, 249 governmental chairmen, and 158 control commission chairmen.[7] By early 1933, not only was the local administration overturned in the North Caucasus, but nearly 45 percent of the entire regional party membership was expelled.[8] The personnel changes imposed by the center would later become an object of contention, when "hidden enemies" were uncovered within these regional organizations.

The 1932 wave of personnel change, similar to the 1930 wave, struck more severely in the non-Russian regions. From the second half of 1932 to early 1933, new regional leaders were appointed in Belorussia, Ukraine, Odessa, Transcaucasia, Azerbaijan, Middle Volga, Tataria, Kazakhstan, and Kirgizia.[9] Central leaders were particularly alert to manifestations of nationalism in reaction to the coercive campaigns to extract ever more grain from the villages. They feared that the regime's class enemies in the countryside were using national identity to rally resistance to procurement efforts. In late 1932, Kuibyshev, for example, drafted legislation that forbade the continued use of the Ukrainian language in official discourse in the North Caucasus and closed all but one Ukrainian language newspaper. The Ukrainian language, he argued, was not in "the cultural interests of the population," but served the interests of "anti-Bolshevik" forces in the region.[10] Postyshev, specifically blamed "nationalist deviations" for unfulfilled agricultural plans in Ukraine.[11] Similar allegations were raised in Belorussia, where dismissed republican leader K. Gei was accused of tolerating a "national deviationist" movement.[12]

Exceptional in this regard was Filipp Goloshchekin, republican leader of Kazakhstan from 1925 to 1933. Instead of displaying tolerance toward nationalism during collectivization, Goloshchekin was criticized explicitly for leading a ruthless campaign to obliterate all vestiges of traditional Kazakh society and culture, including the forced settlement of Kazakhstan's sizable nomadic population.[13] This apparent double standard is explained, in part, by the center's view that Kazkahstan was not one of the major grain-producing regions and, in part, by the assumption that national identity remained generally underdeveloped among native Kazakhs. Goloshchekin, who since the early 1920s had worked as a leader in regional administration, was transferred at this time to a lesser post in the central government.[14] Also noteworthy, the party leaders in several non-Russian provincial enclaves displayed exceptional longevity in office during this period: Betal Kalmykov (1928–37) in Karbadino-Balkaria province, North Caucasus; Mikhnei Erbaniv (1928–37) in Buriat province, Siberia; and, Sergei Petrov (1926–37) in Chuvashia, Middle Volga, whose eleven years was among the longest tenures in regional administration for the interwar period.

Despite the frequent personnel changes in rural and non-Russian regions during the early 1930s, the Provincial Komitetchiki remained entrenched in their positions of power in regional administration. The central leadership, at this time, generally exercised self-restraint toward the Provincial Komitetchiki. The regional leadership, in contrast to lower administrative levels, actually exhibited relative stability in office during these years (see Table 4.1). Stability in leadership was especially notable in Russian regions, where Vareikis, Rumiantsev, Kabakov, and Eikhe demonstrated impressive survival skills considering the extent of political turmoil within regional administration. But even in the non-Russian regions, stability was still evident when informal ties are taken into account. On the 1934 regional leadership list, for example, Nikolai Gikalo in Belorussia and Lev Mirzoian in Kazakhstan were both members of the Transcaucasian network and had strong ties to Ordzhonikidze and Kirov, dating back to the underground and civil war.[15] Khataevich (who does not appear on the 1934 list) simply shifted laterally from the Middle Volga region to the Dnepropetrovsk province in Ukraine.[16]

The personnel changes carried out in the Transcaucasus were notably different from those in other regions. The Transcaucasian region underwent repeated personnel changes from the beginning of the collectivization campaigns. Central leaders combatted Orakhelishvili's subtle obstructions, Lominadze's open defiance as well as interminable factional infighting. In October 1932, Lavrenti Beria was named head of the Transcaucasian region. Although he had network ties to Ordzhonikidze, Beria did not belong to the party's *komitetchik* cohort, but was from the postrevolutionary generation of party workers. He spent most of his career in the regional police bureaucracy. At a regional party meeting, Beria made clear where his loyalties lay: "Did the Transcaucasian leadership fulfill the instructions of the central committee and Comrade Stalin? No, they did not succeed. The Transcaucasian Bolsheviks, in 1930 and 1931, did not manage to achieve the necessary successes in the struggle for the economic and political strengthening of the Transcaucasian federation."[17] Under Beria's direction, members of the old Transcaucasian network were systematically removed from positions of organizational power in the region.[18] This approach to personnel change in the Transcaucasus marked a deliberate effort by the center to decouple informal network ties from the formal structures of power. Of significance, this approach was applied indiscriminately and coercively across the regional administration later in the decade.

The second way in which central leaders sought to secure their power over the regions was to diminish the role of the Provincial Komitetchiki in the policy implementation process. Between 1933 and 1934, central leaders created an alternative organization for agricultural management and scaled back the organizational apparatus for regional administration.

In January 1933, central leaders introduced a new administrative agency for the agricultural sector, the political department of the machine-tractor stations (MTS).[19] The MTS were established across the agricultural regions in the first five-year plan in order to pool tractors and other mechanized equipment. The political departments were concentrated in the major grain-producing regions. They were directed to oversee the implementation of agricultural policies and the fulfillment of procurement plans. The political departments were formally connected to the center by a separate organizational command chain, beyond the administrative jurisdiction of regional and local party organizations. They were administered in the center by Aleksandr Krinitskii, who spent most of his career in regional administration.[20] In citing the advantages of the political departments over the established administrative organs in the countryside, Kaganovich stressed that political department employees were recruited from outside the region and, hence, were not burdened by personal ties or conflicting loyalties. He described them as action-oriented specialists, capable of cutting through the morass of bureaucratic inefficiency that plagued regional administration.[21] Central leaders attempted, through the political departments, to bypass the Provincial Komitetchiki in the agricultural policy process.

Not surprisingly, bureaucratic turf battles soon broke out between the political departments and local party organizations. Despite the center's admonishment to local party leaders "to help the new people," they more often resisted the encroachments of the political departments on their perceived terrain.[22] Local officials were chastised for their petty harassments of political department workers, including the withholding of food rations and housing facilities. One official was even expelled from the party for attempting to arrest the local head of a political department.[23]

The Provincial Komitetchiki adamantly opposed the administrative independence of the political departments and defended the local party organizations in these disputes. They sought solutions that would maintain their dominant position in the agricultural policy process. In June 1933, Pavel Postyshev derided the political departments as "pretenders for power in the districts."[24] During the party congress in February 1934, Postyshev,

Sheboldaev, Vareikis, and Eikhe drew attention to various shortcomings in the performance of the political departments. Sheboldaev was especially harsh in his criticism of the political departments and called for their immediate subordination to the regional party administrative organs.[25] At another party meeting, in June 1934, Kosior and Vareikis complained that the political departments had become entangled in local interests to the detriment of the center's procurement efforts.[26] Even Kirov took up the cause by publicly assailing the performance of the political departments.[27]

Central state leaders finally relented to the Provincial Komitetchiki's steady barrage of criticism. In November 1934, the independent powers of the political departments were curbed and their operations incorporated into the existing regional administrative structure.[28] The dismantling of the political departments also led central leaders to give up their attempt to undercut organizational support to regional administration. This attempt had included, at the regional level, the elimination of the executive staffs and, at the local level, the conversion of departmental staffs into groups of traveling instructors.[29] In this way, the center had sought to undermine the role of implementation teams in regional administration. These organizational changes, however, proved short-lived.[30] During this period of stalemate in center-regional relations, 1933–34, the center failed in its attempt to create alternative organizational forms for regional and agricultural administration. The Provincial Komitetchiki could not be dislodged from their dominant position in the policy implementation process.

Third, central leaders sought to improve the system of checking and control over regional administration. The control system, created in 1922, was a bureaucratic structure that paralleled regional and local levels of administration. Control officials were supposed to monitor the activities of regional and local administrators, reporting their findings to a central control commission. When the center's campaigns for radical restructuring of the countryside initially encountered resistance in 1930, central leaders enlisted the regional control bureaucracy to focus its energies on the implementation process.[31] But the control bureaucracy proved ill-prepared for this assignment. Informal ties were pervasive among regional administrators and control officials, undermining the effectiveness of the control bureaucracy.

In response to this situation, central leaders restructured the system of control to secure its independence from regional and local leaders. In January 1933, an alternative control organ, the central purge commission, was created to conduct a comprehensive review of the rank-and-file party membership in the wake of the disastrous 1932 harvest.[32] Central leaders made a concerted effort to keep the purge commission beyond the reach of the regional leadership. In April 1933, ten special regional purge commissions, responsible only to the central purge commission, were set up to oversee the membership review process.[33] Kaganovich stressed that "it was the duty" of regional purge commission officials "to report to the central committee all violations and defects in the republics, territories, and regions."[34]

Regional leaders, nonetheless, were accused of obstructing the efforts of the purge commissions. Moreover, despite the center's numerous complaints, the regional and local party organizations, not the purge commissions, were subsequently made responsible for organizing the follow-up review and exchange of personal documents for the entire rank-and-file party membership.[35] Between 1935 and 1936, regional leaders oversaw a series of screenings and expulsions of party members.[36] While this process led to mass expulsions of party members, the Provincial Komitetchiki and their personal cliques emerged notably intact. Malenkov later criticized the Provincial Komitetchiki for the "mechanistic" and "passive" way in which they approached the membership review process.[37]

Finally, central leaders attempted to utilize nonbureaucratic means of control. A normative campaign for "inner-party democracy" was organized by the center soon after the initial collectivization problems occurred in 1930. These campaigns sought to employ popular criticism against local officials, but always in controlled settings. Self-criticism sessions, for example, were arranged at which rank-and-file party members as well as nonparty members were provided opportunites to confront and to criticize party leaders.[38] The mass media were enlisted as part of this normative campaign. The press was instructed to uphold "proletarian self-criticism" and "without mercy to strike at the bureaucracy and those who suppress self-criticism."[39] Also, elections for regional and local party leaders were held in the summer of 1930. A *Pravda* editorial at the time stressed that "reelections must strengthen even more so the party organizations in the struggle for the general line of the party and for fighting tempos of socialism."[40] The Provincial Komitetchiki, however, successfully avoided subjecting themselves to self-criticism sessions or reelection campaigns.

In summary, during the early thirties, central leaders responded to their conflict with the regions through a series of mostly benign organizational measures. These tactics – personnel changes, organizational innovations, and normative campaigns – were defined by the constraints of power in the center–regional relationship.[41] The center's response did not directly challenge the parameters of the center-regional relationship as it had evolved during the 1920s. The position and powers of the Provincial Komitetchiki in the postrevolutionary state were for the most part unaltered by the center's tactics. By the mid-1930s, the center's frustration with its inability to achieve its stated goals in the regions became increasingly clear. At this time, central leaders devised a new approach for dealing with the regions. The Provincial Komitetchiki, likewise, sought to redefine the constraints of power in their relations to the center.

II. REDEFINING THE CONSTRAINTS OF POWER IN THE CENTER–REGIONAL RELATIONSHIP

Beginning in 1934, the constraints of power that had shaped center–regional relations early in the decade became the focus of attention of both central and regional leaders. First, several of the Provincial Komitetchiki plotted a palace coup, wherein Stalin would be removed as party general secretary and replaced by their central patron, Sergei Kirov. By forcing a leadership succession, the Provincial Komitetchiki sought to formalize their power and status as the state's regional elite. Their bid to become kingmakers, however, was never put into action. The Provincial Komitetchiki were not able to sustain sufficient cooperation to redefine the constraints of power to their advantage. Central leaders, meanwhile, endeavored to subvert the informal power resources of the regional leadership. Over the next two years, central leaders systematically worked to decouple informal network ties from formal positions of power and to undermine the status image of the Provincial Komitetchiki. By the first half of 1937, central leaders succeeded in removing the regional leadership's informal supports, thus setting the stage for a direct confrontation that ultimately led not just to the political removal, but to the physical destruction of the Provincial Komitetchiki.

The Provincial Komitetchiki acted first to redefine the constraints of power. In February 1934, a party congress convened in Moscow for the first time since 1930. Touted as the "Congress of the Victors," it provided an official occasion to claim victory in the "socialist offensive." While much work still remained to be done, the Bolshevik elite present at the congress celebrated their most recent triumphs in building socialism. Central leaders were more reserved in their praise for what had been accomplished and for the performance of those assembled. Kaganovich strongly criticized individuals "in the ranks of the Bolshevik party, in the ranks of the Central Committee, who, it was discovered, were unable to keep pace with Bolshevik tempos, lagged behind, became emasculated, and lacked sufficient stamina for the new great cause."[42]

In their public statements at the party congress, the Provincial Komitetchiki continued to pay homage to Stalin's leadership, to celebrate socialism's advance, and to laud their own accomplishments. But in private, the Provincial Komitetchiki discussed their conflict with the center and devised a plan to end the center's attacks on them. Meeting in Ordzhonikidze's Kremlin apartment between sessions, several leading members of the Provincial Komitetchiki formed a cabal with the intent of formally limiting Stalin's powers in the center. The existence of this secret cabal was only later confirmed in the memoirs of Anastas Mikoian and Nikita Khrushchev, participants at the congress.[43] Information about the plot is second-hand, although a consensus exists over three important aspects: (1) the participants, (2) the strategy, and (3) its unraveling.

The cabal was instigated and pushed along by Boris Sheboldaev. Iosif Vareikis and Stanislav Kosior were also among the chief conspirators. In addition, the group included Robert Eikhe, Mamia Orakhelishvili, and Grigorii Petrovskii. This particular set of actors is significant for several reasons. First, Sheboldaev, Vareikis, and Kosior represented the major agricultural regions in the country. Thus, the conflict between center and regions over collectivization likely brought these regional leaders together. Second, five of the six named conspirators were connected by personal network ties. Members of the Transcaucasian network were at the heart of the conspiracy. Not only was it initiated by Sheboldaev, Vareikis, and Orakhvelishvili, but the meetings were held in Ordzhonikidze's flat and the plot also involved Sergei Kirov. Kosior and Petrovskii were core members of the Ukrainian network. Third, the conspiracy demonstrated an attempt at interregional cooperation. The regions represented by the participants were the North Caucasus, the Central Black Earth, Ukraine, Transcaucasia, and Siberia. It is especially noteworthy that Eikhe was said to be a participant, since the Ukrainian and Siberian regions often engaged in a bitter competition over the allocation of resources at this time.

The strategy of the conspirators was to use the congress as a legal forum to carry out a nonviolent palace coup against Stalin. According to the party rules, the congress was the body formally empowered to elect party leaders. The last congress had met in 1930.[44] This congress, thus, was the first opportunity to make a formal challenge to the center since the unfolding of the crisis of regional leadership and the intensification of the center–regional conflict during the years 1932 and 1933. The coup entailed three steps. First, the conspirators proposed to make public at the congress Lenin's decade-old request that Stalin be removed as party general secretary. Next, they would orchestrate a no-confidence vote on Stalin's leadership. Finally, the group would nominate Sergei Kirov to replace Stalin and move to vote on appointing Kirov as general secretary. Kirov was arguably the most popular figure in the party leadership at this time. He had received nearly three hundred more votes than Stalin in the election of a new party central committee conducted during the congress. In the conflict between center and regions, he had emerged as a defender of the regional leadership. And, most importantly, he was the central patron of three of the six key participants – Sheboldaev, Vareikis, and Orakhelishvili.

The plot unraveled, however, before reaching step one. When approached by the conspirators, Kirov unequivocally refused to take part in the coup. He reportedly insisted that the removal of Stalin would be seen as a renunciation of all that had been achieved during the past five years. According to Mikoian, Kirov instead argued that he and Ordzhonikidze were already playing a moderating role in the center.[45] Kirov's reluctance to go along may also have been motivated by either loyalty to or, more likely, fear of Stalin.[46] The principal conspirators personally knew and trusted Kirov. Without his participation, the cabal simply collapsed. The conspirators did not try to find an alternative challenger to Stalin's throne.

The aborted coup to unseat Stalin represented the only known instance in which the Provincial Komitetchiki considered taking action to redefine the power constraints in the center–regional relationship. The failure of this conspiracy to move beyond the discussion stage indicated the formidable obstacles that had to be overcome for the regional leaders to redefine these constraints. In regional administration, personal networks and regional interests often placed the Provincial Komitetchiki in competition with one another. The collapse of the conspiracy after Kirov's defection suggested that cooperation was not only difficult to initiate, but even more difficult to sustain. The incident also revealed the boundaries in their perceived role as state actors. The elite identity of the Provincial Komitetchiki included their roles as soldiers of the revolution and also builders of the socialist state, but alas they refrained from taking on the role of kingmakers.

Central leaders, meanwhile, concocted their own plan to redefine the constraints of power to their advantage. The plan focused on the decoupling of informal personal networks from formal state structures. Between the second half of 1934 and the first half of 1937, the central leadership incrementally subverted the informal power resources of the Provincial Komitetchiki. This process entailed: (1) removing core network members from the central leadership, (2) severing the cross-organizational network ties with the organs of control and coercion, (3) breaking the monopoly of the Provincial Komitetchiki on agricultural policy implementation, and (4) undermining the status image of the Provincial Komitetchiki.

First, between 1934 and 1937, core network members Sergei Kirov, Sergo Ordzhonikidze, and Valerian Kuibyshev departed the central leadership as a result of unusual deaths. On 1 December 1934, Kirov was shot to death in the corridor outside his office in the Smolney Institute, headquarters of the Leningrad party organization.[47] The assassin was said to be a disgruntled follower of Zinoviev, the former party leader of Leningrad and one-time rival of Stalin. Few adherents to the official version of the murder exist among scholars, who instead draw attention to the circumstantial evidence and motives that suggest Stalin's complicity.[48] Less than two months later, on 26 January 1935, Valerian Kuibyshev died of heart failure. Although the circumstances of Kuibyshev's death have aroused suspicion, he was reportedly in ill-health prior to being stricken.[49] Finally, on 18 February 1937, Sergo Ordzhonikidze was dead. The official account of Ordzhonikidze's death was heart failure; it was known that he had suffered a heart attack several years earlier. Later it was revealed that Ordzhonikidze, in fact, had committed suicide. Ordzhonikidze shot himself after engaging Stalin in a heated argument over the spreading wave of arrests and executions of the state elite, which included in its reach his own network clients.[50] According to Khrushchev, Ordzhonikidze "realized he could not go on working with Stalin even though he had been one of his closest friends. [H]e could no longer work in a normal manner and, in order to avoid a collision with Stalin or the responsibility of contributing to Stalin's abuses of power, he decided to commit suicide."[51]

The official versions of the deaths of Kirov, Kuibyshev, and Ordzhonikidze were yet another reflection of the informal constraints of power in the state. These individuals were not publicly tried and executed, as were other former Old Bolshevik leaders at this time. Instead, they were accorded "honorable" deaths and, ironically, interred in the Kremlin wall alongside one another directly behind Lenin's mausoleum. Unlike other Old Bolshevik leaders, this group had extensive personal network ties to the Provincial Komitetchiki, the military elite and the industrial elite. The departure of these individuals from the leadership removed a significant informal constraint in the center–regional relationship. Each at times had acted to moderate central economic plans. Ordzhonikidze and Kirov, in particular, served as patrons and protectors for a number of leading actors across the state elite, especially among the Provincial Komitetchiki. While they were active, central leaders demonstrated self-restraint in relations with the regional leadership. Their untimely deaths deprived the Provincial Komitetchiki of an informal power resource and made them more vulnerable to the center's formal organizational and coercive powers.

As Robert Conquest has duly noted, "the murder of Kirov was the overture to 1937."[52]

Second, during the mid-1930s, central leaders succeeded in severing the cross-organizational informal ties between the regional leadership and the organs of control and coercion. This effort began with a comprehensive restructuring of the system of control. The new control agency, the purge commission, created in the wake of the 1932 procurement crisis, eventually usurped the authority over personnel and disciplinary affairs from the existing control bureaucracy, which was relegated to policy implementation issues.[53] In 1934, the police bureaucracy underwent a reorganization that led to a significant expansion of its jurisdiction and powers. The police bureaucracy assumed operative control over special military units, foreign state security, internal secret police, civilian police, border guards, fire departments, and highway patrol. The reorganization, in effect, consolidated under a single administrative framework every coercive organ in the state, except the Red Army.[54]

In September 1936, Nikolai Ezhov was named the chief of the police bureaucracy. A protégé of Lazar Kaganovich, Ezhov had become a prominent central actor overseeing regional administration during the first half of the 1930s.[55] During this time, Ezhov emerged as an outspoken critic of the regional leadership and a firm believer in class war tactics. In December 1935, for example, he complained that the regional leaders "had mastered very badly the repeated orders of the central committee on the need for raising Bolshevik vigilance and discipline."[57] These words recalled the center's confrontation with the Provincial Komitetchiki during the 1932 grain procurement crisis. Ezhov now elaborated the details of a complex conspiracy theory linking the 1932 procurement crisis and the Kirov murder with intraparty factional groupings.[58]

He purged the police bureaucracy of old party hands, who, he asserted, lacked the necessary resolve to prosecute prominent elite figures. Ezhov mocked his predecessors for their treatment of political opponents, suggesting that "it is more like staying at a rest home than in jail."[59] Under Ezhov's direction, relations between the police and the regional leadership immediately turned confrontational. Whereas the police bureaucracy had once exercised restraint in formal relations with the regional leadership, central leaders now openly advocated routine police intervention into regional administration.[60] These organizational and personnel changes signified a successful attempt by the center to mobilize coercive power resources. By 1937, the police bureaucracy was remade into an instrument of Stalin's personal rule.

Following the restructuring of the police bureaucracy, central leaders moved against the military leadership. Similar to the Provincial Komitetchiki, the military elite represented an alternative power center within the institutional framework of the postrevolutionary state. The military elite displayed a professional identity, a distinctive esprit de corps and protocorporatist traits.[61] At least some military leaders demonstrated loyalty and protectiveness toward their accused colleagues. For example, when pressed by Molotov to name specific individuals of wrongdoing at a central committee meeting, Ian Gamarnik, the head of the military–political administration, defiantly refused to implicate any military officers in the alleged conspiracy uncovered by the police.[62]

In the spring of 1937, the revamped police apparat was unleashed on the military elite. A select group of military commanders were quickly and quietly arrested, tried before a secret tribunal, found guilty of treason, and then executed.[63] This act marked the beginning of a wave of terror against the military establishment that by the end of the decade consumed more than two-thirds of the military high command as well as ensnared tens of thousands of middle- and junior-level officers.[64] Among those first targeted for repression were military commanders with the most extensive network ties to the Provincial Komitetchiki, including Tukhachevskii, Iakir, Uborevich, Levandovskii, and Kork. Gamarnik, who had extensive network ties to the Ukrainian political leadership, commited suicide before he could be arrested.

The fall of the military high command in the spring of 1937 removed yet another informal constraint in the center–regional relationship. By subduing the coercive powers of the military, central leaders were further emboldened to confront the Provincial Komitetchiki. While the informal ties that cut across the regional leadership and the military elite presented a potential coercive resource that could be mobilized against the center, no evidence exists to suggest that such a strategy was ever contemplated by regional or military leaders.

Third, central leaders in the mid-1930s acted to dislodge the Provincial Komitetchiki from their strategic location in the policy implementation process. This time, instead of creating alternative channels for policy implementation, central leaders attempted to diminish the formal organizational powers at the disposal of the Provincial Komitetchiki and to ally themselves with a new cohort of regional administrators.

To accomplish the first task, the consolidated administrative–territorial units, which had been formed in the late 1920s, were incrementally dismantled during the mid-1930s. These large administrative–territorial units served as the formal power base of the Provincial Komitetchiki, providing political, economic and organizational resources. Beginning in 1934, a new administrative–territorial structure began to go into place, which directly connected the center to the traditional Russian provinces and the non-Russian republics. In Russia, Boris Sheboldaev had been regional leader of the North Caucasus, but now he presided over the Azov-Black Sea krai, which was less than half the size; Iosif Vareikis had been regional leader of the Central Black Earth region, but now he was responsible for only the Voronezh oblast; and Ivan Kabakov had been regional leader of the Urals, but now he ruled the Sverdlovsk oblast. In such cases, the Provincial Komitetchiki remained leaders in the same region, but their organizational and territorial jurisdictions were significantly reduced. In the non-Russian areas, the overarching Transcaucasian and Central Asian regional committees were dismantled in the mid-1930s as well.

As the territorial domains over which the Provincial Komitetchiki ruled were diminished, their responsibility for the fulfillment of the center's economic plans was decreased accordingly. Further, in an effort to undermine the regional leadership's control over local patronage, central leaders formally assumed responsibility for appointing district level leaders in January 1935.[65] With smaller jurisdictions, the center began to break up the regional leaders' implementation teams. By such means, the center weakened the political machines of the Provincial Komitetchiki.

The restructured administrative–territorial framework provided fresh opportunities for new recruits to advance upward into the ranks of regional administration. A new cadres policy was put into place at this time through which central leaders attempted to ally themselves directly with the cohort of party workers recruited after the civil war. The new policy was intended to promote technically competent and politically reliable cadres into formal positions of power in the regions.[66] Special educational seminars were conducted to cultivate relations between the center and this younger cohort of administrators. For example, in November 1935, a fifteen-month training program was organized by the party's central administrative office for a select group of three hundred regional cadres who were thirty-two years of age or younger.[67] And, in the summer of 1936, a higher party school was set up in Moscow for the express purpose of developing a new elite corps of regional administrators.[68] With the command economic system now in place, central leaders were less dependent on the Provincial Komitetchiki and their cliques for policy implementation. Thus, they engaged in a strategy of coaliton building with this younger generation of regional administrators. Stalin, in particular, welcomed the arrival of the post-civil war generation, claiming that they "would secure three to four times greater results for our country than at present."[69]

The center conducted this recruitment program simultaneously with an "antibureaucratic" campaign, directed against the Provincial Komitet-chiki. By the second half of 1935, the regional leadership as a group was berated on almost a daily basis in the pages of the central press for their false sense of mastery over administrative–economic affairs, lack of concern for political–ideological matters, bureaucratic mentality, and self-aggrandizement.[70] Again, these words echoed the center–regional conflict of the early 1930s. The "antibureaucratic" campaign was a tactic employed by central leaders to politicize the emerging generational cleavage line in regional administration. Stalin, for example, engaged in this tactic when he told an audience of young recruits that "some of our leaders" have become "soulless bureaucrats," who "have yet to learn to value cadres."[71]

Finally, central leaders sought to undermine the status image of the Provincial Komitetchiki. The status of the Provincial Komitetchiki derived partly from their formal position as state actors and partly from their informal elite identity. The elite identity of the Provincial Komitetchiki emphasized above all else their records of service in the defining historical struggles of the Bolshevik party, particularly the underground, revolution, and civil war. This elite identity was reinforced through the official folklore of party history. In the mid-1930s, however, the field of party history underwent a revision that recast the Provincial Komitetchiki in far less prominent roles.

Early in the decade, Stalin personally intervened into the field of party history when he accused the editorial board of a leading journal of "rotten liberalism."[72] By mid-decade, intrusions into the already heavily politicized field of party history had become routine. These interventions led to an official reconstruction of the party's past that redefined the place of the Provincial Komitetchiki in the founding events of the new socialist state. Most significantly, Beria authored a new history of Bolshevism in Transcaucasia, which was serialized in *Pravda*. Beria's version revised earlier histories by Orakhelishvili and Enukidze, which were criticized for obscuring Stalin's contribution. Beria's revision placed Stalin at the forefront of the Bolshevik movement and its triumphs in the region, while Ordzhonikidze and Kirov were mentioned only as minor figures.[73] Stalin, in fact, spent little time in the region during the revolution and civil war. Moreover, in the summer of 1935, central leaders dissolved the two main organizations entrusted with the preservation and publication of party folklore, the Society of Old Bolsheviks and the Society of Former Political Prisoners.[74]

The retelling of personal exploits, which until this time had been common, was now a potentially risky political act. Kosior reportedly decided to withhold the publication of his revolutionary memoirs after being told that Stalin was personally opposed to the project.[75] And, Kirov declined Stalin's personal request to author the new history of the Bolsheviks in Transcaucasia, claiming incompetence as a theorist. By the end of the decade, the story of the Bolshevik party told in officially sanctioned histories had undergone a fundamental revision. The party was no longer depicted as a dynamic sociopolitical force, but as the compliant instrument of Lenin and his "favorite pupil," Stalin.[76] The overshadowing presence of Stalin in official accounts of the new state's founding events contrasted sharply with the elite identity of the Provincial Komitetchiki.

As the informal constraints of power were systematically removed in the mid-1930s, central leaders became more directly confrontational in relations with the regional leadership. In the summer of 1935, central leaders singled out the leadership in the Saratov province for "mistakes in party work and economic leadership."[77] Andrei Zhdanov was sent from Moscow to Saratov to preside over a special meeting where regional leaders were expected to respond to the charges. Excerpts of Zhdanov's report of this meeting were published in *Pravda* for all to read.[78] The harsh criticisms and personal attacks in the report displayed the center's more combative stance toward the regions. Zhdanov admonished the Saratov leadership for "self-assurance," "false self-esteem," "groundless defense of mistakes," "exaggerated successes," and "unprincipled shouting." Zhdanov's report further touched on the very essence of the center–regional conflict when he assailed regional leaders for their "mistaken discussion about dual centers."[79] The next step for the central leaders entailed the physical destruction of rival elite power centers in the postrevolutionary state.

III. DECOUPLING INFORMAL AND FORMAL STRUCTURES: THE FALL OF THE PROVINCIAL KOMITETCHIKI

By early 1937 the central leadership succeeded in mobilizing its formal and coercive power resources as well as undermining the regional leadership's informal power resources. Central leaders next moved to confront directly the Provincial Komitetchiki. The occasion for this confrontation was a party central committee plenum held in late February and early

March 1937. This fateful meeting signaled the onset of a campaign of unbridled coercion to redefine the center–regional relationship and to consolidate a personal dictatorship within the state. Within a year, the Provincial Komitetchiki fell from their positions of power in the regions, victims of the center's reign of terror against the postrevolutionary elite.

In the weeks leading up to the February–March plenum, a series of arrests were carried out within the ranks of the regional organizations. Under Ezhov's direction, the police claimed to have uncovered a widespread network of conspirators working against the Soviet state at the highest levels of regional administration.[80] On the eve of the plenum, *Pravda* published an editorial criticizing the Ukrainian and North Caucasian leaderships for insufficient political vigilance, thus enabling conspirators to infiltrate the party.[81] By singling out the regional strongholds of Kosior, Postyshev, and Sheboldaev, central leaders indicated that they were now prepared to challenge the Provincial Komitetchiki. The plenum was postponed for a week following the sudden death of Sergo Ordzhonikidze. The plenum finally convened in late February and remained in session for ten days, making it the longest in party history and signifying the drama played out on its stage.[82] The Provincial Komitetchiki viewed the plenum as a final opportunity to undercut the growing wave of radicalism and coercion in the party, or at least to redirect its force away from themselves. They sought to end the center's relentless campaigns to expose enemies within party officialdom.[83] But the plenum did not develop in this direction, the die had already been cast for a different outcome.

In their turns, central leaders compiled a case against the Provincial Komitetchiki. This case pieced together themes from the antibureaucracy campaign and the "hidden enemies" conspiracy into a single package. They attacked the Provincial Komitetchiki for their unaccountability, political laxity, and bureaucratic high-handedness. The Provincial Komitetchiki were especially criticized for constructing personal cliques and ensconcing them in positions of power in regional administration. This practice, central leaders argued, fostered the conditions from which a now well-documented conspiracy to destroy Soviet socialism had taken root within the state elite. Central leaders elaborated a chain of myriad informal contacts that connected the Provincial Komitetchiki to this conspiracy. The Provincial Komitetchiki were forced on the defensive throughout the proceedings as their personal network ties were used to imply their own guilt by association. In the first act of the drama, the Provincial Komitetchiki were assailed for the way in which they had made themselves unaccountable by setting up personal cliques within the formal structures of regional administration. The matter of uncovering hidden enemies would come at the end of the plenum.

Andrei Zhdanov, a central party administrator and former head of the Nizhnovgorod region, spoke about personal cliques. Zhdanov was from the Viatka-Volga regional network, which was connected in the center to Viacheslav Molotov.[84] Zhdanov decried how leading cadres in regional administration were selected through a process of "co-optation," by which regional leaders appointed their own personal acquaintances to formal positions of power. "The harmful practice of co-optation," Zhdanov observed, "has deep roots and extends widely."[85] He detailed the pervasiveness of the practice, noting that on average nearly 12 percent of the members of the regional party committees were selected in this fashion. The percentages of co-opted members in the Ukrainian and Belorussian party organizations were reported to be as high as 23 percent and 26 percent, respectively. Moreover, the rates of co-opted members in the local-level party committees on average were much higher, sometimes exceeding 50 percent. Zhdanov remarked that "even in the party's illegal period, when co-optation was a necessity, a series of organizational guidelines were generally followed" when selecting cadres.[86] Stalin was even more critical than Zhdanov when he spoke on the subject. He assailed the Provincial Komitetchiki for building political machines in the regions, surrounding themselves with "friends" and "toadies," and seeking to become "independent from the center."[87]

In response, the Provincial Komitetchiki did not deny the charges of co-optation, but instead defended the practice as an operational necessity given the demands and practices of the center. They complained that their capabilities to implement policy were weakened by the center's constant meddling in regional personnel affairs. Stanislav Kosior elaborated the theme that co-optation was a product of the center's "unstable and unpredictable cadre policies." He argued that if the system of co-optation is to be changed, "then it is necessary also to change the system of transfers and recalls."[88] Likewise, Lev Mirzoian emphasized that "the system of constantly moving and transferring people" was the real source of the cadres problem in regional administration. Citing Kazakhstan's special geographical and ethnic conditions, Mirzoian was unrepentant about the widespread use of co-optation by the republican leadership.[89] Some gallows humor was interjected in the debate when Efim Evdokimov remarked that "co-optation is widespread, as Comrade Stalin noted, including a large number of those who presently sit in the organs of the NKVD."[90]

As a remedy to the widespread practice of co-optation, central leaders proposed holding new elections for the leading positions in regional and local administration. In an indirect reference to the Provincial Komitet-chiki, Zhdanov pointed out that a number of regional leaders, including "senior secretaries," had never once been subjected to a genuine election.[91] The Provincial Komitetchiki urged the center to cancel or to postpone the elections for both practical and political reasons. Iosif Vareikis insisted that elections were an inappropriate solution to the problems of regional admin-istration. He stressed that too much turnover already existed among local cadres and that elections would only exacerbate the problem. Instead, he argued that regional leaders should have more control, not less, over the training, evaluation, and placement of administrative cadres.[92] Mendel Khataevich proposed that the elections be put off until the end of the spring sowing season to ensure the fulfillment of the annual agricultural plan.[93] Mirzoian questioned the political wisdom of holding elections in Kazakhstan given the continued presence of traditional religious elites.[94] Kosior also made a special plea that the regional leaders should not have to submit themselves to an election due to their high status and important roles.[95]

Instead of elections, the Provincial Komitetchiki proposed to conduct political agitation tours. They would barnstorm the regions, engaging workers, collective farmers, and rank-and-file party members in rallies on the domestic and international political situation, the goals and strategies of state policies, and the problems of daily life in the workplace. These political agitation tours would enable the Provincial Komitetchiki to get back to their roots. While making the proposal, they recalled their earlier struggles and triumphs. Vareikis argued that "it is necessary to renew and to expand on those traditions that we, the Bolsheviks, utilized at the time of the civil war, when we routinely delivered speeches to workers about the pressing issues of the moment."[96] Khataevich, meanwhile, conceded that over the past several years "Bolshevik instincts have become dull or been lost for many of us." He called for a revival of "the Bolshevik tradition" of rallying workers and farmers, as had been done at the begin-ning of the five-year plan. "The party in these years," Vareikis reminded, "achieved a great heroic victory in the battle to strengthen the collective farms and to develop Soviet industry."[97]

The Provincial Komitetchiki jealously guarded their position and status within the state. Kosior, in particular, provided a glimpse of the Provincial Komitetchiki's self-perceptions, when he argued that the authority of regional leaders should not be made subject to popular endorsement. The Provincial Komitetchiki saw themselves above such treatment; instead, their authority derived from their rank and status as state actors and from their records of past service. Recalling earlier triumphs, they offered to revive their role as political agitators, instead of elections. Moreover, their response to the center's criticism of the practice of co-optation indicated their protocorporate tendencies. They argued that cadres policy should be recognized as part of the formal institutional jurisdiction of the regional leadership, thereby assuring greater stability and effectiveness in regional administration.

The last days of the plenum were consumed by the alleged conspiracy of hidden enemies uncovered by the police within the postrevolutionary state elite. This part of the proceedings was especially tense as central leaders subjected the Provincial Komitetchiki to a grueling interrogation in order to assess their culpability in allowing this conspiracy to take root at the highest levels of regional administration. Reporting for the center, Georgii Malenkov noted that hundreds of enemies had been uncovered in the party memberships of the regional organizations: 450 enemies in Postyshev's Kievan organization, 500 enemies in Sheboldaev's Azov-Black Sea organization, 177 enemies in Rumiantsev's Western organization, and, 169 enemies in Khataevich's Dnepropetrovsk organization.[98] More seriously, enemies were found to be working side by side with the Provincial Komitetchiki in the regional organizations. Across the regional party apparat, 35 department heads, 13 assistant department heads, and 63 instructors were discovered to be enemies of the regime.[99]

Stalin explained to the assembled how this precarious situation unfolded.[100] He listed three "basic facts" established at the plenum: (1) a network of anti-Soviet enemies, including foreign spies, saboteurs and Trotskyists, had infiltrated the state's political and economic administrative organs; (2) the center was aware that these enemies had crept into the state's administrative apparat and had tried to warn the regional leaders to take action; and (3) regional leaders not only proved unwilling to recognize the enemies in their midst, but actively promoted them into positions of responsibility. This situation, Stalin continued, was a consequence of the regional leadership's lack of political vigilance and blatant disregard of the center's numerous warnings. He directly connected the rise of the conspiracy to the regional leadership's preoccupation with economic affairs. Stalin's remarks were meant to vindicate his position in the collectivization crisis of 1932–3, at which time he argued for the continued application of class warfare. "It is necessary to put an end to the opportunistic complacency," he announced, "which emerges from the mistaken proposition that the growth of our enemy forces has stopped, that they have become tame and harmless. This is not a time for Bolsheviks to rest on their laurels or to loaf. We must not be complacent, but demonstrate vigilance, genuine Bolshevik revolutionary vigilance."[101]

The Provincial Komitetchiki were forced to address questions concerning relations with specific colleagues whom the police had exposed as hidden enemies. The Provincial Komitetchiki displayed three types of responses: disassociation, offense, and defense.[102] Disassociation was the most common response concerning individuals already named in the conspiracy. Regional leaders claimed to have had no personal affiliation with such individuals, nor to have had a direct hand in placing them in positions of responsibility. Stanislav Kosior, for example, stressed that the individuals named in the conspiracy in Ukraine were not promoted by him, but were promoted in early 1933, when at the center's behest Pavel Postyshev took control of cadres policy in the republic. Once in office, these individuals recruited enemy elements into the republican administration through a kind of surreptitious "groupism."[103] In a similar manner, when Boris Sheboldaev was asked to explain his relationship to Chefranov, his former chief of staff who was now exposed as the son of a tsarist police officer, he quickly pointed out that Chefranov was promoted with Kaganovich's approval during the agricultural crisis of 1932.[104] Sheboldaev also explained the presence of another recently exposed enemy, Ronin, in his organization: "We unmasked him and expelled him from the party in 1935, but then he was reinstated by Moscow."[105] These comments implicitly turned the charges back onto the center for its excessive meddling in local cadres policy.

To further disassociate himself from the accused, Kosior admitted his negligence of political–ideological matters and drew attention to his role as an economic manager. He recalled that "it was necessary for us to take the lead in economic work, especially in agriculture. The central committee did not tell us to do this, but we, the leaders, took upon ourselves a large number of technical and practical works in agriculture, which overburdened us and prevented us from following other matters." For this reason, Kosior went on, "these enemies had a full monopoly and sometimes acted in our names. But we did not lead these people, they were completely unchecked." At this point, Stalin interrupted, "But you were the boss of these people?" "I was the boss, Comrade Stalin," Kosior answered, "but I repeat, we spent three-quarters of our time on other matters."[106]

The tactic of disassociating oneself from the political conspiracy by retreating behind economic accomplishments was a common response among the Provincial Komitetchiki. Sheboldaev responded to the charges against two of his associates by pointing out their exemplary records as economic managers. "Take Glebov," Sheboldaev noted, "who from year to year regularly fulfilled the plan at Rostelmash. Take Kolesnikov, who at the factory named for Andreev annually fulfilled the plan and received the Order of Lenin." When Stalin specifically inquired whether Kolesnikov was considered to be in "good account," Sheboldaev replied, "Yes, his work as an indicator was good."[107] Postyshev claimed that if he had let his guard down concerning political enemies, it was only because "it was necessary to direct attention to bolstering agricultural production and to leading the collective farms onto a firm road. To do this, we worked day and night for two years straight."[108]

A second response was to go on the offensive against individuals outside one's own personal network. The Provincial Komitetchiki readily engaged in *kto-kogo* tactics against rival networks. At this time, the central leadership orchestrated a series of transfers among the Provincial Komitetchiki to new regional assignments. In so doing, an opportunity was provided for the Provincial Komitetchiki to demonstrate anew their "revolutionary vigilance" to the center as well as to deflect attention from themselves by exposing enemies. Boris Sheboldaev, for example, was transferred several weeks earlier from the North Caucasus to Kursk, where he confirmed the discovery of eighteen enemies among the provincial leadership.[109] Following the plenum, Postyshev was transferred from Ukraine to Samara, where he displayed a renewed resolve to uncover enemies.[110] Georgii Malenkov noted wryly that "fresh eyes" effectively exposed the shortcomings in regional administrative work.[111]

In another example of an offensive response, Ukrainian leaders ganged up on Pavel Postyshev, accusing him of being the chief patron of a group of "enemies" brought into the republic from outside. The offensive against Postyshev was retribution for the widespread purge of the Ukrainian administrative apparat, which Postyshev oversaw in early 1933. Khataevich, who was also transferred into the region at the same time, reported that Postyshev did not exercise "collective leadership," but acted as a "personal ruler."[112] S. A. Kudriavtsev referred to "a group of workers in the Kiev organization, the so-called Far Easterners. They were well known in the organization as Postyshev's people when he worked in the Far East. Postyshev vigorously supported and promoted them without regard for their professional or political abilities."[113] And, Kosior described how Postyshev's people actively protected Nikolenko, an employee in the republic's propaganda-education bureaucracy accused of political deviance. Nikolenko was slated for expulsion from the party when this information was uncovered in early 1936. But Nikolenko worked directly under Postolovskaia, Postyshev's wife, who intervened on her behalf and defended her against the charges. As a result, Kosior related, Postyshev's people in Kiev, Il'in and Sapov, "considered it their duty to render service to Comrade Postyshev by supporting Postolovskaia, and so Nikolenko was not purged."[114]

Finally, the Provincial Komitetchiki displayed a defensive response when individuals with whom they shared personal network ties were exposed as enemies. They generally avoided direct defenses of those accused, since such an act entailed enormous personal risk for individuals who alas could not be saved. However, the Provincial Komitetchiki indirectly defended such individuals by highlighting the positive contributions they had made to Bolshevism's defining experiences. The defensive response, of course, was also self-serving in that it was used to explain why these particular individuals had not been exposed sooner. Ivan Kabakov of the Urals region, for example, defended his close associate, Kozhevnikov: "he is an old party member, an undergrounder, and considered a faithful defender of the central committee's line." Kabakov further defended two additional accused colleagues, noting that "they participated in the civil war and, in 1923, they fought against the Trotskyists."[115] When Postyshev was questioned about a close assistant, Karpov, who recently had been exposed by the police as an enemy, he responded: "I personally thought that such a robust party worker, who had traveled the long road of bitter struggle for the party and for socialism, to suddenly fall into the camp of the enemies was unreal. I did not believe it."[116] When pushed on the matter by Molotov, however, Postyshev conceded that "he apparently was a worm the whole time."

In another direct confrontation, Sheboldaev was interrogated about the "Rostov affair" in which a number of high-ranking officials in the North Caucasus region were exposed as enemies. Nearly the entire North Caucasus leadership were implicated as political enemies, including: 5 regional political bureau members, 27 regional party committee members, every city party leader and almost every rural district party leader.[117] The case, in particular, involved Gogoberidze and Vardan'ian, with whom Sheboldaev shared personal network ties dating back to the underground and civil war period.[118]

Sheboldaev: About Gogoberidze, I knew only that he was connected with Lominadze, and I knew that they had a personal connection.

Voice: What kind of personal connection?

Sheboldaev: I knew Gogoberidze in the underground.

Stalin: And Baku?

Sheboldaev: And Baku. It is necessary to say that we did not consider him a bad worker in that organization.

Stalin: You considered this to be so.

Sheboldaev: Yes, at that time. After this, I did not work with him for a period.

Stalin: And Vardan'ian?

Sheboldaev: Vardan'ian was recommended to me by Sergo [Ordzhonikidze], although it was said otherwise by the politburo, this is not so. I repeat that Vardan'ian was recommended to me by Sergo.

Beria: And you took in Vardan'ian, when the Transcaucasus had thrown him out, and Gogoberidze, who was already connected to Lominadze.

Sheboldaev: I did not know this.

Voice: You, Comrade Sheboldaev, why do you take in people who have been cast out by other party organizations?

Sheboldaev: Correct. I took in these people who worked in Georgia and Armenia, in particular Gogoberidze and Vardan'ian. But they did not have bad references. For six years, these people were actively connected to me and I supported them. Of course, I thought that they were good workers. I did not think that this strata of people could be enemies and spies. In this matter, I was blind. Stupid trustworthiness led me not even to check them out. It was all because of blind trust.

Sitting in silence during this exchange was Anastas Mikoian who had worked closely with Sheboldaev and Gogoberidze in the Transcaucasian underground. Mikoian ultimately survived Stalin's terror. Years later, after Stalin's death, he would recall fondly the time spent together with Gogo-beridze and Sheboldaev in a Baku prison during the civil war.[119]

In the weeks following the plenum, final preparations were made for the impending assault on the Provincial Komitetchiki. The press continued to publish highly critical reports about the work performance of the regional leadership and to raise suspicion about their political reliability.[120] Continuing a trend which began shortly before the plenum, leading members of the Provincial Komitetchiki were transferred out of the regions where they had long served: Postyshev moved from Ukraine to Samara, Sheboldaev from the North Caucasus to Kursk, and Vareikis from the Central Black Earth to the Far East. The Provincial Komitetchiki were dislodged from their established organizational bases and cut off from their informal cliques. Finally, in the late spring, the center moved against the military high command, many of whom shared strong network ties with the Provincial Komitetchiki.

In the summer of 1937, central leaders began the process of physically removing the Provincial Komitetchiki and uprooting their personal cliques from regional administration. The process typically involved the arrival in the provincial capital of a central plenipotentiary, who would convene a special meeting of the party organization to announce the arrest of several prominent regional officials.[121] Georgii Malenkov was sent to Belorussia and the Transcaucasus, Lazar Kaganovich was sent to Ukraine, the Western region and the Central Industrial region; Andrei Zhdanov was sent to the Urals and the Middle Volga; and, Mikhail Shkiriatov was sent to the North Caucasus. So would begin a series of public denunciations and accusations that would fan the investigation outward, implicating more and more officials. In a matter of weeks or sometimes days, the entire regional political administrative leadership (including party, government and control officials), and in some cases the economic administrative leadership, would be removed from their posts. Quite often the individuals promoted to replace those removed soon became the victims of subsequent waves of denunciations and arrests. It was not until early 1938 that stability in office returned to regional administration, signaled by a central resolution criticizing the "heartless bureaucratic attitude toward the people and the members of the party."[122]

Nearly all the regional leaders removed at this time, in turn, were arrested in connection with some aspect of the conspiracy that allegedly took root in the state elite in the 1930s. A similar pattern of arrest was employed in which an individual was summoned to Moscow on the pretext of urgent business and instructed to travel by special train. On the outskirts of Moscow, the train was stopped and the individual was arrested by the secret police. Unlike past party leaders, the Provincial Komitetchiki were not put on public trial, but were sentenced to death in secret and shot by the secret police, sometimes on the same day. The first set of regional leaders to be executed, in October 1937, included: B. Sheboldaev, M. Khataevich, I. Rumiantsev, I. Kabakov, A. Krinitskii, M. Razumov (Eastern Siberia), and I. Kodatskii (Leningrad). In 1938, R. Eikhe, I. Vareikis, L. Mirzoian, and L. Kartvelishvili were sentenced and shot to death. The leaders of Ukraine – S. Kosior, P. Postyshev, V. Zatonskii, and V. Chubar – were arrested in early 1938 and executed a year later, in February 1939.[123]

The Provincial Komitetchiki were simply no match for the coercive and radical forces that the central leadership unleashed on them. While they had been able to contest the center within the established constraints of power earlier in the decade, the Provincial Komitetchiki proved unable to defend themselves from the center's lethal assault later in the decade. The Provincial Komitetchiki, like so many others before them, were simply overwhelmed by the dynamics of the terror process. The striking irony, of course, was that these same individuals had witnessed this process earlier, but from the opposite side. Yet when it was their turn, they submitted to the process without mustering any significant forms of resistance.

Upon receiving the news of Tukhachevskii's arrest, Iosif Vareikis, for example, reportedly telephoned Stalin personally to urge a further review of the facts in the case.[124] Stalin was enraged and threatened Vareikis: "This is not your business. Do not interfere in what does not concern you. The NKVD knows what it is doing. Only an enemy of the people would defend Tukhachevskii." Within days of this conversation, Vareikis received a telegram informing him to report at once to Moscow. He immediately complied. Vareikis was arrested en route at a small train station outside Moscow. How does one explain why an individual such as Vareikis, in this situation and at this point in time, obeyed this order apparently so willingly?

The fall of the Provincial Komitetchiki was a direct consequence of the center's success in redefining the constraints of power in the center–regional relationship. Once the informal constraints were removed, the center was able to apply coercion against the regional leadership. The "great purges" were, in effect, an extreme response to the constraints of power in the new state as a result of the intersection of informal and formal structures. The physical assault against the regional leadership, above all else, represented a concerted effort by central state actors to decouple informal social networks from formal political structures and to transform the sources of elite status. In so doing, the distribution of power resources in the new state was fundamentally reordered.

But why were the Provincial Komitetchiki unsuccessful in their attempt to redefine the constraints of power? And, more importantly, why were the Provincial Komitetchiki incapable of coordinating a defense against the center during the purges? When the constraints of power of the first half of the 1930s were in place, the Provincial Komitetchiki demonstrated an ability to cooperate. At a party meeting in January 1933, leaders from different regions and different networks demonstrated a united front against the center's position in the 1932 grain procurement crisis. As a result, they succeeded to force some policy concessions from the center. And, at the party congress in February 1934, a small group of regional leaders cooperated to the point of plotting a coup against Stalin. But while they had won several policy battles, they were incapable of the level of cooperation that would enable them to remove the party leader.

In the second half of the decade, when the informal constraints had been removed, the Provincial Komitetchiki no longer proved capable of cooperation at all. At the party meeting in February–March 1937, central leaders effectively turned the regional leaders against one another. The Provincial Komitetchiki were constrained from acting in concert by their own formal and informal cleavage lines. In their capacity as regional governors, they constantly found themselves in competition with one another over the distribution of resources in the state. As members of personal networks, they belonged to discrete informal social groupings that rewarded inward-directed behavior. Personal network rivalries reinforced the formal administrative–territorial arrangement, creating a formidable cleavage line. The personalistic structure of regional administration created an environment which did not support interregional and internetwork cooperation. In the end, the Provincial Komitetchiki were easily divided and conquered by the center.

Finally, to return to the more specific question above, why does Vareikis board the train to his own execution? The fall of the Provincial Komitetchiki can also be explained by the constraints of their elite identity. The elite identity of the Provincial Komitetchiki was so completely defined by their service to Bolshevism that when the party's leader turned against them, they were incapable of operating beyond its realm, even to preserve their own lives. The case of Levon Mirzoian, Kazakhstan republican leader, is illustrative in this regard. Mirzoian was a member of the old Transcaucasian personal network, a close friend of Kirov and Ordzhonikidze, and a veteran of the crucial civil war battles for Baku and Astrakhan. In May 1938, shortly before execution, Mirzoian reportedly declared: "I have faithfully served the party and the people for twenty-two years. I have never betrayed the party's interests. I swear on my last breath, on the life of my children, that I was never an enemy of the party or the people"[125] Mirzoian's final plea, of course, was made under extreme duress, but it also reveals the perception among these actors that their perceived status image might earn them a reprieve. In the end, the Provincial Komitetchiki fell victim to Stalin's terror still clinging to their records of service, which by this time had been rendered meaningless.

Once the center succeeded in redefining the constraints of power, its formal power resources could be applied against the regional leaders. As a result, the structure and identity of the Provincial Komitetchiki were effectively neutralized as informal power resources. The fall of the Provincial Komitetchiki marked the end of one of the most dramatic episodes in the ongoing struggle throughout Russian history between ruler and elite.

8

CONCLUSION: STATE BUILDING AND THE SOVIET RUSSIAN CASE RECONSIDERED

Soviet Russia was long considered by Western scholars to be a strong state. The underlying source of its strength was presumed to be the formal structure of the Bolshevik party, the "organizational weapon" forged by Lenin in the revolutionary struggle to depose Russia's old regime. The subsequent collapse of the Soviet state ultimately laid bare the conceptual limitations of this long-standing conventional wisdom. The case study presented here offered a reconceptualization of the Soviet state, emphasizing its informal sources of power – personal networks and elite identity. This concluding chapter suggests that the findings of the case study offer a solution to three puzzles found in the scholarly literature on Soviet Russia and comparative state theory: (1) Does reconstructing personal network ties and uncovering sources of elite status among the Bolsheviks contribute something new to an understanding of state building in postrevolutionary Soviet Russia? (2) Does this reexamination of the building process provide insight into the subsequent collapse of the Soviet state? and (3) Does this reexamination of the Soviet Russian case offer anything new to the recent efforts of comparative theorists to explain state-building outcomes?

To begin, the case study focused attention on the informal power resources of an intrastate elite cohort, the Provincial Komitetchiki. Moreover, it showed how these informal power resources were deployed to facilitate the process of building a state capacity for territorial administration in the postrevolutionary state. Finally, it provided insight into an intra-state elite conflict, whose outcome determined the particular type of authoritarianism found in the postrevolutionary state. A summary of the empirical findings and their analytical implications are presented first.

The case study represented the first examination of the new state's first generation of regional leaders. The Provincial Komitetchiki played the role of field generals in the new state's campaign to build the command–administrative system in the Soviet Russian periphery. Yet despite this prominent role, they have remained a neglected group in Western area studies.

The Provincial Komitetchiki, it was found, did not just hold formal positions of power in the new state, but also were members of informal personal networks. These networks originated in the prerevolutionary underground and became more coherently defined in the civil war. Personal networks arose along the major battle fronts of the civil war, centered around political commissars and their revolutionary–military committee staffs. These civil war networks of fighter-organizers represented a kind of Bolshevik *druzhina*. The Bolshevik *druzhina* resembled in several ways the *druzhina* of Russia's Muscovite past, which were composed of soldier-servitors bound by personal loyalty to the household of a warrior prince. Following the civil war, when the formal internal structures of the new state were still poorly defined, the Bolshevik *druzhina* emerged as a politically dominant force in regional administration. Powerful central patrons enabled these particular networks to gain access to scarce organizational and material resources. By such means, they eventually displaced or subsumed regional network rivals. The rise of the Provincial Komitetchiki to positions of regional leadership in the new state occurred along personal network lines. The Transcaucasian regional network, it was shown, was especially well represented among the Provincial Komitetchiki.

The case study also reconstructed the elite identity of the Provincial Komitetchiki. A sketch was drawn of the early life, underground, and civil war experiences of the Provincial Komitetchiki, based on autobiographical materials prepared at the time when they first arrived as regional leaders. These materials were not significant for their realistic depiction of the life experiences of the Provincial Komitetchiki. Rather, they offered a glimpse into the sources of elite status in the postrevolutionary state. In this regard, the Provincial Komitetchiki stressed above all else their records of service to the party in the underground and civil war. On the basis of this service, they saw themselves as a distinctive status group within the rapidly expanding state elite. Of course, they were not the only members of the postrevolutionary elite to have worked in the prerevolutionary underground or to have fought in the civil war. Members of the military, industrial and police elites also boasted similar records of service. All of these actors, however, could distinguish themselves from other elite sub-groups in the new state: the *intelligenty*, who fled abroad after 1905, rather than continue to serve in the underground; the post-civil war party recruits, who were either too young or too late to participate in the battles of the civil war; and, the former tsarist civil servants, who despite their technical-administrative expertise were tainted by their previous political affiliations.

By focusing on personal network ties and sources of elite status, the case study shed light on two defining features of the postrevolutionary state elite that have been largely ignored by Western scholars. More importantly, the focus on personal network ties and elite identities revealed the informal power resources that the Provincial Komitetchiki sought to exploit in relations with central state leaders. These informal resources existed independent of central state leaders and, at least for a short period, afforded regional leaders a degree of autonomy from the center.

Second, central state leaders in the 1920s presided over an "infrastructurally" weak state. The Bolsheviks had reclaimed most of the old tsarist empire, but they lacked the technical and material means to administer a territory that spanned eleven time zones and included huge tracts of land beyond the reach of railways or telegraphs. They were determined to push ahead with a program of rapid economic development, but had access to only meager and unreliable sources of revenue. They were treated as a pariah and scourge by the world's great powers, but lacked the capability to engage in even minor geopolitical competition. To overcome these obstacles, central state leaders employed one of the few resources at their disposal – personal network ties. In the early postrevolutionary state, a "patrimonial" system was favored over a "bureaucratic" system as the means to strengthen the infrastructural powers of the new state.

This finding helps to answer a question that has long nagged area specialists. If the formal bureaucratic lines of command remained ill defined and fluid for more than a decade after the civil war, how did such an "infrastructurally" weak state carry out such a comprehensive economic reform in the early 1930s? Yet it was precisely at this time that the new state successfully developed its capacities for territorial administration and revenue extraction. While both coercion and social forces no doubt played an important part in this process, neither explains sufficiently how the new state constructed and managed the command-administrative system in the regions.

The study elaborated an alternative explanation to the field's ongoing "forces from above" versus "forces from below" debate. It argued that personal network ties represented the missing piece to the Soviet state-building puzzle. More specifically, the intersection of informal network ties with formal organizational structures enabled the new state to extend its administrative reach across the vast rural and multiethnic periphery. The study demonstrated that network ties were stretched horizontally across territorial and institutional lines as well as vertically from region to center. Moreover, it was shown that these outwardly extended ties were used as an informal social structure by which information was exchanged, resources were obtained and activities were coordinated. By such means, the new state enhanced its capacities for territorial administration and revenue extraction.

Finally, while the "patrimonial" system succeeded to strengthen the infrastructural powers of the state, it came at a high price for central leaders. The intersection of informal and formal structures constrained the "despotic" powers of central state leaders. The Provincial Komitetchiki indirectly asserted their interests into the state's decision-making process by means of central patrons. The cross-organizational reach of personal network ties effectively muted the center's bureaucratic mechanisms of coercion and control. And, their strategic position in the policy implementation process enabled them to gain access to centrally allocated resources, which in turn were used to solidify their own personal political machines in the regions. These underlying constraints of power shaped the interactions between central and regional actors in the early 1930s and became the target of efforts by both sides to redefine these constraints in the mid- to late 1930s.

The conflict between central and regional leaders arose over the implementation of collectivization policies. These policies called on the Provincial Komitetchiki to restructure the agricultural sector in order that the state could directly extract grain and other agricultural resources from the countryside. The Provincial Komitetchiki in principle supported collectivization and in practice ruthlessly strove to bring it to reality. But efforts to realize these radical policies created a crisis for regional leaders, which overwhelmed their administrative capabilities and threatened the survival of their political machines. In response to this crisis, the Provincial Komitetchiki clashed with central leaders over issues related to the implementation of collectivization.

But this conflict was not simply a policy dispute. Rather, it represented an intrastate power struggle, whose outcome would determine the particular regime type of the postrevolutionary state. It was not a state-societal conflict over democratic or authoritarian regime types. Instead, it was a fight over variant forms of authoritarianism, distinguished by the formal division of power between ruler and elite. In this contest, the Provincial

Komitetchiki sought to establish a protocorporatist regime, while Stalin wanted to consolidate a bureaucratic absolutist regime.

The protocorporatist regime type was defined by routinized and checked despotic power and personalized and unchecked infrastructural power. To realize this arrangement, the Provincial Komitetchiki sought to impose order on what they saw to be an arbitrary rule-making process and to be granted discretionary control over the conduct of regional administration. These were the terms of service that the Provincial Komitetchiki sought to secure from central state leaders. Sheboldaev's plea, for example, to organize a permanent working committee of central and regional representatives to work out collectivization policies represented an attempt to persuade the center to share its decision-making power. Kosior's resistance to the center's proposal for regional elections, meanwhile, captured perfectly the proprietary claim that the Provincial Komitetchiki tried to make on their formal position as regional governors. It was an attempt, in effect, to gain tenure in the state's "patrimonial" system of infrastructural power.

In the state center, Stalin sought to establish a bureaucratic absolutist regime for the new state. This regime type was defined by personalized and unchecked despotic power and rationalized and checked infrastructural power. In their attempt to construct such a regime, central leaders were resisted not just by the Provincial Komitetchiki, but by several other elite subgroups. In particular, the Red Army high officer corps and the Red directors of the industrial administrative bureaucracy demonstrated similar "protocorporatist" tendencies as did the Provincial Komitetchiki.[1] And, like the Provincial Komitetchiki, these actors had access to informal power resources: personal network ties, strategic location in the policy process, and elite status image based on civil war service. They preferred a regime type in which power was formally allocated to discrete corporate bodies within the framework of the state.

In the center-regional conflict of the 1930s, both sides sought to redefine the underlying constraints of power in the relationship in order to realize their preferred regime type. The study showed that in the early 1930s the Provincial Komitetchiki at several pivotal junctures demonstrated cooperation in dealings with the center. These instances, it is argued, represented the first tentative steps toward the formation of a corporate consciousness and the realization of an elite power sharing arrangement with the center. But a bolder gambit to redefine in a more fundamental way the constraints of power by removing Stalin from the central leadership collapsed in utter failure. By contrast, central leaders fared much better with their incremental strategy to undermine the informal power resources of the Provincial Komitetchiki. In so doing, they succeeded in redefining the constraints of power to their advantage. At this point, the Provincial Komitetchiki no longer demonstrated cooperative behavior. Divided against themselves, they were incapable of restraining the center's formal bureaucratic and coercive powers. The "great purges" of the late 1930s, in which the Provincial Komitetchiki along with the military and industrial elites were the principal targets, were an extreme measure by which the center was able to decouple personal network ties from formal organizational structure in the postrevolutionary state.

The cohort of regional leaders who emerged in the wake of the "great purges" lacked the same informal power resources of the Provincial Komitetchiki. In particular, the sources of elite status underwent a transformation. Whereas elite status was previously associated with services rendered to the party in the heroic events of the march to power, it was now strictly a prerequisite of formal position and no longer attained independently from central leaders. The new cohort of regional leaders did not contest the center for a share in the despotic powers of the state. Despotic power remained personalized and unchecked. Power was allocated on the basis of who was in favor in Stalin's court. With the constraints of power redefined, central leaders were now able to employ their formal bureaucratic and coercive powers with considerably less resistance from the second generation of regional leaders.

But though the bureaucratic lines of command in the state were more clearly defined than at any time in the previous two decades, central leaders still did not abandon the practice of employing a "patrimonial" system of infrastructural power. Three structural features of the post-revolutionary state contributed to the perpetuation of "patrimonial" administrative practices: (1) the basis of authority of regional leadership; (2) the system of resource allocation; and (3) the pattern of rule making.

First, as in the tsarist period, a dilemma existed for state leaders who sought, on the one hand, to concentrate power in the center and, on the other hand, to administer an expansive periphery. The dilemma was reconciled by creating a system in which the power of regional leaders in principle derived from a central source. Whereas in the tsarist period, the authority of regional governors was based on the personal authority of the Tsar, in the Soviet period regional governors were considered the agents of the party's central leadership. They were appointed by and answered to central leaders. As the personal representative of a central source of authority, regional leaders played the role of viceroys or prefects. They remained for the most part unchecked by any regionally based institutional or popular constraints.

Second, related to this first solution, organizational, financial and other valued resources continued to be distributed through a system of central allocation to strategic bureaucratic points. In exchange, the recipients of these resources were responsible for overseeing the process of policy implementation at the regional level. Regional administration, thus, still featured patron-client implementation teams, which formed around these resource distribution points. For this reason, the system of reward and advancement for regional elites remained personalized.

Finally, the pattern of rule making in the center contributed to the survival of personal networks in regional administration. Stalin himself proved to be the greatest obstacle to the construction of a "bureaucratic" system of infrastructural power. The general secretary opposed a system of power allocation, operating on legally defined rules and roles. Such a rationalized system of infrastructural power could not coexist with his personalized system of despotic power. Stalin preferred the system of court politics. Roles and titles remained fluid in this arrangement, as when Stalin declared himself to be prime minister during the war. Stalin did not discourage the existence of intraparty cliques, rather he promoted them in a kind of "balance of power" checking game. Just as Molotov's Viatka-Volga network, Kuibyshev's Middle Volga network and Ordzhonikidze's Transcaucasian network had once acted as intraelite rivals, personal cliques persisted to intrigue against one another and to vie for power, patronage, and privilege in Stalin's court.

Next, do the case findings provide any clues to solving the puzzle of the sudden demise of the Soviet Russian state? Throughout the 1970s and 1980s, area specialists debated whether the sources of state strength were located "above" in coercive and bureaucratic organs or "below" in strategic bases of social support.[2] When Gorbachev attempted a radical break from the foreign and domestic policies of the past, area specialists did not seriously envision that his reform course would lead to the collapse of the state. Instead, they debated which of the following outcomes was the most likely scenario: failed reform and political reaction, successful reform and liberalization, or partial reform and gradual decline. For area specialists, conceptualizations of state strength in either the formal organs from above or in social forces from below obscured the underlying constraints of power created by the intersection of informal personal networks with formal organizational structures. Consequently, it was not apparent just how weak the state had become.

Ironically, the emerging literature on the collapse of the Soviet state continues to reflect the earlier "forces from above" versus "forces from below" debate. In an example of the former approach, Jerry Hough has written: "Clearly the key to the outcome is to be found at the top of the political system or the state."[3] As the general secretary, it was simply assumed that Gorbachev had access to sufficient coercive and organizational resources to maintain the state, but he simply did not use them wisely. In effect, the state collapsed when the top leader did not render the proper rewards and sanctions both to ensure popular compliance and to discourage elite defection. By contrast, another group of scholars has focused on "forces from below" to explain the Soviet state collapse. This approach stresses the revival of civil society, the proliferation of informal groups, and the mobilization of movement politics.[4] It has been especially popular in studies of the fall of communist regimes in the non-Russian national republics and Eastern Europe.[5] In this approach, the collapse is generally explained as the victory of a reinvigorated society against a moribund state.

An alternative conceptualization of power exists in the field, although it has not received the same level of attention from scholars. Instead of formal organs from above or social forces from below, this alternative approach looks at informal forces "from within." This approach emphasizes the personalistic ways in which power was manifested in the Soviet state, most often in patron–client formations. The pioneering work of Rigby served as the foundation of this alternative approach. Following his trail, Gill, Willerton and Urban provided illuminating detailed case studies of the informal side of the Soviet state. Jowitt's concept of "neotraditionalism," emphasizing the personalistic flow of power under Brezhnev, deftly captured the essential features of this alternative conceptualization of the state.[6] While the "forces from within" has steadily gained greater acceptance among area specialists, no study yet exists that attempts to explain Soviet state collapse from this perspective. Andrew Walder, however, recently applied the "forces from within" approach to the question of state collapse in China and Eastern Europe.[7] Walder and other scholars directed attention to the ways in which informal social structures, existing within the formal political structures, incrementally undermined the strength of these states, mainly by diverting economic resources from the state center.

The findings of this study showed that the contraints of power in the Soviet command-administrative state were rooted in the informal "forces from within." This observation not only applies to Soviet state building, but also helps to understand better the dynamics of Soviet state collapse. As was shown during the building phase, the constraints of power did not remain fixed, but they could be redefined to the advantage of one side or the other. And this is, in fact, what occurred throughout the Soviet period.

Following Stalin's death, the regime underwent a second leadership succession contest from which Nikita Khrushchev emerged victorious. Khrushchev secured his triumph by means similar to those that Stalin had employed in 1920s, particularly trading organizational resources for personalistic resources with regional leaders. And just as Stalin had earlier discovered, Khrushchev found that regional leaders were able to constrain the despotic powers of the state center. On this occasion, however, the conflict between ruler and elite had a different outcome. Whereas in 1934 regional leaders failed to unseat Stalin, thirty years later, in 1964, an elite cabal succeeded in ousting Khrushchev in a palace coup. The new ruler, Leonid Brezhnev, was a long-time veteran of the regional administrative elite.

Khrushchev's removal signaled that the constraints of power in the state had again been redefined, but this time to the advantage of the elites. The division of power between ruler and elite now more closely resembled a "protocorporatist" regime type, similar to that favored by the Provincial Komitetchiki in the 1930s. Under Brezhnev, the state exhibited a personalized and unchecked system of "infrastructural" power, while its system of "despotic" power became more routinized and checked. Regional leaders benefitted from this arrangement by gaining access to the same powers and privileges that had been sought by the Provincial Komitetchiki three decades earlier. First, regional leaders secured a proprietary claim on their positions as provincial governors. Brezhnev's "trust-in-cadres" policy, in effect, gave regional leaders lifelong tenure in office. Second, regional leaders were granted a much greater degree of discretionary power over their internal affairs, including personnel matters. In this way, personal political machines became more firmly entrenched in their regions. Third, through the extensive reach of their political machines, regional leaders gained access to the economic resources of the state. Regional administration under Brezhnev was notable for pervasive economic corruption. Centrally allocated resources were diverted into private hands and locally produced economic resources were seized by rent-seeking regional officials.[8] Finally, regional leaders were formally included in the state's rule-making process in policy matters that directly concerned their areas of jurisdiction. The term "collective leadership" was employed to describe this practice, which distinguished Brezhnev's style of rule from both Stalin's and Khrushchev's. In this way, the state's system of despotic power resembled a coporate-like, elite power sharing arrangement.

Under Brezhnev, the infrastructural capabilities of the state were weakened by a change in the structure of network ties. During this period, the career patterns of regional leaders displayed a marked decrease in vertical and horizontal movement.[9] As a result, informal network ties exhibited a more limited cross-regional reach and core network members remained located in their host regions. This inward structure contrasted with the state-building phase, when informal network ties exhibited an outward structure through their extensive cross-regional reach and the relocation of core network members to central posts. By the early 1980s, the regional administrative elite had become more insular and particularist. Moreover, personal network ties were routinely used to capture political and economic resources from the state center.

These were the constraints of power that Gorbachev inherited when he came to power in the spring of 1985. Gorbachev moved quickly to reclaim "despotic" power from various state elite groups. The "infrastructural" powers of the state, however, remained weakened as a result of a long-term, gradual process of the diffusion of power away from the center along informal lines. Thus, Gorbachev was successful in securing control over the state's policy-making process and in short order he defined a program of radical reform. But he was far less successful in bringing his reform policies into reality. Just as Gorbachev had sought to introduce market mechanisms into the planned economy and to liberalize the political system, he also attempted to uproot the "patrimonial" system of infrastructural power and to replace it with a "bureaucratic" system. Gorbachev's political institutional reforms – introducing elections, restructuring the legislature and removing the party bureaucracy from the policy process – successfully undermined the "patrimonial" system of infrastructural power. But he did not, indeed he could not, immediately replace it with a "bureaucratic" system. As a result, the state was left without its underlying, informal administrative support structure.

This study does not dispute that social forces and coercion, or more accurately, the lack of coercion were important factors in the collapse of the Soviet state. But these factors do not indicate the extent to which the state's infrastructural powers had already been weakened as a result of informal forces from within. The inward structure of informal network ties, in particular, diminished the state's capacity to implement policies in the periphery. The state's "patrimonial" system of infrastructural power and "protocorporatist" system of despotic power had negative long-term implications for state survival. In the end, the Soviet state lacked the capacity to stave off its own territorial demise. In this way, the diffusion of power along informal lines was a precondition of state collapse. From this perspective it can be argued that the Soviet state eventually fell apart along the same lines upon which it had been built six decades earlier.

Finally, what are the implications of the empirical findings for comparative state-building theory? The case study builds on the "state-in-society" approach to explain state-building outcomes. It sought to uncover the microlevel social foundations of macrolevel political institutions. Toward this end, the case study showed that the structure of informal network ties as they intersected with formal organizational lines had a direct influence on the development of a state capacity for territorial administration in Soviet Russia. The findings suggest that previous depictions of Soviet state building, which stressed formal organization, are in need of revision. The findings, moreover, have broader implications for comparative state-building theory, which earlier directly borrowed from the Soviet area studies literature to explain successful state building outcomes. But while this particular depiction of Soviet state building was subsequently found to be incomplete, the study maintains that the Soviet Russian case did provide a model for twentieth-century postcolonial state builders.

The twentieth century has witnessed three waves of intensive state building activities related to the fall of empires. For comparative theorists, these historical changes have yielded an abundance of cases for the study of state building. Among the many cases, Soviet Russia for many years was considered a paradigm of successful state building. According to this argument, Soviet state leaders, in response to macrolevel international pressures, built a territorial administrative bureaucracy, which facilitated revenue extraction and enabled the state to employ coercion and wage war. In this regard, Soviet Russia fit a more general state-building pattern in which geopolitical competition precipitated the development of increasingly more complex and rational formal organizations, through which administrative, extractive and coercive functions were realized.

But this depiction of Soviet Russia was flawed on two counts. First, more-recent comparative studies have identified variant historical patterns in which state capacities are realized by means other than rational, formal organizational structures. Ertman, for example, has shown how patrimonial, as opposed to bureaucratic, relations provided the infrastructural underpinnings for the first successful early modern states in France and Spain.[11] And Barkey has shown how the Ottoman state developed a capacity for territorial administration through a process of negotiation and bargaining with soldier-bandit elites.[12] Second, comparative theorists relied on a picture of the Soviet Russian state-building process that was drawn in the early area studies literature. This picture emphasized formal organizational structure as the principal means by which Soviet Russia developed its capacities for rule. Area studies scholars, however, would only later compile convincing evidence to show that formal organizational structures were not yet operative during the main period in which the state developed its capacities for territorial administration and revenue extraction. Ironically, the Soviet state collapsed at a time when its formal organizational structures were better defined and more stable than they had been at any previous point in Soviet history.

The case study presented an alternative explanation of the process of Soviet state-building, emphasizing the role of personal networks. To this extent, the study is unique in its attempt to employ network analysis to the study of political institution building. By stressing the role of personal networks, the findings seemingly contradict a well-documented position in comparative theory that personal networks tend to obstruct or undermine state building attempts.[13] One way or another, it seems, networks do matter. Yet the role of personal networks in state-building processes has not been adequately conceptualized and incorporated into comparative state theory.

What then are the conditions under which personal networks either enhance or constrain state capacity? Personal network ties provide an informal social mechanism along which resources are exchanged, information is obtained, and collaborative actions are planned. But whether this results in enhanced or constrained administrative capacities depends on the structure of informal network ties as they intersect with formal organizational lines. The Soviet case demonstrated that when this intersection exhibited an "outward" structure the state's administrative capacity was strengthened, but when it exhibited an "inward" structure it was weakened. An outward or inward structure was determined by the cross-organizational reach of network ties as well as the location of core network members.

Most postcolonial states and especially single-party states displayed similar structural features as those that sustained informal personal networks in the Soviet state, including the centralization of the sources of political authority, the system of resource allocation to strategic bureaucratic points, and the unchecked and centralized patterns of policy making. Single-party states of various regime types employed personal network ties in order to realize their capacities of rule, from economic development in Japan and South Korea to territorial integration in India and Indonesia. Empirical findings from other cases suggest that outwardly structured network ties were a necessary element of successful state building. Israel and Communist China, for example, represent two of the more successful state building cases in the twentieth century. In both cases, cadres who actually participated in the state-building process, as in Soviet Russia, were veterans of illegal underground experiences. Similarly, China's Communist party and Israel's Histadrut Labor Federation and Mapai Workers party were compelled to utilize informal network ties to carry out basic political tasks in the early years, before the formal organizational structures of the new states were operative. In a study of the Israeli Mapai party, Peter Medding argued that in the post independence period the party was sustained by a "chain of personal contact," which served as a "mechanism for the centralization of political power."[14] And, Victor Nee, in a study of the Communist Chinese state's effort to develop an administrative capacity in the rural countryside, noted "the existence of an 'old boy' network of subcounty cadres." "Not only did this network enhance the power of the party-state," he contended, "but it also laid the basis for a new relationship between center and locality."[15]

More recently, communism's collapse has generated new state-building experiences in Eastern Europe and the former Soviet Union. Some scholars have already noted the formative role of personal network ties, especially among the former communist nomenklatura elite, in shaping postcommunist economic institutions.[16] Postcommunist Russia, moreover, is presently undergoing center-regional power struggles reminiscent of the postrevolutionary Soviet period. In a study of contemporary regional politics, Peter Kirkow described "a revitalization of power exerted by former nomenklatura members and an activization of previous social networks."[17] This development is a direct consequence of the intersection of informal and formal structures in the former communist states. As the formal structures of power collapsed or were dismantled, informal personal networks were left standing. Members of these personal networks were placed in an advantageous position in the ensuing competition over political and economic resources. For the former communist nomenklatura, personal network ties have provided an informal social structure along which information is exchanged, resources are obtained, and collaborative actions are coordinated. In this way, personal networks are shaping the emergence of institutional forms in Russia's postcommunist transition, just as they did earlier in its postrevolutionary period.

The Soviet Russian state was a virtual labyrinth of bureaucratic structures, but it was a far cry from a rational–legal bureaucratic state. Beneath the formal facade of the monolithic party and the planned economy existed an informal world of cliques, factions, networks and *druzhina*. Power and status within the state elite derived as much from the workings of these informal groupings as they did from the formal lines of command. Soviet Russia indeed represented a paradigmatic case for twentieth-century state building, but not for the creation of a "modern" bureaucratic order. Rather, the Soviet Russian case was an early model of a process in which personalistic patterns of political authority and organization were adapted to new formal–legalistic structures within the institutional framework of hastily constructed post colonial states. If comparative theorists and area specialists were caught off guard by the collapse of the twentieth century's most feared state, perhaps the reason in part can be found in their lack of attention to this underworld of personalistic relations. Lenin once exhorted, "Give me an organization of revolutionaries, and I will overturn Russia!" He might just as well have said, "a network of revolutionaries."

NOTES

1. INTRODUCTION

1. In the mid-1970s, the Social Science Research Council organized a working group devoted to comparative historical analysis of "States and Social Structures." Also, several benchmark works on the state were published in the mid-1970s. Charles Tilly, ed., *The Formation of the National States in Western Europe* (Princeton, NJ: Princeton University Press, 1975); the English-language translation of the edited works of the German sociologist Otto Hintze, *The Historical Essays*, ed. Felix Gilbert (New York: Oxford University Press, 1975); Perry Anderson, *Lineages of the Absolutist State* (London: New Left Books, 1974); and Gianfranco Poggi, *The Development of the Modern State* (Stanford, CA: Stanford University Press, 1978).

2. See, for example, Stephen Krasner, *Defending the National Interest: Raw Material Investments and US Foreign Policy* (Princeton, NJ: Princeton University Press, 1978); Theda Skocpol, *States and Social Revolutions: Comparative Analysis of France, Russia and China* (New York: Cambridge University Press, 1979); and Eric Nordlinger, *On the Autonomy of the Democratic State* (Cambridge, MA: Harvard University Press, 1981).

3. Gabriel Almond, *A Discipline Divided: Schools and Sects in Political Science* (Newbury Park, CA: Sage Publications, 1989), ch. 8.

4. See, for example, Samuel Huntington, *Political Order in Changing Societies* (New Haven, CT: Yale University Press, 1968); S. N. Eisenstadt, *The Political Systems of Empires* (New York: The Free Press, 1969); and Leonard Bender et al., *Crises, Sequences and Political Development* (Princeton, NJ: Princeton University Press, 1973).

5. Bob Jessop, *State Theory: Putting Capitalist States in Their Place* (University Park: Pennsylvania State University Press, 1990), p. 2.

6. For an excellent overview of this literature, see Theda Skocpol, "Bringing the State Back In: Strategies of Analysis in Current Research," in *Bringing the*

State Back In, eds., P. Evans, D. Rueschmeyer, and T. Skocpol (New York: Cambridge University Press, 1985), pp. 3–35.

7. Michael Mann, "The Autonomous Power of the State: Its Origins, Mechanisms and Results," in *States in History*, ed. John Hall (Oxford: Basil Blackwell, 1986), ch. 4.

8. The classic definition is found in Max Weber, *Economy and Society: An Interpretive Outline of Sociology* (Berkeley and Los Angeles: University of California Press, 1978), vol. 2, pp. 901–5.

9. The literature produced many rich case studies of state building in various regional and historical contexts. For a sample of this work, see Vivienne Shue, *The Reaches of the State: Sketches of the Chinese Politic* (Stanford, CA: Stanford University Press, 1988); John Brewer, *The Sinews of Power: War, Power and the English State, 1688–1783* (Cambridge: Harvard University Press, 1988); Lisa Anderson, *The State and Social Transformation in Libya and Tunisia* (Princeton, NJ: Princeton University Press, 1986); Peter Katzenstein, *Small States in World Markets* (Ithaca, NY: Cornell University Press, 1985); Stephen Skorownek, *Building a New American State: Expansion of National Administrative Capacities* (New York: Cambridge University Press, 1982); and Peter Hall, *Governing the Economy: The Politics of State Intervention in England and France* (New York: Oxford University Press, 1986).

10. For a good discussion of these concepts, see Joel Migdal, *Strong Societies, Weak States: State–Societal Relations and State Capabilities in the Third World* (Princeton, NJ: Princeton University Press, 1988), pp. 4–7. A good critique of the way in which the "statists," defined and measured these concepts is found in Robert Jackman, *Power Without Force: The Political Capacity of Nation–States* (Ann Arbor: University of Michigan Press, 1993), ch. 3.

11. R. Kent Weaver and Bert Rockman, eds., *Do Institutions Matter? Government Capabilities in the United States and Abroad* (Washington, DC: The Brookings Institution, 1993); and G. John Ikenberry, *Reasons of State: Oil Politics and the Capacities of the American Government* (Ithaca, NY: Cornell University Press, 1988).

12. Skocpol, *States and Social Revolutions*, pp. 19–33; Charles Tilly, *Coercion, Capital and the Formation of the European States* (Oxford: Basil Blackwell, 1990); and John Hall and G. John Ikenberry, *The State* (Minneapolis: University of Minnesota Press, 1989).

13. Dietrich Rueschmeyer and Peter Evans, "The State and Economic Transformation," in *Bringing the State Back In*, eds., Evans, Rueschmeyer, and Skocpol, pp. 44–77; and Alice Amsden, *Asia's Next Giant: South Korea and Late Industrialization* (New York: Oxford University Press, 1989).

14. Barbara Geddes, "Building State Autonomy in Brazil, 1931–1964," *Comparative Politics* 22 (January 1990), p. 217.

15. A recent attempt to bring together the state-building and transitions literatures is Yossi Shain and Juan Linz, *Interim Governments and Democratic Transitions* (New York: Cambridge University Press, 1996).

16. Margaret Levi, *Of Rule and Revenue* (Berkeley and Los Angeles: University of California Press, 1988).

17. Barbara Geddes, *Politician's Dilemma: Building State Capacity in Latin America* (Berkeley and Los Angeles: University of California Press, 1994).

18. Joel Migdal, Atul Kohli, and Vivienne Shue, eds., *State Power and Social Forces: Domination and Transformation in the Third World* (New York: Cambridge University Press, 1994), introduction and ch. 1.

19. Peter Evans, *Embedded Autonomy: States and Industrial Transformation* (Princeton, NJ: Princeton University Press, 1995).

20. Robert Jackman, *Power Without Force: The Political Capacity of Nation–States* (Ann Arbor: University of Michigan Press, 1993).

21. Leonard Schapiro, *The Communist Party of the Soviet Union* (New York: Vintage Books, 1971, rev. ed.); Robert V. Daniels, "The Secretariat and the Local Organizations in the Russian Communist Party, 1921–1923," *American Slavonic and East European Review* (March 1967); and Robert Service, *Bolshevik Party in Revolution: A Study in Organizational Change, 1917–1923* (London: Macmillan, 1979).

22. Adam Ulam, *Stalin: The Man and His Era* (New York: Viking, 1973), pp. 258–259.

23. Philip Selznick, *The Organizational Weapon: A Study of Bolshevik Strategy and Tactics* (Glencoe, IL: The Free Press, 1960).

24. Samuel Huntington and Clement Moore, eds., *Authoritarian Politics in Modern Society: The Dynamics of Established One-Party Systems* (New York: Basic Books, 1970).

25. Huntington, *Political Order in Changing Societies*, pp. 1, 137, 336–41, 400 (quote).

26. Skocpol, *States and Social Revolutions*, pp. 162, 215, 226 (quote).

27. Huntington, *Political Order in Changing Societies*, p. 400.

28. J. Arch Getty, *Origins of the Great Purges: The Soviet Communist Party Reconsidered, 1933–1938* (New York: Cambridge University Press, 1986); Roger Pethyridge, *One Step Backwards, Two Steps Forward* (Oxford: Clarendon Press, 1990); Graeme Gill, *The Origins of the Stalinist Political System* (New York: Cambridge University Press, 1990); and James Hughes, *Stalin, Siberia and the Crisis of the New Economic Policy* (New York: Cambridge University Press, 1991).

29. Pethyridge, *One Step Backwards*, p. 294.

30. The classic treatment is Sheila FitzPatrick, *The Russian Revolution* (New York: Oxford University Press, 1982).

31. See Mark Von Hagen's review article in *Slavic Review* 48 (Winter 1989), pp. 637–640.

32. See Migdal, *Strong Societies, Weak States*. It does not accept Jackman's assertion that "political capacity" is a better indicator of state strength and, ultimately, state survival. The legitimacy of a political regime is not the same phenomenon as the capabilities of a state.

33. Sydney Tarrow, *Between Center and Periphery: Grassroots Politicians in Italy and France* (New Haven, CT: Yale University Press, 1977), ch. 1.

34. See, for example, Shue, *Reach of the State*; and Karen Barkey, *Bandits and Bureaucrats: The Ottoman Route to State Centralization* (Ithaca, NY: Cornell University Press, 1994).

35. Some excellent examples include Jerry Hough, *Soviet Prefects: Local Party Organs in Industrial Decision-making* (Cambridge, MA: Harvard University Press, 1969); T. H. Rigby and Bohdan Harasymiw, eds., *Leadership Selection and Patron–Client Relations in the USSR and Yugoslavia* (London: George Allen

& Unwin, 1983); Andrew Walder, *Communist Neo-Traditionalism: Work and Authority in Chinese Industry* (Berkeley and Los Angeles: University of California Press, 1986); Jean Oi, *State and Peasant in Contemporary China* (New York: Oxford University Press, 1989); and John Willerton, *Patronage and Politics in the USSR* (New York: Cambridge University Press, 1992).

36. A noteworthy exception is Gill, *The Origins of the Stalinist Political System*.

37. W. Lloyd Warner and P. S. Lunt, *The Social Life of a Modern Community* (New Haven, CT: Yale University Press, 1941), p. 110.

38. David Knoke, *Political Networks: The Structural Perspective* (New York: Cambridge University Press, 1990), pp. 11–16.

39. Weber, *Economy and Society,* vol. 1, pp. 305–7.

40. Mann, "The Autonomous Power of the State."

41. For a good discussion of the limits of the "European" model of state building, see Barkey, *Bandits and Bureaucrats*, ch. 1.

42. Thomas Ertman, *Birth of the Leviathan: Building States and Regimes in Medieval and Early Modern Europe* (New York: Cambridge University Press, 1997), pp. 6–10.

43. Gerald M. Easter, "Personal Networks and Post-revolutionary State Building: Soviet Russia Reexamined," *World Politics* 48, no. 4 (July 1996), pp. 551–578.

44. Two notable recent studies include Sven Steinmo, Kathleen Thelen and Frank Longstreth, eds., *Structuring Politics: Historical Institutionalism in Comparative Perspective* (New York: Cambridge University Press, 1992); and Jack Knight, *Institutions and Social Conflict* (New York: Cambridge University Press, 1992).

45. *Pravda*, 1 April 1937.

46. Iosif Stalin, *Voprosy leninizma* (Moscow: Partizdat TsK VKP(b), 1934, 10th ed.) pp. 592–3.

47. John Reshetar Jr., *A Concise History of the Communist Party of the Soviet Union* (New York: Praeger Publishers, 1960), p. 200; and Isaac Deutscher, *Stalin: A Political Biography* (New York: Vintage Books, 1960), pp. 363–4.

48. Getty, *Origins of the Great Purges*; and Gill, *The Origins of the Stalinist Political System*.

49. See, for example, Lynn Viola, *The Twenty-Five Thousanders* (New York: Oxford University Press, 1988).

50. The journal *Voprosy istorii KPSS* became the principal source for the historical revision of the Provincial Komitetchiki in a series of rehabilitation articles published in the early to mid-1960s.

51. See, for example, the draft chapter covering the radical economic campaigns of the 1930s proposed for a new history of the Soviet period. V. V. Lel'chuk, "Istoriia sovetskogo obshchestva: kratkii ocherki (1917–1945 gg.)," *Istoriia SSSR*, no. 4 (July–August 1990), p. 13.

52. Stephen Cohen, *Bukharin and the Bolshevik Revolution: A Political Biography* (New York: Knopf, 1973), p. 327.

53. Barry Wellman and S. D. Berkowitz, "Introduction: Studying Social Structures," in *Social Structures: A Network Approach*, ed. B. Wellman and S. D. Berkowitz (New York: Cambridge University Press, 1988), p. 4.

54. Some of the best-known works from this literature are presented in J. Clyde

Mitchell, ed., *Social Networks in Urban Situations* (Manchester: Manchester University Press, 1969).

55. Harrison White, "Where Do Markets Come From?" *American Journal of Sociology* 87 (November 1981); Ron Burt, *Corporate Profits and Cooptation: Networks of Market Constraints and Directorate Ties in the American Economy* (New York: Academic Books, 1983); and Mark Granovetter, "The Strength of Weak Ties," *American Journal of Sociology* 78 (May 1973).

56. Edward Laumann and Franz Pappi, *Networks of Collective Action: A Perspective on Community Influence Systems* (New York: Academic Press, 1976).

57. Edward Laumann and David Knoke, *The Organizational State: Social Choice in National Policy Domains* (Madison: University of Wisconsin Press, 1987).

58. For a similar approach for determining personal network ties within the Soviet elite, see John Willerton, "Patronage Networks and Coalition Building in the Brezhnev Era," *Soviet Studies* 39, no. 2 (April 1987), pp. 177–178.

59. The principal source materials consulted for individual members of the Provincial Komitetchiki are listed in footnote 53 in Chapter 2.

60. John Scott, *Social Network Analysis* (Newbury Park, CA: Sage Publications, 1991), p. 86.

61. The archive of the Society of Old Bolsheviks is located in the Russian Center for the Preservation and Investigation of Documents of Recent History (hereafter RTsKhIDNI), formerly the Institute of Marxism-Leninism attached to the central committee of the Communist party of the Soviet Union.

2. ANATOMY OF A REGIONAL ELITE

1. Two notable exceptions are: Don Karl Rowney, *Transition to Technocracy: The Origins of the Soviet Administrative State* (Ithaca, NY: Cornell University Press, 1989); and Stephen Sternheimer, "Administration for Development: The Emerging Bureaucratic Elite, 1920–1930," in *Russian Officialdom: The Bureaucratization of Russian Society from the Seventeenth to the Twentieth Century*, ed. Don Karl Rowney and Walter Pintner (Chapel Hill: University of North Carolina Press, 1980), pp. 317–54.

2. Leon Trotsky, *The Revolution Betrayed: What Is the Soviet Union and Where Is It Going?* (New York: Pathfinder Press, 1972 [1936]), ch. 5.

3. Ibid., pp. 92, 93. In later writings, Trotsky modified this view, placing more emphasis on the individual role of Stalin. Leon Trotsky, *Stalin: An Appraisal of the Man and His Influence* (New York: Stein & Day, 1967 ed.), suppl. 1.

4. Trotsky, *Revolution Betrayed*, pp. 94–105.

5. Some of the best early work on regional administration was done by Robert V. Daniels. See especially Daniels, "The Secretariat and the Local Organizations in the Russian Communist Party, 1921–1923," *The American Slavonic and East European Review*, no. 1 (March 1967), pp. 32, 33. John A. Armstrong, *The Politics of Totalitarianism: The Communist Party of the Soviet Union from 1934 to the Present* (New York: Random House, 1961), p. 11; and, more recently, Robert Service, *Bolshevik Party in Revolution: A Study in Organizational Change, 1917–1923* (London: Macmillan, 1979), p. 184.

6. Leon Trotsky, *My Life: An Attempt at an Autobiography* (New York: Pathfinder Press, 1970), p. 506.

7. Daniels, "Secretariat and the Local Organizations," p. 49.

8. Trotsky, *Revolution Betrayed*, pp. 88, 89.

9. John Reshetar Jr., *A Concise History of the Communist Party of the Soviet Union* (New York: Praeger Publishers, 1960), p. 200; and Isaac Deutscher, *Stalin: A Political Biography* (New York: Vintage Books, 1960), pp. 363, 364.

10. Merle Fainsod, *Smolensk Under Soviet Rule* (Cambridge: Harvard University Press, 1958), p. 448 (quote), ch. 23. Fainsod's Smolensk case study was the first major work in Western historiography that utilized archival sources. In its emphasis on the limits of central bureaucratic control, the Smolensk case study went further than Fainsod's earlier classic text, although the theme can be found there as well. See Merle Fainsod, *How Russia Is Ruled* (Cambridge: Harvard University Press, 1967 rev. ed.), pp. 234–7; 417–20.

11. Jerry Hough, *Soviet Prefects: The Local Party Organs in Industrial Decision-making* (Cambridge: Harvard University Press, 1969).

12. J. Arch Getty, *Origin of the Great Purges: The Soviet Communist Party Reconsidered, 1933–1938* (New York: Cambridge University Press, 1986), p. 25.

13. See Roger Pethyridge, *One Step Backwards, Two Steps Forward* (Oxford: Clarendon Press, 1990); and James Hughes, *Stalin, Siberia and the Crisis of the New Economic Policy* (New York: Cambridge University Press, 1991).

14. T. H. Rigby, "Early Provincial Cliques and the Rise of Stalin," *Soviet Studies* 33, no. 1 (January 1981), pp. 3–28.

15. Graeme Gill, *The Origins of the Stalinist Political System* (New York: Cambridge University Press, 1990), pp. 23–6, ch. 3.

16. Andrew Walder, *Communist Neo-traditionalism: Work and Authority in Chinese Industry* (Berkely and Los Angeles: University of California Press, 1986); John Willerton, *Patronage and Politics in the USSR* (New York: Cambridge University Press, 1992); and Victor Nee and David Stark, eds., *Remaking the Economic Institutions of Socialism: China and Eastern Europe* (Stanford, CA: Stanford University Press, 1989).

17. T. H. Rigby, "Was Stalin a Disloyal Patron?" *Soviet Studies* 38, no. 3 (July 1986), pp. 311–324.

18. Gill, *Origins of the Stalinist Political System*, pp. 44, 128, 129, 217.

19. David Knoke, *Political Networks: The Structural Perspective* (New York: Cambridge University Press, 1990).

20. Gill, *Origins of the Stalinist Political System*, pp. 40, 41, 216.

21. See, for example, Chester Barnard's classic work, *The Functions of the Executive* (Cambridge: Harvard University Press, 1937); Peter Blau, *The Dynamics of Bureaucracy* (Chicago: University of Chicago Press, 1963); and Michel Crozier, *The Bureaucratic Phenomenon* (Chicago: University of Chicago Press, 1964).

22. The following section provides an analytical overview of the role of personal networks in the prerevolutionary underground, civil war, and postrevolutionary provincial administration. See Chapter 4 for an empirical study of the Transcaucasian regional network.

23. The underground existence remains a largely neglected topic in Western historiography. A noteworthy exception is Ralph C. Elwood, *Russian Social-Democrats in the Underground: A Study of the RSDRP in the Ukraine* (Assen, the

Netherlands: Van Gorcum, 1974). The following overview is drawn from Elwood's in depth study.

24. Russian Center for the Preservation and Investigation of Documents of Recent History (hereafter RTsKhIDNI), f. 79, op. 1, d. 74.

25. Ibid., d. 3, ll. 1–4.

26. Anastas Mikoyan, *Memoirs of Anastas Mikoyan: The Path of Struggle* (Madison, WI: Sphinx Press, 1988), p. 450.

27. Ibid.

28. For different systems of trust, see James Coleman, *Foundations of Social Theory* (Cambridge: Harvard University Press, 1990), ch. 8.

29. Diego Gambeta, ed., *Trust: Making and Breaking Cooperative Relations* (Oxford: Basil Blackwell, 1988).

30. For an excellent single-volume work on the military campaigns of the civil war, see Evan Mawdsley, *The Russian Civil War* (Boston: Allen & Unwin, 1987).

31. RTsKhIDNI, f. 79, op. 1, d. 7, l. 1.

32. Ibid., d. 110, ll. 36–38.

33. See T. H. Rigby, "Early Provincial Cliques and the Rise of Stalin," *Soviet Studies* 33, no. 1 (January 1981); and Graeme Gill, *Origins of the Stalinist Political System*.

34. For the persistence of patronage networks throughout the Soviet period, see the excellent study by John Willerton, *Patronage and Politics in the USSR* (New York, UK: Cambridge University Press, 1992).

35. For example, Nikolai Kubiak, RTsKhIDNI, f. 124, op. 1, d. 1004, 1. 6; Gaia Gai, RTsKhIDNI, f. 124, op. 1, d. 429, 1. 16.

36. Domenic Lieven, *Russia's Rulers Under the Old Regime* (New Haven: CT: Yale University Press, 1989), p. 9. Also, on the term *druzhina*, see John LeDonne, *Absolutism and Ruling Class: The Formation of the Russian Political Order* (New York: Oxford University Press, 1991), pp. x, 5, 15.

37. W. E. Mosse, "Makers of the Soviet Union," *The Slavonic and East European Review* 46, no. 106 (January 1968), pp. 141–154.

38. Ibid., p. 152.

39. Sheila FitzPatrick, "The Bolsheviks' Dilemma: Class, Culture, and Politics in the Early Soviet Years," *Slavic Review* 47, no. 4 (Winter 1988), pp. 604, 605.

40. Alexander Shlyapnikov, *On the Eve of 1917* (London: Allison & Busby, 1982), p. 6. Also, see Elwood, *Russian Social–Democrats*, pp. 60, 61.

41. Leopold Haimson, "Yuri Petrovich Denike, 1887–1964," *Slavic Review* 24, no. 2 (June 1965), p. 371.

42. Nadezhda Krupskaya, *Memories of Lenin* (New York: International Publishers, 1930), pp. 137, 138.

43. Trotsky, *Stalin*, p. 41.

44. Feliks Chuev, ed., *Sto sorok besed s Molotovym* (Moscow: Terra, 1991), p. 304.

45. N. A. Vasetskii, "L. D. Trotskii: politicheskii portret," *Novaia i noveishaia istoriia*, no. 3 (May–June 1991), p. 157.

46. V. I. Lenin, *KPSS: ob ustavii partii* (Moscow: Politizdat, 1981), p. 221.

47. *Izvestiia TsK RKP(b)*, no. 4 (April 1923), p. 45.

48. Ibid., no. 3 (March 1922), p. 20.

49. *Trinadtsatyi s'ezd RKP(b): stenograficheskii otchet* (Moscow: Gospolizdat, 1963), p. 118. The percentage of komitetchiki serving as heads of the organizational-instructional departments in provincial party committees increased slightly in this period, from 27.5 percent to 30 percent; meanwhile, the percentage of komitetchiki serving as heads of the agitation-propaganda departments declined, from 31 percent to 23 percent.

50. *Piatnadtsatyi s'ezd VKP(b): stenograficheskii otchet* (Moscow: Gospolizdat, 1961), vol. 1, p. 115.

51. For a full description of the issues, personalities and events in the succession, see Deutscher, *Stalin*; and Robert Tucker, *Stalin as Revolutionary, 1879–1929* (New York: Norton, 1973), chs. 8–11.

52. Robert V. Daniels, "Soviet Politics Since Khrushchev," in *The Soviet Union Under Brezhnev and Kosygin*, ed. John Strong (New York: Van Nostrand Reinhold, 1971), p. 20.

53. The information presented in Tables 2.1–2.4 was obtained from the following sources: (1) autobiographical statements submitted by the Provincial Komitetchiki to the Society of Old Bolsheviks; (2) responses to a personal questionnaire also submitted to the Society of Old Bolsheviks; (3) posthumous rehabilitation obituaries; and (4) published memoirs, biographies and histories. The main sources consulted for the individuals included in these tables are listed below:

A. Andreev: RTsKhIDNI, f. 73, op. 1, foreword (*predislovie*); A. A. Andreev, *Vospominaniia, pis'ma* (Moscow: Politizdat, 1985).

R. Eikhe: RTsKhIDNI, f. 124, op. 1, d. 2215, ll. 1–6; *Voprosy istorii KPSS*, no. 7 (1965), 92–97.

I. Gamarnik: *Vospominaniia druzei i soratnikov* (Moscow: Voenizdat, 1978).

N. Gikalo: RTsKhIDNI, f. 85, op. 15, d. 34, ll. 1–5; Ibid., f. 80, op. 8, d. 25, ll. 3–9.

F. Goloshchekin: RTsKhIDNI, f. 124, op. 1, d. 484, ll. 1–12.

V. Ivanov: *Izvestiia TsK KPSS,* no. 12 (December 1988), p. 90.

I. Kabakov: RTsKhIDNI, f. 124, op. 1, d. 784, ll. 3, 4.

M. Khataevich: RTsKhIDNI, f. 124, op. 1, d. 2043, ll. 2–6; *Voprosy istorii KPSS*, no. 6 (1963), 98–101.

S. Kosior: RTsKhIDNI, f. 124, op. 1, d. 951, l. 1; *Vospominaniia, ocherki,stat'i* (Moscow: Politizdat, 1989).

A. Krinitskii: *Voprosy istorii KPSS*, no. 12 (1964).

N. Kubiak: RTsKhIDNI, f. 124, op. 1, d. 1004, ll. 1–7.

L. Mirzoian: RTsKhIDNI, f. 80, op. 7, d. 3, l. 1; *Voprosy istorii KPSS*, no. 1 (1965), 101–4.

P. Postyshev: RTsKhIDNI, f. 124, op. 1, d. 1560, ll. 1, 2.

I. Rumiantsev: RTsKhIDNI, f. 124, op. 1, d. 1662, ll. 3–5.

B. Sheboldaev: RTsKhIDNI, f. 124, op. 1, d. 2138, ll. 1, 2.

I. Vareikis: RTsKhIDNI, f. 124, op. 1, d. 302, ll. 1–5; D. Lappo, *Iuozas Vareikis* (Voronezh: Tsentral'no-chernozemnoe izdatel'stvo, 1989).

54. For a good overview of the regional bureaus, see N. E. Petukhova, "Sozdanie oblastnykh biuro TsK RKP(b) i nekotorye storonye ikh deiatel'nosti, 1920–1922," *Voprosy istorii KPSS,* no. 4 (April 1965), pp. 74–81.

55. The Central Black Earth region, for example, had a total population of nearly

12 million, of whom over 90 percent were peasants. *Ocherki istorii voronezhskoi organizatsii KPSS* (Voronezh: Tsentral'no-chernozemnoe knizhnoe izdatel'stvo, 1967), pp. 260, 261.

56. RTsKhIDNI, f. 124, op. 1, d. 484, l. 1 (F. Goloshchekin); Ibid., d. 2138, l. 2 (B. Sheboldaev); and Ibid., d.2043, l. 2 (M. Khataevich).

57. RTsKhIDNI, f. 124, op. 1, d. 2215, ll. 3, 4.

58. Ibid., d. 302, 1. 5 (Vareikis); *Voprosy istorii KPSS*, no. 12 (1964), pp. 96–99 (Krinitskii).

59. *Izvestiia TsK KPSS,* no. 9 (September 1990), pp. 186, 189.

60. Richard Robbins, *The Tsar's Viceroys: Russian Provincial Governors in the Last Years of the Empire* (Ithaca, NY: Cornell University Press, 1987), p. 4.

3. CONSTRUCTING AN ELITE IDENTITY

1. Leopold Haimson, "The Problems of Social Identities in Early Twentieth Century Russia," *Slavic Review* 47, no. 1 (Spring 1988), p. 4. Haimson's seminal article remains the most illuminating discussion of identity formation in the early postrevolutionary state.

2. Domenic Lieven, *Russia's Rulers Under the Old Regime* (New Haven, CT: Yale University Press, 1989).

3. John Armstrong, *The European Administrative Elite* (Princeton, NJ: Princeton University Press, 1976).

4. Robert Crummey, *Aristocrats and Servitors: The Boyar Elite in Russia, 1613–1689* (Princeton, NJ: Princeton University Press, 1983), p. 12.

5. The archive of the Society of Old Bolsheviks is found in the Russian Center for the Preservation and Investigation of the Documents of Recent History (hereafter RTsKhIDNI).

6. Sheila FitzPatrick, "Ascribing Class: The Construction of Social Identity in Soviet Russia," *Journal of Modern History* 65 (December 1993), pp. 745–770.

7. See Reginald Zelnick's insightful analysis of this literature in *Law and Disorder on the Narova* (Stanford, CA: Stanford University Press, 1992).

8. See, for example, the experiences of Pavel Postyshev, RTsKhIDNI, f. 124, op. 1, d. 1560, l. 1; Ivan Ruminatsev, RTsKhIDNI, f. 124, op. 1, d. 1662, ll. 3–5; and Robert Eikhe, RTsKhIDNI, f. 124, op. 1, d. 2215, l. 3.

9. RTsKhIDNI, f. 124, op. 1, d. 2043, ll. 4, 5.

10. Ibid., d. 784, l. 4.

11. Ibid.

12. Ibid., d. 1004, l. 5.

13. Maksim Kartvelishvili worked as a lower party official in Georgia in the early twenties. His brother was Lavrenti Kartvelishvili, who held several major regional posts in the twenties and thirties. RTsKhIDNI, f. 124, op. 1, d. 835, ll. 3, 15.

14. See, for example, the autobiographical statements of Ivan Rumiantsev, RTsKhIDNI, f. 124, op. 1, d. 1662, ll. 4, 5; Pavel Postyshev, RTsKhIDNI, f. 124, op. 1, d. 1560, l. 1; and Ivan Kabakov, RTsKhIDNI, f. 124, op. 1, d. 784, l. 4.

15. RTsKhIDNI, f. 124, op. 1, d. 1004, l. 5.

16. Ibid., d. 302, l. 3. D. Lappo, *Iuozas Vareikis* (Voronezh: Tsentral'no-chernozemnoe knizhnoe izdatel'stvo, 1989), pp. 18–25.

17. RTsKhIDNI, f. 124, op. 1, d. 2043, l. 4.

18. Ibid., 1004, ll. 5, 6.

19. Ibid., d. 302, l. 3.

20. Ibid., d. 2215, ll. 3, 4.

21. *0 stanislav kosiore: vospominaniia, ocherki, stat'i* (Moscow: Politizdat, 1989), p. 236.

22. RTsKhIDNI, f. 124, op. 1, d. 2215, l. 4.

23. Georges Haupt and Jean-Jacques Marie, *Makers of the Russian Revolution: Biographies of Bolshevik Leaders* (Ithaca, NY: Cornell University Press, 1974), p. 166.

24. See, for example, B. Sheboldaev, RTsKhIDNI, f. 124, op. 1, d. 2138, l. 2; S. Kosior, RTsKhIDNI, f. 124, op. 1, d. 951, l. 1; I. Rumiantsev, RTsKhIDNI, f. 124, op. 1, d. 1662, l. 3; and, M. Khataevich, f. 124, op. 1, d. 2043, l. 2.

25. RTsKhIDNI, f. 124, op. d. 2215, l. 1.

26. Ibid., d. 1004, l. 6.

27. Ibid., d. 484, ll. 10, 11.

28. Ibid., d. 302, l. 1.

29. Anastas Mikoyan, *Memoirs of Anastas Mikoyan: The Path of Struggle* (Madison, WI: Sphinx Press, 1988), pp. 413, 414.

30. RTsKhIDNI, f. 124, op. 1, d. 951, l. 1.

31. *Pravda,* 6 May 1937.

32. *Voprosy istorii KPSS,* no. 6 (1963), pp. 98–101.

33. RTsKhIDNI, f. 124, op. 1, d. 2043, ll. 5, 6.

34. Ibid., d. 302, ll. 4, 5.

35. *Voprosy istorii KPSS,* no. 2 (1963), pp. 101–6.

36. RTsKhIDNI, f. 80, op. 2, d. 1, ll. 2, 3.

37. Ibid., op. 3, d. 31, l. 1.

38. Ibid., f. 124, op. 1, d. 2138, l. 2.

39. Mikoyan, *Memoirs of Anastas Mikoyan*, p. 440.

40. RTsKhIDNI, f. 124, op. 1, d. 1560, l. 2.

41. The best early source of this heroic literature was the memoir section of the historical journal, *Proletarskaia revoliutsiia.* This literary style survived in official publications until the end of the Soviet state.

42. RTsKhIDNI, f. 79, op. 1, d. 123, l. 61.

43. Ibid., f. 85, op. 1, d. 117, ll. 5–19; and ibid., d. 133, ll. 1–9.

44. Ibid., f. 124, op. 1, d. 429, ll. 13–18.

45. Ibid., l. 32.

46. *Izvestiia TsK KPSS,* no. 7 (July 1991), pp. 130, 131.

47. Ante Ciliga, *The Russian Enigma* (London: Ink Links, 1979), p. 74.

48. RTsKhIDNI, f. 17, op. 2, d. 612, vyp. III, l. 73.

49. Ibid., vyp. I, ll. 19, 20.

50. Ibid., d. 514, vyp. II, l. 33.

51. Ibid., vyp. I, l. 60.

52. Ibid., d. 612, vyp. I, l. 38.

53. Ibid., d. 514, vyp. I, l. 80.

54. Ibid., d. 612, vyp. III, l. 11; ibid. d. 514, vyp. I, l. 62.

55. Ibid., d. 612, vyp. I, l. 22.

56. Iosif Stalin, *Voprosy leninizma (Moscow:* Partizdat TsK VKP(b), 1934, 10th ed.), pp. 592, 593 (emphasis added).

4. EXTENDING THE REACH OF THE STATE

1. T. H. Rigby, *Lenin's Government: Sovnarkom, 1917–1922* (New York: Cambridge University Press, 1979); E. G. Gimpel'son, *Iz istorii stroitellstvo sovetov, noiabr 1917 g.–iuli 1918 g.* (Moscow: Gosiurizdat, 1958) and, V. Z. Drobizhev, *Lenin vo glave sovetskogo pravitel'stva* (Moscow, 1970).

2. N. Sukhanov, *The Russian Revolution: A Personal Record* (Princeton, NJ: Princeton University Press, 1984), pp. 209–11.

3. Efim Gorodetskii and Iurii Sharapov, *Sverdlov* (Moscow: Molodaia gvardiia, 1971), pp. 174–181; E. M. Stasova, *Vospominaniia* (Moscow: Izdatel'stvo mysl', 1969).

4. An excellent study of Sverdlov's role in organizing center–local relations within the party is Robert Service, *Bolshevik Party in Revolution: A Study in Organizational Change, 1917–1923* (London: Macmillan, 1979), chs. 3, 4.

5. *0 Iakove Sverdlove: vospominaniia, ocherki, stat'i sovremenikov* (Moscow: Politizdat, 1985), pp. 123–279.

6. Ia. M. Sverdlov, *Izbrannye stat'i i rechi* (Moscow: Gosizdat, 1939), p. 92.

7. This group included Tsiurupa, Podvoiskii, and Stuchka in the center; and Kuibyshev and Goloshchekin in the regions. See the Russian Center for the Preservation and Investigation of Documents of Recent History (hereafter RTsKhIDNI). RTsKhIDNI, f. 86, op. 1, d. 27, ll. 1–14; ibid., d. 33, l. 88.

8. *Pravda,* 16 March 1939.

9. Gorodetskii and Sharapov, *Sverdlov,* p. 182.

10. Leon Trotsky, *My Life: An Attempt at an Autobiography* (New York: Pathfinder Books, 1970), p. 341.

11. Ibid., p. 277.

12. Leon Trotsky, *Stalin: An Appraisal of the Man and His Influence* (New York: Stein & Day, 1967 ed.), pp. 344, 345.

13. V. I. Lenin, *Speeches to the Party Congresses* (Moscow: Progress, 1971), pp. 73, 74

14. RTsKhIDNI, f. 124, op. 1, d. 978, l. 6; and, N. Popov, "Nikolai Krestinskii: byl i ostaius kommunistom," in *Reabilitirovan posmertno,* ed. S. Panov (Moscow: Iuridicheskaia literatura, 1989), pp. 143–145.

15. See the organizational report delivered at the Tenth Party Congress in 1921. *Desiatyi s'ezd RKP(b): stenograficheskii ochet* (Moscow: Gospolizdat, 1963), p. 56. Janice Ali, "Aspects of the RKP(в) Secretariat, March 1919 to April 1922," *Soviet Studies* 26, no. 3 (July 1974), pp. 396–416.

16. RTsKhIDNI, f. 124, op. 1, d. 978, l. 2.

17. Alexander Shlyapnikov, *On the Eve of 1917* (London: Allison & Busby, 1982), p. 25.

18. See Krestinskii's organizational report to the Tenth Party Congress. *Desiatyi s'ezd: sten. otchet,* pp. 53, 54. Also, see Mark Neuweld, "The Origins of the Central Control Commission," *The American Slavic and East European Review*

18, no. 3 (October 1959), pp. 317–19; and Leonard Schapiro, *The Communist Party of the Soviet Union* (New York: Vintage Books, 1971, rev. ed.), pp. 259, 260.

19. *Desiatyi s'ezd: sten. otchet*, pp. 92, 293. The quote is by David Riazanov.

20. Krestinskii needed 240 votes of a possible 479 to remain a Central Committee member; he received 161 votes. V. I. Startsev, "Politicheskie rukovoditeli sovetskogo gosudarstva v 1922 nachale 1923 g.," *Istoriia SSSR*, no. 5 (September–October 1988), p. 102.

21. RTsKhIDNI, f. 124, op. 1, d. 1321, l. 6; Feliks Chuev, ed., *Sto sorok besed s Molotovym* (Moscow: Terra, 1991).

22. Ibid., l. 3. See Molotov's discussion of his prerevolutionary and early administrative roles in the party. Chuev, *Sto sorok besed*, pp. 121–239.

23. See Molotov's speech to the Eleventh Party Congress and the Secretariat's annual report. *Odinnadtsatyi s'ezd RKP(b): stenograficheskii otchet* (Moscow: Gospolizdat, 1961), pp. 54–57, 659. Also, see Robert V. Daniels, "The Secretariat and the Local Organizations in the Russian Communist Party, 1921–1923," *The American Slavonic and East European Review* 16, no. 1 (March 1967), pp. 41–44.

24. *Odinnadtsyi s'ezd: sten. otchet,* p. 62.

25. Ibid., p. 61.

26. *V. I. Lenin, KPSS: o rabote patiinogo i gosudarstvennogo apparata* (Moscow: Politizdat, 1976), p. 139.

27. Stalin was named to the first informal bureau of the central committee (November 1917), the executive committee of the Council of Peoples' Commissariats (November 1917), the Revolutionary Military Council (October 1918), the Presidium of the Supreme Executive Committee (November 1918), and the first politburo and orgburo (March 1919).

28. Robert Tucker, *Stalin as Revolutionary, 1879–1929: A Study in History and Personality* (New York: Norton & Co., 1973), p. 221.

29. T. H. Rigby, *Stalin* (Englewood Cliffs, NJ: Prentice Hall, 1966), p. 72.

30. *Odinnadtsatyi s'ezd: sten. otchet*, pp. 84, 85.

31. Lenin, *Speeches*, pp. 225, 226. Lenin's letters to A. D. Tsiurupa, another member of his inner circle of troubleshooters, from January and February 1922. "0 perestroike raboty SNK, STO i Malogo SNK," *V. I. Lenin, KPSS: 0 rabote part. i gos. apparata*, pp. 133–138.

32. For an alternative view of Lenin's approach to state bureaucracy, see Moshe Lewin, *Lenin's Last Struggle* (New York: Monthy Review Press, 1968), pp. 123–128.

33. G. V. Kuibysheva, et al, *Valerian Vladimirovich Kuibyshev:biografiia* (Moscow: Politizdat, 1966), pp. 53–152.

34. I. M. Dubinskii-Mukhadze, *Kuibyshev* (Moscow: Molodaia gvardiia, 1971), pp. 298, 299.

35. A. I. Zevelev, *Istoki stalinizma* (Moscow: Vysshaia shkola, 1990), p. 76.

36. Service, *Bolshevik Party in Revolution*, p. 107.

37. Boris Bazhanov, *Vospominaniia byvshego sekretia stalina* (Paris: Izdatel'stvo Tretlia Volna, 1983), p. 25.

38. Ibid., p. 26.

39. Chuev, *Sto sorok besed*, p. 319.

40. Nikita Khrushchev, *Khrushchev Remembers* (Boston: Little, Brown, 1970), p. 34.

41. Kuibyshev's personal archive showed that he continued to monitor and to intervene in the affairs of the Samaran organization after he had been transferred out of the region. RTsKhIDNI, f. 79, op. 1, d. 122, ll. 1–32.

42. Anastas Mikoian, *V nachale dvadtsatykh* (Moscow: Politizdat, 1975), ch. 2.

43. N. E. Petukhova, "Sozdanie oblastnykh biuro TsK RKP(в) i nekotorye storonye ikh deiatel'nosti, 1920–1922 gg.," *Voprosy istorii KPSS*, no. 4 (April 1965), pp. 74–81.

44. Donald Raleigh, "Revolutionary Politics in Provincial Russia: the 'Tsaritsyn Republic' in 1917," *Slavic Review*, vol. 40, no. 2 (1981).

45. John P. LeDonne, "From Gubernia to Oblast: Soviet Administrative-Territorial Reform, 1917–1923" (Ph.D. thesis, Columbia University, 1962), p. 42.

46. *Izvestiia TsK RKP(b)*, no. 24 (October 1920).

47. *Vos'moi s'ezd RKP(b), mart 1919 goda: protokoly* (Moscow: Politizdat, 1959), p. 429.

48. Merle Fainsod, *How Russia Is Ruled* (Cambridge: Harvard University Press, 1967, rev. ed.), p. 92.

49. "Polozhenie ob oblastnykh biuro," *Izvestiia TsK RKP(b)*, no. 33 (October 1921), pp. 21, 22. For a good overview of the regional bureaus, see N. E. Petukhova, "Sozdanie oblastnykh biuro," *Voprosy istorii KPSS*, no. 4 (April 1965), pp. 74–81.

50. Petukhova, "Sozdanie oblastnykh biuro," p. 77. Among those selected to lead regional bureaus in the early twenties were: Sergo Ordzhonikidze and Sergei Kirov (later head of the Northwest bureau) in the Caucasus; Lazar Kaganovich and Ian Rudzutak in Central Asia; Stanislav Kosior and Emilian Iaroslavskii in Siberia, Filipp Goloshchekin and Hungarian communist, Bela Kun, in the Urals; Nikolai Kubiak and Pavel Postyshev in the Far East; and Anastas Mikoian and Kliment Voroshilov in the Southeast.

51. Ibid., p. 79.

52. A. V. Osipova, "Bor'ba Dal'biuro TsK RKP(в) za ukreplenie dal'nevostochnoi partorganizatsii," *Voprosy istorii KPSS*, no. 2 (February 1962), pp. 107, 108; and A. P. Shurygin, "Dal'biuro TsK RKP(в) v gody grazhdanskoi voiny, 1920–1922 gg.," *Voprosy istorii KPSS*, no. 8 (August 1966), pp. 60–62.

53. Osipova, "Bor'ba Dal'biuro TsK RKP(в)," p. 105.

54. V. S. Kirillov and A. Ia. Sverdlov, *Grigorii Konstantinovich Ordzhonikidze: biografiia* (Moscow: Gospolizdat, 1962), pp. 154–159.

55. S. Nazarov, *Iz istorii sredazbiuro TsK RKP(b), 1922–1924* (Tashkent: Izdatel'stvo Uzbekistana, 1965), pp. 80–92; A. A. Rosliakov, *Sredazbiuro TsK RKP(b): voprosy strategii i taktiki* (Ashkhabad: Izdatel'stvo Turkmenistana, 1975) pp. 13, 14; and, B. A. Tulepbaev, *Sotsialisticheskie agrarnye preobrazovaniia v srednei azii i kazakhstane* (Moscow: Izdatel'stvo Nauka, 1984), ch. 2.

56. P. M. Alampiev, *Ekonomicheskoe raionirovanie SSSR* (Moscow: Gosplanizdat, 1959), p. 65; and P. S. Pavlovskii and M. A. Shafir, *Administrativno-territorial'noe ustroistvo sovetskogo gosudarstva* (Moscow, 1961), p. 58.

57. M. F. Vladimirskii, "Osnovnye polozheniia ustanovleniia granits administrativno-khoziaistvennykh raionov," in *Voprosy ekonomicheskogo raionirovaniia*

SSSR: sbornik materialov i statei, 1917–1929 gg., ed. G. M. Khrzhizhanovskii (Moscow: Gospolizdat, 1957), pp. 55–64.

58. See, for example, the recommendations issued by the State Planning Commission's head of regionalization. I. G. Aleksandrov, "O raionirovanii," in *Voprosy ekonomicheskogo raionirovaniia*, ed. Krzhizhanovskii, pp. 87–96. LeDonne, "From Gubernia to Oblast," pp. 78–83.

59. *KPSS v rezoliutsiakh i reshcheniiakh s'ezdov, konferentsii i plenumov TsK*, vol. 1 (Moscow: Gospolizdat, 1954), p. 718. The North Caucasus was also targeted as an experimental region at this time, but implementation there was delayed for over two years.

60. LeDonne, "From Gubernia to Oblast," pp. 209–213; and, *Ocherki istorii kommunisticheskikh organizatsii urala* (Sverdlovsk: Sredne-ural'skoe knizhnoe izdatel'stvo, 1974), pp. 16–24.

61. Walker Connor, *The National Question in Marxist-Leninist Theory and Strategy* (Princeton, NJ: Princeton University Press, 1984), ch. 3; and Richard Pipes, *The Formation of the Soviet Union* (New York: Atheneum, 1968, rev. ed.), ch. 6.

62. Ibid., p. 76. The quote is from K. Zavlialov at the Ninth Party Congress.

63. Quoted in Shurygin, "Dal'biuro Tsk RKP(b)," p. 60.

64. *Izvestiia TsK RKP(b)*, no. 33 (October 1921), p. 22.

65. Daniel Brower, "The Smolensk Scandal and the End of NEP," *Slavic Review*, vol. 45, no. 4 (winter 1986).

66. The central leadership refers to full and candidate members of the politburo, the main policy-making organ, and the secretariat, the organizational head of the territorial party apparatus. For another analysis of patronage politics that employs the same definition of "the center," see John Willerton, "Patronage Networks and Coalition Building in the Brezhnev Era," *Soviet Studies* 39, no. 2 (April 1987), p. 177. A regional leader refers to an individual who worked for at least two years in a particular region during the civil war (1918–21) and/or the postwar political consolidation (1920–23).

67. A network tie is determined by two criteria: (1) evidence of a working relationship (two or more years) in at least one of three milieux (prerevolutionary underground, civil war, postwar consolidation); and/or (2) evidence of friendship or family relationship. Below are the source materials used to determine the informal ties of the regional leadership listed in Table 4.2. They include personal correspondence, memoirs and biographies.

A. Andreev: RTsKhIDNI, f. 73, op. 1, d. ll. 1–9; *Vospominaniia, pis'ma* (Moscow: Politizdat, 1985).

L. Beria: RTsKhIDNI, f. 80, op. 24, d. 166, ll. 1, 2.

R. Eikhe: RTsKhIDNI, f. 124, op. 1, d. 2215, ll. 1–6; *Voprosy istorii KPSS*, no. 7 (1965), 92–97.

I. Gamarnik: *Vospominaniia druzei i soratnikov* (Moscow: Voenizdat, 1978).

N. Gikalo: RTsKhIDNI, f. 85, op. 15, d. 34, ll. 1–5; ibid., f. 80, op. 8, d. 25, ll. 3–9.

F. Goloshchekin: RTsKhIDNI, f. 124, op. 1, d. 484, ll. 1–12.

A. Ikramov: RTsKhIDNI, f. 79, op. 1, d. 708, ll. 1–7; *Pravda*, 9 April 1964.

L. Kartvelishvili: RTsKhIDNI, f. 80, op. 29, l. 1; ibid., f. 124, op. 1, d. 835, ll. 16–17.

M. Khataevich: RTsKhIDNI, f. 124, op. 1, d. 2043, ll. 2–6; *Voprosy istorii KPSS*, no. 6 (1963), 98–101.

S. Kosior: RTsKhIDNI, f. 124, op. 1, d. 951, l. 1; *Vospominaniia, ocherki, stat'i* (Moscow: Politizdat, 1989).

A. Kostanian: *Kommunist* (Erevan), 28 July 1967.

A. Krinitskii: *Voprosy istorii KPSS*, no. 12 (1964).

L. Mirzoian: RTsKhIDNI, f. 80, op. 7, d. 3, l. 1; *Voprosy istorii KPSS*, no. 1 (1965), 101–4.

M. Orakhelashvili: RTsKhIDNI, f. 85, op. 11, d. 28, ll. 1–4; *Mamiia Orakhelashvili* (Tbilisi: Izdatel'stvo sabchota sakartvelo, 1986).

I. Rumiantsev: RTsKhIDNI, f. 124, op. 1, d. 1662, ll. 3–5.

B. Semenov: *Izvestiia TsK KPSS*, no. 12 (1989), p. 110.

B. Sheboldaev: RTsKhIDNI, f. 124, op. 1, d. 2138, ll. 1, 2.

V. Shubrikov: *Izvestiia TsK KPSS*, no. 12 (1989), p. 112.

I. Vareikis: RTsKhIDNI, f. 124, op. 1, 302, ll. 1–5; D. Lappo, *Iuozas Vareikis* (Voronezh: Tsentral'no-chernozemnoe knizhnoe izdatel'stvo, 1989).

68. *Voprosy istorii KPSS*, no. 1 (1965), 101–104.

69. The archival sources are from the former Central Party Archive of the Institute of Marxism-Leninism, which has been renamed the Russian Center for the Preservation and Investigation of Documents of Recent History.

70. Ron Grigor Suny, *The Making of the Georgian Nation* (Bloomington: Indiana University Press, 1988).

71. For Ordzhonikidze's official appointments, see RTsKhIDNI, f. 85, op. 1, d. 15, l. 1; ibid., op. 1, d. 18, l. 1; for Kirov's official appointments, see RTsKhIDNI, f. 80, op. 3, d. 34, l. 1; ibid., op. 4, d. 47, l. 1; ibid., op. 5, d. 24, l. 1.

72. For Kirov, see RTsKhIDNI, f. 80, op. 4, d. 44, ll. 1–4; ibid., d. 94, ll. 2–4; ibid., op. 5, d. 13, ll. 1–4; d. 20, l. 1; ibid., d. 25, l. l.; ibid., f. 85, op. 11. d. 8, ll. 1–7. For Kvirikeli, see RTsKhIDNI, f. 85, op. 11, d. 13, ll. 3–18; ibid., d. 14, ll. 1–3; ibid., d. 19, l. 1, 2; d. 34, ll. 2–7. For Gikalo, see RTsKhIDNI, f. 85, op. 11, d. 28, ll. 1–4; ibid., d. 34, ll. 1–5; ibid., d. 59, ll. 1, 2.

73. For the coordination of military and political tasks, see RTsKhIDNI, f. 85, op. 15, d. 57, l. 1; ibid., d. 61, l. 1; ibid., d. 71, ll. 1, 2; ibid., d. 103, l. 1. For the placement of network members in positions of power, see RTsKh-IDNI, f. 85, op. 15, d. 182, ll. 4–9; ibid., d. 243, l. 1; ibid., d. 246, ll. 1–5.

74. RTsKhIDNI, f. 80, op. 22, d. 11, ll. 3–7; d. 15, ll. 1–10.

75. Ibid., op. 3, d. 20, ll. 1–8.

76. Oleg Khlevniuk, *In Stalin's Shadow: The Career of Sergo Ordzhonikidze* (Armonk, NY: M. E. Sharpe, 1995), p. 16.

77. RTsKhIDNI, f. 85, op. 24, d. 114, ll. 1, 2.

78. Ibid., d. 261, l. 1.

79. RTsKhIDNI, f. 80, op. 3, d. 15, ll. 1, 4; ibid., op. 4, d. 7, ll. 3–7.

80. RTsKhIDNI, f. 85, op. 11, d. 28,   ll. 1–4; ibid., op. 15, d. 246, ll. 2–5.

81. *Pravda*, 10 June 1963.

82. G. K. Dolunts, *Kirov v revoliutsii* (Krasnodar: Krasnodarskoe knizhnoe izdatel'stvo, 1967), p. 65.

83. For evidence of Nazaretian's close ties with Ordzhonikidze, see RTsKhIDNI,

f. 85, op. 11, d. 85, ll. 2–5; for Nazaretian's ties with Kirov, see RTsKh-IDNI, f. 80, op. 4, d. 117, l. 1.

84. RTsKhIDNI, f. 80. op. 7, d. 3, l. 1; ibid., op. 8, d. 25, ll. 3–9.

85. Khlevniuk, *In Stalin's Shadow*, p. 33.

86. See the remarks of politburo member Lazar Kaganovich delivered to the sixteenth party congress in the summer of 1930. *Shestnadtsatyi s'ezd vsesoiuznoi kommunisticheskoi partii (b): stenograficheskii otchet* (Moscow: Gospolizdat, 1935), p. 156.

87. *Spravochnik partiinogo rabotnika* (Moscow: Partizdat, 1934, vol. 8), pp. 272, 273.

88. RTsKhIDNI, f. 85, op. 27, d. 127, ll. 2–12; ibid., d. 140, ll. 1, 2; ibid., d. 300, ll. 1–26.

89. Ibid., d. 304, l. 1.

90. Ibid., d. 308, ll. 5–52; ibid., op. 1, d. 317, ll. 1–17; ibid., op. 27, d. 321, ll. 1–9.

91. Ibid., f. 80, op. 25, d. 11, ll. 1–14; ibid., op. 26, d. 40, ll. 1–5.

92. Ibid., op. 12, d. 29, l. 1.

93. Ibid., op. 15, d. 45, l. 1.

94. See, respectively, ibid., f. 80, op. 10, d. 42, ll. 1; ibid, op. 12, d. 22, ll. 1, 2; ibid., op. 13, d. 16, l. 1.

95. Ibid., f. 85, op. 27, d. 307, ll. 3–15; ibid., d. 308, ll. 16–29, 33–50; ibid., d. 312, ll. 10–18; ibid., d. 315, ll. 1, 2; ibid., d. 321, ll. 1–9. Also, see Amy Knight's excellent biography of Lavrenti Beria, Stalin's secret police chief, who worked in Transcaucasia at this time and was a protégé of Ordzhonikidze, Amy Knight, *Beria: Stalin's First Lieutenant* (Princeton, NJ: Princeton University Press, 1993), chs. 2, 3.

96. RTsKhIDNI, f. 85, op. 27, d. 308, ll. 36–48; ibid., d. 317, ll. 8, 9; ibid., f. 80, op. 15, d. 13, ll. 1–8.

97. RTsKhIDNI, op. 14, d. 10, ll. 9–64.

98. Ibid., op. 15, d. 45, l. 1; ibid., op. 17, d. 58, l. 1.

99. Ibid., op. 17, d. 55, l. 1; ibid., op. 18, d. 103, ll. 1, 2; ibid., d. 105, l. 1.

100. Ibid., 80, op. 18, d. 107, ll. 1, 2.

101. R. W. Davies, *The Soviet Economy in Turmoil* (Cambridge: Harvard University Press, 1989), 283–309.

102. RTsKhIDNI, f. 80, op. 15, d. 51, l. 1; ibid., d. 49, l. 1; ibid., op. 17, d. 57, l. 1; ibid., op. 14, d. 49, l. 1.

103. For Sheboldaev, see ibid., f. 124, op. 1, d. 2138, l. 1; for Rumiantsev, see ibid., d. 1662, l. 5; for Vareikis, see Lappo, *Iuozas Vareikis*, 85–99.

104. RTsKhIDNI, f. 80, op. 16, d. 45, l. 1.

105. Ibid. op. 17, d. 58, l. 1.

5. THE CONSTRAINTS OF POWER

1. Stalin was exceptional in that he identified more with the *komitetchiki* than with the *intelligenty*. He was responsible for nationalities policy and regional affairs. Stalin never actually served in postwar regional administration.

2. They replaced Nikolai Bukharin and Mikhail Tomskii.

3. *Izvestiia TsK KPSS*, no. 12 (December 1988), p. 82.

4. The existence of a "moderate bloc" within the politburo, in the early 1930s,

has always remained a puzzle to observers. It was first suggested by Boris Nikolaevsky in a publication entitled "The Confessions of an Old Bolshevik." The "confessions" were allegedly those of Nikolai Bukharin, who apparently spoke openly and pessimistically about high-level party politics during an official visit to London in 1935. The position is supported by Western scholars, such as Robert Conquest and Moshe Lewin. J. Arch Getty is a strong opponent of the view that a moderate bloc existed.

5. A. Vaksberg, "Kak zhivoi s zhivyni," *Literaturnaia gazeta*, 29 June 1988, p. 13.

6. Russian Center for the Preservation and Investigation of Documents of Recent History RTsKhIDNI, f. 85, op. 27, d. 304, l. 1; ibid., d. 308, ll. 36–49; ibid., d. 316, ll. 1–22; ibid., d. 317, ll. 6–10.

7. See, for example, the remarks of Boris Sheboldaev. RTsKhIDNI, f. 17, op. 2, d. 514, vyp. I, l. 81.

8. Eugene Zaleski, *Stalinist Planning for Economic Growth, 1933–1952* (Chapel Hill, NC: University of North Carolina Press, 1980), pp. 115–29.

9. For evidence of Kirov's support for a more moderate economic plan, see F. Benevenuti, "Kirov in Soviet Politics, 1933–1934," CREES papers on Soviet Industrialization, no. 8 (Birmingham, UK, 1977).

10. Moshe Lewin, "Taking Grain: Soviet Policies of Agricultural Procurements Before the War," *The Making of the Soviet System: Essays in the Social History of Interwar Russia* (New York: Pantheon Books, 1985), pp. 158, 159. Also, see his report on the agricultural plan for 1933. RTsKhIDNI, f. 80, op. 17, d. 15, l. 20.

11. RTsKhIDNI,, f. 80, op. 18, d. 19, ll. 1–20.

12. S. M. Kirov, *Izbrannye, stat'i i rechi, 1905–1934* (Leningrad: OGIZ, 1939), p. 663.

13. RTsKhIDNI, f. 79, op. 1, d. 744, l. 2.

14. Ibid., d. 381, l. 1.

15. V. M. Selunskaia, "Kommunisticheskaia partiia v bor'be za kollektivizatsiiu sel'skogo khoziaistva v SSSR," *Voprosy istorii KPSS*, no. 9 (September 1987), p. 51. Kuibyshev drafted a secret politburo communication, dated 23 May 1932, that urged a more "realistic" course regarding grain collections. RTsKhIDNI, f. 79, op. 1, d. 375, l. 1.

16. Hiroaki Kuromiya, *Stalin's Industrial Revolution: Politics and Workers, 1928–1932* (New York: Cambridge University Press, 1988), p. 142.

17. *Pravda*, 17 November 1964; *Izvestiia TsK KPSS*, no. 11 (1989); *Pravda*, 28 January 1991; and Amy Knight, *Beria: Stalin's First Lieutenant* (Princeton, NJ: Princeton University Press, 1993).

18. Oleg Khlevniuk, *In Stalin's Shadow: The Career of Sergo Ordzhonikidze* (Armonk, NY: M. E. Sharpe, 1995), p. 35.

19. S. Z. Ginzburg, "O gibeli Sergo Ordzhonikidze," *Voprosy istorii KPSS*, no. 3 (March 1991), pp. 91–93; and I. M. Dubinskii-Mukhadze, *Ordzhonikidze* (Moscow: Molodaia gvardiia, 1967), p. 294.

20. Three inner-party oppositon groups arose in this period: Lominadze-Syrtsov, Eismont-Tolmachev and Riutin-Slepkov. A discussion of the platform and supporters of the Riutin group is found in *Izvestiia TsK KPSS*, no. 3 (March 1990), pp. 150–178.

21. S. M. Kirov: *Izbrannye stat'i i rechi, 1905–1934* (Leningrad: OGIZ, 1939).

22. L. M. Kaganovich, "Moskovskie bol'sheviki v bor'be za pobedu piateletki," (Moscow, pamphlet, 1932).

23. See, for example Kuibyshev's remarks concerning Ordzhonikidze's report on industrial development. RTsKhIDNI, f. 79, op. 1, d. 372, ll. 1–22. Also, see Sheila FitzPatrick, "Ordzhonikidze's Takeover of Vesenkha: A Case Study in Soviet Bureaucratic Politics," *Soviet Studies* 37, no. 2 (April 1985).

24. RTsKhIDNI, f. 80, op. 3, d. 10, ll. 1, 2; ibid., op. 22, d. 5, l. 1; ibid., f. 79, op. 1, d. 142, ll. 2–13.

25. Ibid., f. 79, op. 1, d. 343, ll. 1–22; ibid., f. 80, op. 19, d. 5, ll. 1–9.

26. Ibid., f. 79, op. 1, d. 780, ll. 1, 2; ibid., f. 80, op. 16, d. 22, l. 1; ibid., op. 17, d. 60, l. 1.

27. Ibid., f. 80, op. 3, d. 15, l. 4.

28. See the reminiscences of Ordzhonikidze's wife, Zinaida Gavrilovna. *Trud,* 1 December 1964.

29. RTsKhIDNI, f. 80, op. 13, d. 32, ll. 1, 2; ibid., op. 15, d. 80, ll. 1, 2; ibid., op. 18, d. 150, l. 1.

30. Anastas Mikoian, "V pervyi raz bez Lenina," *Ogonek,* no. 50 (December 1989), p. 6.

31. My understanding of the tsarist origins of this organizational structure was influenced by David McDonald.

32. S. I. Ikonnikov, *Sozdanie i deiatel'nost' ob'edinennykh organov TSKK-RKI, v 1923–1934 gg.* (Moscow: Nauka, 1971), pp. 34–65.

33. For Kuibyshev, see RTsKhIDNI, f. 79, op. 1, d. 5, ll. 1–5; for Ordzhonikidze, see ibid., f. 85, op. 1, d. 1, ll. 1–6.

34. Ibid., f. 79, op. 1, d. 110, l. 26.

35. Paul Cocks, "The Politics of Control: The Historical and Institutional Role of the Party Control Organs of the CPSU," (Ph.D., Harvard University, 1968), p. 171. These findings were in contrast to earlier scholarly depictions of the regional control commissions as the "disciplined cogs of the central machine." Mark Neuweld, "The Origins of the Central Control Commission," *The American Slavic and East European Review* 18, no. 3 (October 1959), p. 329.

36. *KPSS v rezoliutsiiakh i resheniiakh s'ezdov, konferentsii i plenumov TsK,* vol. 4 (Moscow: Politizdat, 1970), p. 428.

37. *XVII s'ezd: sten otchet,* p. 286.

38. Cocks, "Politics of Control," p. 172.

39. Timothy Colton, *Commissars, Commanders and Civilian Authority: The Structure of Soviet Military Politics* (Cambridge: Harvard University Press, 1979), pp. 11–14; Merle Fainsod, *Smolensk Under Soviet Rule* (Cambridge: Harvard University Press, 1958), p. 68.

40. *Istoriia kommunisticheskoi partii sovetskogo soiuza,* vol. 4, pt. 1 (Moscow: Politizdat, 1970), p. 400.

41. For Gusev, see RTsKhIDNI, f. 124, op. 1, d. 551, ll. 2–8; Kuibyshev, see ibid., f. 79, op. 1, d. 8, l. 1. Kuibyshev cooperated with Gusev to set the agenda for these administrative changes. Ibid., d. 282, l. 1; ibid., d. 291, ll. 1, 2.

42. For Kuibyshev's tie to Bubnov, see RTsKhIDNI, f. 79, op. 1, d. 127, l. 1; and *Voprosy istorii KPSS,* no. 4 (1963), pp. 784, 785.

43. RTsKhIDNI, f. 124, op. 1, d. 263, l. 4.

44. *Geroi grazhdanskoi voiny* (Moscow: Molodaia gvardiia, 1963).

45. RTsKhINDI, f. 124, op. 1, d. 302, l. 4.

46. Boris Levytsky, *The Stalinist Terror in the Thirties: Documentation from the Soviet Press*, (Stanford, CA: Stanford University Press, 1974), p. 150.

47. *Pravda,* 7 July 1932. Also, see Molotov's remarks to a special meeting of the Ukrainian leadership in *Pravda*, 14 July 1932.

48. *Pravda*, 9 July 1932; also, see Kosior's correspondence with Kuibyshev, RTsKhIDNI, f. 79, op. 1, d. 381, l. 1.

49. Hryhory Kostiuk, *Stalinist Rule in the Ukraine* (New York: Praeger, 1960), pp. 18–21.

50. *Za tempy, kachestvo, proverky*, no. 4 (1933), pp. 69, 70.

51. James E. Mace, "Famine and Nationalism in the Soviet Ukraine," *Problems of Communism* (May–June 1984), p. 45.

52 V. P. Zatonskii, "Iz vospominanii ob ukrainskoi revoliutsii," *Letopisi revoliutsii*, nos. 5–6 (1929), pp. 128–141.

53. Levytsky, *Stalinist Terror in the Thirties*, p. 66.

54. *Ian Gamarnik: Vospominaniia, druzei i soratnikov* (Moscow: Voenizdat, 1978), pp. 66–78; *Krasnaia zvezda*, 2 June 1964.

55. Lars Lih, Oleg Naumov, and Oleg Khlevniuk, eds., *Stalin's Letters to Molotov, 1925–1936* (New Haven, CT: Yale University Press, 1995), p. 177.

56. James W. Heinzen, "Alien Personnel in the Soviet State: The People's Commissariat of Agriculture under Proletarian Dictatorship, 1918–1929," *Slavic Review* 56, no. 1 (Spring 1997), pp. 73–100.

57. R. W. Davies, *The Socialist Offensive: The Collectivisation of Soviet Agriculture, 1929–1930* (Cambridge: Harvard University Press, 1980), pp. 32, 33.

58. Heinzen, "Alien Personnel," p. 100.

59. *KPSS v rezoliutsiiakh i reshenniiakh s'ezdov, konferentsii i plenumov TsK*, vol. 4 (Moscow: Politizdat, 1970), p. 386.

60. *0 Stanislave Kosiore: Vospominaniia, ocherki, stat'i* (Moscow: Politizdat, 1989), pp. 77–79, 119, 120.

61. B. A. Abramov, "0 rabote komissi politburo TsK VKP (b) po voprosam sploshnoi kollektivizatsii," *Voprosy istorii KPSS*, no. 1 (January 1964), pp. 32–43.

62. RTsKhIDNI, f. 124, op. 1, d. 1004, l. 7.

63. B. A. Abramov, "Kollektivizatsiia sel'skogo khoziaistva v RSFSR," in *Ocherki istorii kollektivizatsii sel'skogo khoziaistva v SSSR, 1929–1932 gg.*, ed. V. P. Danilov (Moscow: Gospolizdat, 1963), pp. 130, 131.

64. I. F. Ganzha, I. I. Slinyko, and P. V. Shostak, "Ukrainskoe selo na puti k sotsializmu," in *Ocherki istorii kollektivizatsii*, ed. Danilov, p. 188.

65. RTsKhIDNI, f. 80, op. 15, d. 27, l. 1; ibid., d. 46, l. 1; ibid., op. 16, d. 26, l. 1.

66. Ibid., f. 17, op. 2, d. 612, vyp. I, l. 20.

67. Lih, Naumov, and Khlevniuk, *Stalin's Letters to Molotov*, p. 200.

68. RTsKhIDNI, f. 17, op. 2, d. 612, l. 71.

69. Ibid.

70. Merle Fainsod, *How Russia Is Ruled* (Cambridge: Harvard University Press, 1967, rev. ed.), pp. 236, 237.

71. *Pravda*, 1 April 1937.

6. CENTER AND REGIONS IN CONFLICT I

1. Alec Nove, *An Economic History of the USSR* (New York; Penguin Books, 1969); V. P. Danilov, *Sovetskaia dokolkhoznaia derevnia: sotsial'naia struktura, sotsial'naia otnosheniia* (Moscow: Nauka, 1979).

2. E. H. Carr and R. W. Davies, *Foundations of a Planned Economy*, vol. 1 (New York: Macmillan, 1969), table 7.

3. Stephen Cohen, *Bukharin and the Bolshevik Revolution: A Political Biography* (New York: Knopf, 1973), ch. 8.

4. See William Chase, *Workers, Society and the Soviet State: Labor and Life in Moscow* (Urbana: University of Illinois Press, 1987), pp. 105–21, 136–72.

5. *KPSS v rezoliutsiiakh i resheniiakh: s'ezdov, konferentsii i plenumov TsK*, vol. 4 (Moscow: Politizdat, 1970), p. 12. Moshe Lewin, *Peasants and Soviet Power* (Evanston, IL: Northwestern University Press, 1968); R. W. Davies, *The Socialist Offensive: The Collectivisation of Soviet Agriculture, 1929–1930* (Cambridge: Harvard University Press, 1980).

6. See Moshe Lewin's excellent article, "Taking Grain: Soviet Policies of Agricultural Procurements Before the War," *The Making of the Soviet System: Essays in the Social History of Interwar Russia* (New York: Pantheon Books, 1985), pp. 142–177.

7. *Pravda*, 17 January 1930.

8. N. I. Nemakov, *Kommunisticheskaia partiia: organizator massogo kolkhoznogo dvizheniia, 1929–1932 gg.* (Moscow: Moskovskogo universiteta, 1966), 82.

9. P. N. Sharova, ed., *Kollektivizatsiia sel'skogo khoziaistva: vazhneishie postanovleniia kommunisticheskoi partii i sovetskogo pravitel'stva, 1927–1935 gg.* (Moscow: AN SSSR, 1957); N. A. Ivnitskii, *Klassovaia bor'ba v derevne i likvidatsiia kulachestva kak klassa, 1929–1932 gg.* (Moscow: Nauka, 1972); V. P. Danilov and N. A. Ivnitskii, eds., *Dokumenty svidetel'stvuiut: iz istorii derevni nakune i vkhode kollektivizatsii, 1927–1932 gg.* (Moscow: Politizdat, 1989).

10. Nemakov, *Kommunisticheskaia partiia*, p. 10.

11. *Bol'shevik*, no. 22 (December 1929), pp. 10–23; N. A. Ivnitskii, "0 nachale etap sploshnoi kollektivizatsii," *Voprosy istorii KPSS*, no. 4 (April 1962), p. 65.

12. *Pravda*, 7 November 1929.

13. B. A. Abramov, "Kollektivizatsiia sel'skogo khoziaistva v RSFSR," in *Ocherki istorii kollektivizatsii sel'skogo khoziaistva v soiuznykh respublikakh, 1929–1932 gg.*, ed. V. P. Danilov (Moscow: Gospolizdat, 1963), p. 98.

14. *Molot*, 4 October 1929.

15. Danilov and Ivnitskii, eds., *Dokumenty*, pp. 288, 289.

16. For Sheboldaev, see *Pravda*, 9 May 1929; for Khataevich and Kosior, see Danilov and Ivnitskii, eds., *Dokumenty*, pp. 286, 288, 289; for Vareikis, see Lewin, *Russian Peasants*, pp. 431, 432.

17. *Istoriia SSSR*, no. 3 (May–June 1989), p. 42.

18. Ivnitskii, *Klassovaia bor'ba*.

19. *Bol'shevik*, no. 22 (December 1929), pp. 12–18; *Pravda*, 7 November 1929. The quote is from Stalin's remarks in *Pravda*.

20. For Vareikis, in the Central Black Earth region, see *Pravda*, 9 May 1929; for Eikhe, in Western Siberia, see Danilov and Ivnitskii, eds., *Dokumenty*, p. 287.

21. Danilov and Ivnitskii, eds., *Dokumenty*, p. 287.

22. Ibid., p. 284.
23. For an overview of this question, see Moshe Lewin, "Who Was the Soviet Kulak?" *Making of the Soviet System*, pp. 121–41.
24. Danilov and Ivnitskii, eds., *Dokumenty*, pp. 284, 285.
25. Abramov, "Kollektivizatsiia sel'skogo khoziaistva," p. 98.
26. B. A. Abramov, "0 rabote kommissi politbiuro TsK VKP(b) po voprosam sploshnoi kollektivizatsii," *Voprosy istorii KPSS*, no 1 (January 1964)," pp. 34, 35.
27. Ibid., p. 40.
28. Iosif Stalin, *Voprosy leninizma* (Moscow: Partizdat TsK VKP(b), 1934, 10th ed.), pp. 313, 314. Stalin's strong line was supported by Vareikis and Kosior, but opposed by Khataevich. Ivnitskii, *Klassovaia bor'ba*, pp. 162, 163, 171, 172.
29. *KPSS v rez.*, vol. 4, pp. 383–386.
30. RTsKhIDNI, f. 73, op. 1, d. 66, l. 26; and *Pravda*, 15 January 1930.
31. RTsKhIDNI, f. 73, op. 1, d. 66, l. 27.
32. *Ocherki istorii saratovskoi organizatsii KPSS, 1918–1937* (Saratov: Privolzhskoe knizhnoe izdatel'stvo, 1965), p. 263.
33. *Ocherki istorii voronezhskoi organizatsii KPSS* (Voronezh: Tsentral'no-chernozemnoe knizhnoe izdatel'stvo, 1967), p. 286; P. N. Sharova, *Kollektivizatsiia sel'skogo khoziaistva v tsentral'no-chernozemnoi oblasti, 1928–1932 gg.* (Moscow: AN SSSR, 1963), p. 137.
34. *Ocherki istorii kommunisticheskikh organizatsii urala, 1921–1973 gg.* (Sverdlovsk: Sredne-ural'skoe knizhnoe izdatel'stvo, 1974), vol. 2, p. 96.
35. *Ocherki istorii kommunisticheskoi partii belorussii, 1921–1966 gg.* (Minsk: Belorus, 1967), vol. 2, p. 143.
36. F. I. Goloshchekin, "Ob osedanii kazakov," in idem., *Kazakstan na putiakh sotsialisticheskogo pereustroistva: sbornik statei i rechi* (Kazakhstan: Kraigiz, 1931), pp. 24–46.
37. *Pravda*, 26 April 1930.
38. *Pravda*, 2 March 1930.
39. *KPSS v rez.*, vol. 4, pp. 394–7; Danilov and Ivnitskii, eds., *Dokumenty*, pp. 387–94.
40. Ivnitskii, *Klassovaia bor'ba*, p. 220.
41. B. A. Abramov, *Organizatorskaia rabota partii* (Moscow, 1956), p. 103.
42. R. W. Davies, "The Syrtsov-Lominadze Affair," *Soviet Studies* 33, no. 1 (January 1981), pp. 30–3.
43. For an overview of this debate, see Davies, *Socialist Offensive*, pp. 311–330.
44. Lewin, "Taking Grain," p. 166.
45. *KPSS v rez.*, vol. 4, pp. 452, 453; *Pravda*, 24 January 1931; I. E. Zelenin, "O nekotorykh 'belykh piatnakh' zavershaiushgo etapa sploshnoi kollektivizatsii," *Istorii SSSR*, no. 2 (March–April 1989) p. 4.
46. Between the regions and the villages existed the *okrug* (district) and the *raion* (county) administrative–territorial units.
47. *Spravochnik partiinogo rabotnika* (Moscow: Partizdat, 1934), vol. 8, pp. 272, 273.
48. *Chetyrnadtsatyi s'ezd VKP(b): stenograficheskii otchet* (Moscow: Gospolitizdat, 1958), pp. 215, 235.

49. N. A. Zolotarev, *Vazhnyi etap organizatsionnogo ukreplieniia kommunisticheskoi partii, 1929–1937 gg.* (Moscow: Partizdat, 1979), ch. 1. Merle Fainsod, *Smolensk under Soviet Rule* (Cambridge: Harvard University Press, 1958), pp. 62–74.

50. *KPSS v rez.*, vol. 4, pp. 414–18.

51. L. Maleiko, "Iz istorii razvitiia apparata partiinykh organov," *Voprosy istorii KPSS*, no. 2 (February 1976), p. 115. See Mendel Khataevich's criticisms of the decision in *Pravda*, 19 January 1930.

52. Maleiko, "Iz istorii razvitiia," p. 113.

53. *Pravda*, 17 January 1930. For a good description of these reforms, see Merle Fainsod, *How Russia Is Ruled* (Cambridge: Harvard University Press, 1967, rev. ed.), pp. 192–4.

54. L. M. Kaganovich, "Moskovskie bol'sheviki v bor'be za pobedu piatiletki," pamphlet (Moscow, 1932), p. 112.

55. See the remarks of Khataevich, Rumiantsev, and Razumov in *Pravda*, 19 January 1930.

56. *Spravochnik partiinogo rabotnika*, vol. 8, p. 277. V. K. Beliakov and N. A. Zolotarev, *Organizatsiia udesiateriaet sily: razvitie organizatsionnoi struktury KPSS* (Moscow: Politizdat, 1975), p. 58. In the Moscow regional organization, nine territorial–production sectors were formed: dairy–livestock (24 districts), light industry (23 districts), potatoes–livestock (20 districts), grain (20 districts), cottage industry (15 districts), heavy industry (10 districts), fuel and energy (9 districts).

57. Fainsod, *How Russia Is Ruled*, pp. 194, 195.

58. *Partiinoe stroitel'stvo*, no. 16 (August 1930), pp. 18–29; ibid., no. 11 (June 1931), p. 13; ibid., no. 1–2 (January 1932), p. 14.

59. Lynne Viola, "Bab'i Bunty and the Peasant Women's Protest During Collectivization," *Russian Review* 45, no. 1 (January 1986); Davies, *Socialist Offensive*, pp. 256–61;

60. Davies, *Socialist Offensive*, pp. 255, 256.

61. Danilov and Ivnitskii, eds., *Dokumenty*, pp. 466, 467.

62. *Ocherki istorii kommunisticheskoi Partii ukrainy* (Kiev: Politizdat Ukrainy, 1977), p. 425; *Ocherki istorii moskovskogo organizatsii KPSS: 1883–1965* (Moscow: Moskovskii Rabochii, 1966), p. 469. For a general overview, see Ivnitskii, *Klassovaia bor'ba*, pp. 247–260.

63. N. V. Teptsov, "Pravda o raskulachivanii: dokumental'nyi ocherk," *Kentvar* (March–April 1992), p. 51.

64. Danilov and Ivnitskii, eds., *Dokumenty*, pp. 456, 476,

65. RTsKhIDNI, f. 79; op. 1. d. 821; ll. 2–8.

66. Ivnitskii, *Klassovaia bor'ba*, p. 248.

67. A. A. Andreev, *Vospominaniia, pis'ma* (Moscow: Politizdat, 1985), p. 178.

68. Teptsov, "Pravda o raskulachivanii," pp. 46–62.

69. RTsKhIDNI, f. 73, op. 1, d. 83, ll. 42, 43, 49, 58, 59; ibid., d. 97, l. 13.

70. Mark Von Hagen, *Soldiers in the Proletarian Revolution: The Red Army and the Soviet Socialist State, 1917–1930* (Ithaca, NY: Cornell University Press, 1990), pp. 308–25.

71. Danilov and Ivnitskii, eds., *Dokumenty*, p. 393; Fainsod, *Smolensk Under Soviet Rule*, pp. 165, 166, 242.

72. Lewin, "Taking Grain," p. 166.
73. *Partiinoe stroitel'stvo*, nos. 17–18 (September 1932), p. 5.
74. For the state's procurement totals between 1928 and 1940, see Lewin, "Taking Grain," pp. 142–177, table 6.1.
75. Iu. A. Moshkov, *Zernovaia problema v gody sploshnoi kollektivizatsii sel'skogo khoziaistva SSSR, 1929–1932 gg.* (Moscow: Moskovskogo universiteta, 1966), pp. 164, 165.
76. Lewin, "Taking Grain," p. 153.
77. Zelenin, "0 nekotorykh 'belykh piatnakh,' " pp. 5–8.
78. Khataevich raised this particular point to central leaders. *Pravda*, 13 March 1930.
79. Robert Conquest, *The Harvest of Sorrow: Soviet Collectivization and the Terror Famine* (New York: Oxford University Press, 1986), chs. 11–13; Zelenin, "0 nekotorykh 'belykh piatnakh,' " pp. 8–17.
80. Moshkov, *Zernovaia problema*, p. 224.
81. Stalin, *Voprosy leninizma*, pp. 301, 302.
82. *Pravda*, 9 July 1932.
83. Ibid., 14 July 1932.
84. *Istoriia SSSR*, no. 3 (May–June 1989), p. 48.
85. *Pravda*, 7 September 1932.
86. V. M. Selunskaia, "Kommunisticheskaia partiia v bor'be za kollektivizatsiiu sel'skogo khoziaistva v SSSR," *Voprosy istorii KPSS*, no. 9 (September 1987), p. 51.
87. RTsKhIDNI, f. 79, op. 1, d. 375, l. 1.
88. Lewin, "Taking Grain," p. 153; Moshkov, *Zernovaia problema*, pp. 202, 203.
89. *Spravochnik partiinogo rabotnika*, vol. 8, pp. 567–568.
90. Lewin, "Taking Grain," p. 154.
91. Zelenin, "0 nekotorykh 'belykh piatnakh,' " pp. 8–17. Central plenipotentiaries were Kaganovich in the North Caucasus, Molotov in Ukraine and Postyshev in the Lower Volga.
92. *Istoriia SSSR*, no. 3 (May–June), p. 50.
93. Ibid., pp. 50, 51.
94. *Pravda*, 2 March 1930.
95. For Kosior's remarks, see *Pravda*, 26 April 1930. In his article, Kosior quoted from Stalin's "Dizzy with Success" editorial.
96. RTsKhIDNI, f. 17, op. 2, d. 514, vyp. I, l. 83.
97. Ibid., vyp. II, l. 35.
98. Stalin, *Voprosy leninizma*, p. 334.
99. Ibid., pp. 509, 518,
100. Selunskaia, "Kommunisticheskaia partiia v bor'be," p. 45.
101. *Pravda*, 27 April 1930.
102. *XVI s'ezd: sten. otchet*, p. 320.
103. Stalin, *Voprosy leninizma*, pp. 491, 492.
104. Danilov and Ivnitskii, eds., *Dokumenty*, pp. 481, 482.
105. See comments of: Goloshchekin in Kazakhstan, RTsKhIDNI, f. 17, op. 2, d. 514, vyp. I, l. 83; Vlas Chubar, governmental head of Ukraine, RTsKhIDNI, f. 17, op. 2, d. 514, vyp. I, ll. 98, 99; and Vareikis in Central Black Earth region, RTsKhIDNI, f. 17, op. 2, d. 514, vyp. I, l. 60.

106. RTsKhIDNI, f. 17, op. 2, d. 514, vyp. I, l. 65.
107. Ibid., ll. 60, 61. Other regional leaders agreed that weather conditions had undermined the procurement campaign. See Khataevich, RTsKhIDNI, f. 17, op. 2, d. 514, vyp. II, l. 30; and, Vlas Chubar, Ukrainian head of government, RTsKhIDNI, f. 17, op. 2, d. 514, vyp. I, l. 60.
108. RTsKhIDNI, f. 17, op. 2, d. 514, vyp. I, l. 65.
109. Ibid., f. 79, op. 1, d. 381, ll. 1–6.
110. *Molot*, 8 November 1932; *Pravda*, 19 November 1932.
111. RTsKhIDNI, f. 17, op. 2, d. 514, vyp. II, l. 35.
112. See the remarks of Khataevich, *Pravda*, 13 March 1930; and E. Riabnin, head of the government in Central Black Earth region, *Pravda,* 28 March 1930.
113. RTsKhIDNI, f. 17, op. 2, d. 514, vyp. I, ll. 81, 82.
114. See comments of Vareikis, RTsKhIDNI, f. 17, op. 2, d. 514, vyp. I, l. 60; of Kosior, RTsKhIDNI, f. 17, op. 2, d. 514, vyp. I, l. 65; and of Khataevich, RTsKhIDNI, f. 17, op. 2, d. 514, vyp. II, l. 31.
115. *Pravda*, 13 March 1930.
116. RTsKhIDNI, f. 17, op. 2, d. 514, vyp. I, l. 80.
117. Ibid., f. 17, op. 2, d. 500, l. 45. Also, see remarks by Eikhe, RTsKhIDNI, f. 17, op. 2, d. 500, l. 46; and Kosior RTsKhIDNI, f. 17, op. 2, d. 500, ll. 50, 51.
118. RTsKhIDNI, f. 17, op. 2, d. 514, vyp. I, l. 60.
119. Zelenin, "0 nekotorykh 'belykh piatnakh,' " p. 17. Although Postyshev was employed in regional administration for most of his career, he worked as a central committee secretary between 1930 and 1932. Beginning in 1933, however, he returned to regional administration as a party leader in Ukraine. On this issue, his views reflected those of the Provincial Komitetchiki.
120. Stalin, *Voprosy leninizma*, p. 509.
121. B. A. Abramov, "Iz istorii bor'by KPSS za osushchestvlenie politiki," *Voprosy istorii KPSS*, no. 9 (September 1981), p. 66.
122. Lewin, "Taking Grain," p. 157, 158.
123. RTsKhIDNI, f. 17, op. 2, d. 500, ll. 195, 196.
124. Ivnitskii, *Klassovaia bor'ba*, pp. 299, 300.
125. Iosif Vareikis, *Usloviia uspekha i organizatsiia sotsialisticheskogo stroia v derevne* (Stalingrad: Kraevoe knigoizdatel'stvo, 1936), p. 62.
126. *Soviet Ukraine Today* (Moscow-Leningrad: Cooperative Publishing Society of Foreign Workers in USSR, 1934), pp. 24–26.
127. Lecture at Harriman Institute, Columbia University, 21 April 1989.

7. CENTER AND REGIONS IN CONFLICT II

1. *Shestnadtsatyi s'ezd vsesoiuznoi kommunisticheskoi partii (b): stenograficheskii otchet* (Moscow: Gospolitizdat, 1935), p. 81. The center's main personnel office was the cadres department of the central party apparat, which at this time was called the Organizational-Distribution Department (*orgraspred*).
2. RTsKhIDNI, f. 124, op. 1, d. 140, ll. 2–5; and *Bol'shaia sovetskaia entsiklopediia* (Moscow: Izdatel'stvo sovetskaia entsiklopediia, 1970, 3rd ed.), vol. 3, p. 48. Kaganovich assumed control of the Moscow organization and conducted a thorough personnel turnover, bringing in nearly 150 new workers. See *Ocherki*

istorii moskovskoi organizatsii KPSS, 1883–1965 (Moscow: Moskovskii rabochii, 1966), p. 470.

3. *Ocherki istorii partii azerbaidzhana* (Baku: Azerbaidzhanskoe gosudarstvnnoe izdatel'stvo, 1963), p. 472; *Ocherki istorii kommunisticheskoi partii armenii* (Erevan: Izdatel'stvo aiastan, 1967), p. 338; *Ocherki istorii kommunisticheskoi partii gruzii* (Tbilisi: Izdatel'stvo TsK KP Gruzii, 1971), pp. 509, 526. For an overview of the numerous personnel changes in the Transcaucasus, see Ronald Grigor Suny, *The Making of the Georgian Nation* (Bloomington: University of Indiana Press, 1988), ch. 11.

4. R. W. Davies, "The Syrtsov-Lominadze Affair," *Soviet Studies* 33, no. 1 (January 1981), p. 41.

5. *Ocherki istorii kommunisticheskoi partii belorussii* (Minsk: Izdatel'stvo belarus, 1967), vol. 2, pp. 121, 126, 148.

6. RTsKhIDNI, f. 124, op. 1, d. 2138, l. 1.

7. *Soviet Ukraine Today* (Moscow-Leningrad: Cooperative Publishing Society of Foreign Workers in the USSR, 1934), pp. 11, 12.

8. I. E. Zelenin, "0 nekotorykh 'belykh piatnakh' zavershaiushchego etapa sploshnoi kollektivizatsii," *Istoriia SSSR*, no. 2 (March–April 1989), p. 12.

9. The new appointees included: N. Gikalo (Belorussia); P. Postyshev, M. Khataevich, and I. Akulov (Ukraine); E. Veger (Odessa); L. Beria (Transcaucasus); Bagirov (Azerbaijan); A. Lepa (Tataria); L. Mirzoian (Kazakhstan); M. Belotskii (Kirgizia).

10. RTsKhIDNI, f. 79, op. 1, d. 381, l. 4.

11. James E. Mace, "Famine and Nationalism in the Soviet Ukraine," *Problems of Communism* (May–June 1984), p. 47. This movement was alleged to have centered around Mykola Skrypnik, a Ukrainian politburo member and education head.

12. *Ocherki istorii kommunisticheskoi partii belorussi*, p. 169. The Belorussian "nationalist deviationist" movement was alleged to have been organized by the Belorussian communist, V. M. Ignatovski.

13. Zelenin, "0 nekotorykh 'belykh piatnakh,' " pp. 5, 6.

14. RTsKhIDNI, f. 124, op. 1, d. 484, l. 11.

15. Ibid., f. 80, op. 3, d. 15, ll. 1, 4; *Voprosy istorii KPSS*, no. 1 (1965), pp. 101–104.

16. These lateral transfers were sometimes misinterpreted by Western analysts. For example, Khataevich moved from the Middle Volga region to the Dnepropetrovsk province in Ukraine. Khataevich was wrongly described as having been "sent from Moscow to the Ukraine." In fact, Khataevich had previously worked in regional administration, where he had emerged as a critic of central policies in the countryside. Robert Sullivant, *Soviet Politics and the Ukraine, 1917–1957* (New York: Columbia University Press, 1962), p. 190.

17. *VII kommunisticheskikh organizatsii zakavkaz'ia: stenograficheskii otchet* (Tbilisi: Zakpartizdat, 1934), p. 9.

18. Suny, *Making of the Georgian Nation*, p. 264. He appointed thirty-two police officials to district level party leadership posts; meanwhile, the new leader of Azerbaijan, Bagirov, was also from the regional police bureaucracy.

19. *Bol'shevik*, nos. 1–2 (January 1933), pp. 1–21; *Partiinoe stroitel'stvo*, nos. 13–14 (July 1933), pp. 62, 63. Robert F. Miller, *One Hundred Thousand Tractors:*

The MTS and the Development of Controls in Soviet Agriculture (Cambridge: Harvard University Press, 1970), ch. 2.

20. *Voprosy istorii KPSS*, no. 12 (1964), pp. 96–99.
21. *Shestnadtsatyi s'ezd vsesoiuznoi kommunisticheskoi partii (b): stenograficheskii otchet* (Moscow: Gospolizdat, 1934), p. 559.
22. Kaganovich, "Tseli i zadachi," p. 21.
23. *Pravda*, 12 June 1933; 20 June 1933.
24. Ibid., 22 June 1933.
25. *Shestnadtsatyi s'ezd: sten otchet*, p. 150.
26. B. A. Abramov, "Kollektivizatsiia sel'skogo khoziaistva v RSFSR," in *Ocherki istorii kollektivizatsii sel'skogo khoziaistva v soiuznykh respublikakh, 1929–1932 gg.*, ed. V. P. Danilov (Moscow: Gospolizdat, 1963), pp. 145, 146.
27. RTsKhIDNI, f. 80, op. 18, d. 19, ll. 1–20.
28. *KPSS v rezoliutsiiakh i resheniiakh s'ezdov, konferentsii i plenumov TsK, 1931–1941* (Moscow: Politizdat, 1971), vol. 5, pp. 198–203.
29. *Shestnadtsatyi s'ezd: sten. otchet*, p. 672; L. A. Maleiko, "Iz istorii razvitiia apparata partiinykh organov," *Voprosy istorii KPSS*, no. 2 (February 1976), p. 119.
30. *Partiinoe stroitel'stvo*, no. 7 (March 1935), p. 47; L. Maleiko, "Iz istorii razvitiia apparata," p. 119.
31. *KPSS v rezoliutsiiakh*, vol 4, p. 428; Paul Cocks, "The Politics of Party Control: The Historical and Institutional Role of Party Control Organs of the CPSU" (Ph.D., Harvard University, 1968), p. 166; and S. I. Ikonnikov, *Sozdanie i deiatel'nost' ob'edinennvkh organov TskK–RKI v 1923–1934 gg.* (Moscow: Nauka, 1971), pp. 455–68.
32. *KPSS v rezoliutsiakh*, vol. 5, p. 89.
33. *Pravda*, 29 April 1933. E. Iaroslavski, "Za bol'shevistkuiu proverku i chistku riadov partii," pamphlet (Moscow, 1933).
34. *Shestnadtsatyi s'ezd: sten. otchet*, p. 562.
35. For an excellent overview of this comprehensive membership review, see J. Arch Getty, *Origins of the Great Purges: The Soviet Communist Party Reconsidered, 1933–1938* (New York: Cambridge University Press, 1985), chs. 2, 3. Also, see N. A. Zolotarev, *Vazhnyi etap organizatsionnogo ukrepleniia kommunisticheskoi partii, 1929–1937* (Moscow: Partizdat, 1979), pp. 167–74.
36. *Partiinoe stroitel'stvo*, no. 9 (May 1936), pp. 51–66; ibid., no. 24 (December 1936), p. 58.
37. RTsKhIDNI, f. 17, op. 2, d. 612, vyp. III, l. 72.
38. Iosif Stalin, *Voprosy leninizma* (Moscow: Partizdat TsK VKP(b), 1934, 10th ed.), p. 419; *Pravda*, 8 May 1930; 16 May 1930.
39. *Pravda*, 10 May 1930.
40. Ibid., 17 May 1930.
41. These tactics were characteristic of later reform from above efforts by Khrushchev and Gorbachev, reflecting the persistence of these constraints.
42. See Kaganovich's speech to the partry congress. *Semnadtsatyi s'ezd: sten. Otchet.*
43. Anastas Mikoian, "Iz pervyi raz bez Lenina," *Ogonek*, no. 50 (December 1989), p. 6; and Nikita Khrushchev, *Khrushchev Remembers: The Glasnost Tapes* (Boston: Little, Brown, 1990), pp. 20–2. The incident is also confirmed by Molotov in Feliks Chuev, ed., *Sto sorok besed s Molotovym* (Moscow: Terra,

1991), pp. 307, 308. Also see *Znamia*, no. 7 (July 1988), p. 89; and Robert Conquest, *Stalin and the Murder of Kirov* (New York: Oxford University Press, 1989), pp. 27–9.

44. Following the 1934 party congress, only two additional congresses were convened over the next eighteen years of Stalin's rule. Perhaps the reason was that Stalin was reluctant to provide the opportunity for state elites to meet and discuss issues informally.

45. Mikoian, "Iz pervyi raz bez Lenina," p. 6.

46. According to Mikoian, Kirov later reported the incident to Stalin. Ibid.

47. A detailed description of Kirov's last hours is found in Krasnikov, *S. M. Kirov v Leningrade* (Leningrad: Lenizdat, 1964), p. 20.

48. For a reconstruction of the crime and a compilation of the circumstantial evidence, see Robert Conquest, *Stalin and the Kirov Murder*. The case against Stalin's involvement is well argued by J. Arch Getty, *Origins of the Great Purges*, pp. 207–10.

49. Robert Conquest, *The Great Terror: A Reassessment* (New York: Oxford University Press, 1990), pp. 70, 71. One persistent rumor among Soviet historians was that Stalin, knowing that Kuibyshev had a weak heart, ordered that the elevator in his Kremlin apartment be turned off.

50. *Literaturnaia gazeta*, 7 September 1988; Conquest, *The Great Terror*, pp. 167–73.

51. *XXII s'ezd Kommunisticheskoi partii sovetskogo soiuza: stenograficheskii otchet (Moscow: Gosizdat, 1962), vol. 3,* , pp. 587.

52. Conquest, *Stalin and the Kirov Murder*, p. 129.

53. *Semnadtsatyi s'ezd: sten otchet*, pp. 562, 563; *Spravochnik partiinogo rabotnika* (Moscow: Partizdat, 1934), vol. 8, p. 241.

54. Merle Fainsod, *How Russia Is Ruled* (Cambridge: Harvard University Press, 1967, rev ed.), p. 433.

55. *Pravda*, 26 September 1936.

56. Boris Starkov, "Narkom Ezhov," in *Stalinist Terror: New Perspectives*, ed. J. Arch Getty and Roberta Manning (New York: Cambridge University Press, 1993), pp. 21–3.

57. *Pravda*, 26 December 1935.

58. RTsKhIDNI, f. 17, op. 2, d. 613, ll. 13, 14; *Izvestiia TsK KPSS*, no. 9 (1989), pp. 35–39; Starkov, "Narkom Ezhov," pp. 24–26.

59. RTsKhIDNI, f. 17, op. 2, d. 613, l. 13.

60. *Bol'shevik*, no. 8 (March 1937); *Argumenty i fakti*, 18–24 March 1989; and Merle Fainsod, *Smolensk Under Soviet Rule* (Cambridge: Harvard University Press, 1958), p. 166.

61. Mark Von Hagen, *Soldiers in the Proletarian Revolution: The Red Army and the Soviet Socialist State, 1917–1930* (Ithaca, NY: Cornell University Press, 1990), conclusion.

62. RTsKhIDNI, f. 17, op. 2, d. 612, vyp. III, ll. 41–43.

63. *Pravda*, 11 June 1937. This group included M. N. Tukhachevskii, N. E. Iakir, I. P. Uborevich, V. M. Primakov, B. M. Feldman, A. I. Kork, R. P. Eideman, V. P. Putna. Ian Gamarnik committed suicide shortly before his own arrest.

64. John Erickson, *The Soviet High Command: A Military-Political History, 1918–*

1941 (London: Macmillan, 1962); Vitaly Rapoport and Yuri Alexeev, *High Treason: Essays on the History of the Red Army, 1918–1938* (Durham, NC: Duke University Press, 1985).

65. RTsKhIDNI, f. 17, op. 2, d. 612, vyp. III, l. 72.

66. *Partiinoe stroitel'stvo*, no. 17 (October 1935), pp. 73–78.

67. Ibid., no. 21 (November 1935), p. 56.

68. Ibid., no. 14 (July 1936), p. 40.

69. *Pravda*, 6 May 1935.

70. Getty, *Origins of the Great Purges*, pp. 58–136.

71. *Pravda*, 6 May 1935.

72. Stalin, *Voprosy leninizma*, p. 475. The journal was *Proletarskaia revoliutsiia*, which had served as one of the leading publications in cultivating a hero status for veterans of the underground and civil war.

73. L. Beria, *K voprosy ob istorii bol'shevistskikh organizatsii v za kavkaz'e* (Gosizdat, 1948).

74. *Pravda*, 26 May 1935; *Partiinoe stroitel'stvo*, no. 11 (1935), p. 47.

75. *Znamia*, no. 6 (June 1964).

76. For an excellent discussion of this historical revision as part of the intrastate power struggle, see Graeme Gill, "Political Myth and Stalin's Quest for Authority in the Party," in *Authority, Power and Policy in the USSR*, ed. T. H. Rigby, Archie Brown, and Peter Reddaway (London: Macmillan, 1988).

77. *Ocherki istorii saratovskoi organizatsii KPSS* (Saratov: Privilzhskoe knizhnoe izdatel'stvo, 1965), vol. 2, p. 340.

78. *Pravda*, 12 July 1935.

79. Ibid.

80. RTsKhIDNI, f. 17, op. 2, d. 613, ll. 13–15.

81. *Pravda*, 8 February 1937.

82. The first item on the agenda was the fate of Nikolai Bukharin, one of the party's most popular former leaders. Stephen Cohen, *Bukharin and the Bolshevik Revolution: A Political Biography* (New York: Alfred Knopf, 1973).

83. G. A. Chigrinov, "Pochemu stalin, a ne drugie?" *Voprosy istorii KPSS*, no. 6 (June 1990), pp. 91, 92.

84. RTsKhIDNI, f. 124, op. 1, d. 1321, l. 6; and *Izvestiia TsK KPSS*, no. 12 (December 1989), p. 90.

85. RTsKhIDNI, f. 17, op. 2, d. 612, vyp. I, ll. 5–8.

86. Ibid.

87. *Pravda*, 1 April 1937.

88. RTsKhIDNI, f. 17, op. 2, d. 612, vyp. I, ll. 20, 21.

89. Ibid., l. 28.

90. Ibid., l. 37.

91. Ibid., l. 7.

92. Ibid., ll. 11, 12.

93. Ibid., l. 22.

94. Ibid., ll. 28, 29.

95. Ibid., l. 21.

96. Ibid., ll. 11, 12.

97. Ibid., l. 22.

98. Ibid., vyp. III, l. 69.

99. Ibid., l. 72.
100. Ibid., vyp. II, ll. 3–6.
101. Ibid., l. 3.
102. These categories are roughly based on those defined by Timothy Colton in his depiction of the responses of the military political elite to the 1937 terror. See *Commissars, Commanders and Civilian Authority: The Structure of Soviet Military Politics* (Cambridge: Harvard University Press, 1979), pp. 144–51.
103. RTsKhIDNI, f. 17, op. 2, d. 612, vyp. II, ll. 10–12.
104. Ibid., l. 24.
105. Ibid., vyp. III, l. 25.
106. Ibid., vyp. II, ll. 11, 12.
107. Ibid., l. 24.
108. Ibid., vyp. III, l. 27.
109. Ibid., vyp. II, l. 25.
110. Ibid., d. 630, ll. 6, 15.
111. Ibid., d. 612, vyp. II, ll. 72, 73.
112. Ibid., vyp. III, ll. 88, 89.
113. Ibid., ll. 50–53.
114. Ibid., ll. 12, 13.
115. Ibid., vyp. II, l. 33.
116. Ibid., vyp. III, ll. 26, 27.
117. Ibid., l. 57.
118. Ibid., vyp. II, ll. 24, 25.
119. Anastas Mikoyan, *Memoirs of Anastas Mikoyan: The Path of Struggle* (Madison: Sphinx Press, 1988), pp. 473–77.
120. *Pravda*, 17 March 1937 and 13 April 1937.
121. For a description of this process, see Conquest, *The Great Terror*, ch. 8; and, Getty, *Origins of the Great Purges*, pp. 163–71.
122. RTsKhIDNI, f. 17, op. 2, d. 630, ll. 6–12. The report was delivered by Georgii Malenkov. The official resolution is found in *KPSS v rez.*, vol. 5, pp. 303–312.
123. *Izvestiia TsK KPSS*, no. 12 (December 1989), pp. 87–113.
124. D. Lappo, *Iuozas Vareikis* (Voronezh: Tsentral'no-chernozemnoe knizhnoe izdatel'stvo, 1989).
125. Ibid., no. 1 (January 1965), pp. 101–4.

8. CONCLUSION

1. Mark Von Hagen, *Soldiers in the Proletarian Dictatorship: The Red Army and the Soviet Socialist State, 1917–1930* (Ithaca, NY: Cornell University Press, 1990); and, Jeremy Azrael, *Industrial Managers and Soviet Power* (Cambridge: Harvard University Press, 1966).
2. For strategic bases of support, see Seweryn Bialer, *Stalin's Successors* (New York: Cambridge University Press, 1980).
3. Jerry Hough, *Democratization and Revolution in the Soviet Union, 1985–1991* (Washington, DC: The Brookings Institute Press, 1997), p. 15.
4. M. Steven Fish, *Democracy from Scratch* (Princeton, NJ: Princeton University Press, 1994).

5. For national movements in the USSR, see Jane Dawson, *Econationalism: Anti-Nuclear Activism and National Identity in Russia, Lithuania and Ukraine* (Durham, NC: Duke University Press, 1996); for the revival of civil society in Eastern Europe, see Vladimir Tismaneau, *Reinventing Politics: Eastern Europe from Stalin to Havel* (New York: The Free Press, 1993).

6. Ken Jowitt, "Soviet Neo-Traditionalism: The Political Corruption of a Leninist Regime," *Soviet Studies* 35 (1983).

7. Andrew Walder, ed., *The Waning of the Communist State: Economic Origins of Political Decline in China and Hungary* (Berkeley and Los Angeles: University of California Press, 1995).

8. Peter Rutland, *The Politics of Economic Stagnation: The Role of Local Party Organs in Economic Management* (New York: Cambridge University Press, 1993).

9. William Clark, *Soviet Regional Elite Mobility After Khrushchev* (New York: Praeger, 1989); Michael Urban, *An Algebra of Soviet Power: Elite Circulation in Belorussia* (New York: Cambridge University Press, 1989); and John Willerton, *Patronage and Politics in the USSR* (New York: Cambridge University Press, 1992).

10. Theda Skocpol, *States and Social Revolutions: Comparative Analysis of France, Russia and China* (New York: Cambridge University Press, 1979); Charles Tilly, *Coercion, Capital and the Formation of the European States* (Oxford: Basil Blackwell, 1990); Brian Downing, *The Military Revolution and Political Change* (Princeton, NJ: Princeton University Press, 1992).

11. Thomas Ertman, *Birth of the Leviathan: Building States and Regimes in Medieval and Early Modern Europe* (New York: Cambridge University Press, 1997).

12. Karen Barkey, *Bandits and Bureaucrats: The Ottoman Route to State Centralization* (Ithaca, NY: Cornell University Press, 1994).

13. See the classic article by Guenther Roth, "Personal Rulership, Patrimonialism and New States," *World Politics* 20 (January 1968).

14. Peter Medding, *Mapai in Israel: Political Organization and Government in a New Society* (New York: Cambridge University Press, 1972), pp. 136, 137.

15. Victor Nee, "Between Center and Locality: State, Militia and Village," in *State and Society in Contemporary China*, ed. Victor Nee and David Mozingo (Ithaca: Cornell University Press, 1983), pp. 232, 242.

16. David Stark and Victor Nee, "Toward an Institutional Analysis of State Socialism," in *Remaking the Economic Institutions of Socialism: China and Eastern Europe*, ed. Victor Nee and David Stark (Stanford: Stanford University Press, 1989), p. 15. Also, see Dorothy Solinger, "Urban Reform and Relational Contracting in Post-Mao China: An Interpretation of the Transition from Plan to Market," in *Reform and Reaction in Post-Mao China*, ed. Richard Baum (New York: Routledge, 1991), pp. 104–123.

17. Peter Kirkow, "Regional Warlordism in Russia: The Case of Primorskii Krai." *Europe-Asia Studies* 47, no. 6 (1995), p. 923.

BIBLIOGRAPHY

ARCHIVAL SOURCES
Archival sources employed in this study came from the Russian Center for the Preservation and Investigation of Documents of Recent History (hereafter RTs-KhIDNI), formerly the Institute of Marxism-Leninism attached to the Central Committee of the Communist Party of the Soviet Union. The main archival fonds used in the study included:

Fond 17: The Organizational-Personnel Department of the Central Committee of the Communist Party.

Fond 79: Personal archive of Valerian V. Kuibyshev.

Fond 80: Personal archive of Sergei M. Kirov.

Fond 85: Personal archive of Grigorii K. Ordzhonikidze.

Fond 124: Society of Old Bolsheviks.

RUSSIAN NEWSPAPERS AND JOURNALS
Argumenty i fakti
Bol'shevik
Istoriia SSSR
Izvestiia TsK RKP(b)
Izvestiia TsK KPSS
Krasnaia zvezda
Literaturnaia gazeta
Molot
Partiinoe stroitel'stvo
Pravda
Trud
Voprosy istorii KPSS
Znamia

COLLECTIONS OF DOCUMENTS, SPEECHES, AND POLICY STATEMENTS

XXII s'ezd: kommunisticheskoi partii sovetskogo soiuza : stenographicheskii otchet. Moscow: Gosizdat, 1962.

VII kommunisticheskikh organizatsii zakavkaz'ia: stenograficheskii otchet. Tbilisi: Zakpartizdat, 1934.

Danilov, V. P., and N. A. Ivnitskii, eds. *Dokumenty svidetel'stvuiut: iz istorii derevni nakune i vkhode kollektivizatsii, 1927–1932 gg.* Moscow: Politizdat, 1989.

Desiatyi s'ezd RKP(b): stenograficheskii otchet. Moscow: Gospolizdat, 1963.

Goloshchekin, F. I. *Kazakstan na putiakh sotsialisticheskogo pereustroistva: sbornik stat'i i rechi.* Kazakhstan: Kraigiz, 1931.

Kaganovich, L. M. "Moskovskie bol'sheviki v bor'be za pobedu piateletki." pamphlet. Moscow, 1932.

Kirov, S. M. *Izbrannye, stat'i i rechi, 1905–1934.* Leningrad: OGIZ, 1939.

KPSS v rezoliutsiakh i resheniiakh s'ezdov, konferentsii i plenumov TsK. vols. 4, 5. Moscow: Politizdat, 1954.

Lih, Lars, Oleg Naumov, and Oleg Khlevniuk, eds. *Stalin's Letters to Molotov, 1925–1936.* New Haven, CT: Yale University Press, 1995.

Odinnadtsatyi s'ezd RKP(b): stenograficheskii otchet. Moscow: Gospolizdat, 1961.

Piatnadtsatyi s'ezd VKP(b): stenograficheskii otchet. Moscow: Gospolizdat, 1961.

Semnadtsatyi s'ezd vesesoiuznoi kommunisticheskoi partii (b): stenograficheskii otchet. Moscow: Gospolizdat, 1934.

Sharova, P. N., ed. *Kollektivizatsiia sel'skogo khoziaistva: vazhneishie postanovleniia kommunisticheskoi partii i sovetskogo pravitel'stva, 1927–1935 gg.* Moscow: AN SSSR, 1957.

Shestnadtsatyi s'ezd vsesoiuznoi kommunistickeskoi partii (b): stenograficheskii otchet. Moscow: Gospolizdat, 1935.

Soviet Ukraine Today. Moscow-Leningrad: Cooperative Publishing Society of Foreign Workers, 1934.

Spravochnik partiinogo rabotnika. vol. 8. Moscow: Partizdat, 1934.

Stalin, Iosif. *Voprosy leninizma.* Moscow: Partizdat TsK VKP(b), 1934, 10th ed.

Sverdlov, Ia. M. *Izbrannye stat'i i rechi.* Moscow: Gospolizdat, 1939.

Trinadtsatyi s'ezd RKP(b): stenograficheskii otchet. Moscow: Gospolitizdat, 1963.

V. I. Lenin, KPSS: o rabote partiinogo i gosudarstvennogo apparata. Moscow: Politizdat, 1976.

V. I. Lenin, KPSS: ob ustavii partii. Moscow: Politizdat, 1981.

Vareikis, I. M. *Usloviia uspekha i organizatsiia sotsialisticheskogo stroia 1936.*

Vosmoi s'ezd RKP(b), mart 1919 goda: protokoly. Moscow: Politizdat, 1959.

MEMOIRS AND BIOGRAPHICAL SOURCES

Andreev, A. A. *Vospominaniia, pis'ma.* Moscow: Politizdat, 1985.

Bazhanov, Boris. *Vospominaniia byshego sekretia stalina* Paris: Izdatel'stvo Tret'ia Volna, 1983.

Bol'shaia sovetskaia entsiklopediia. Moscow: Izdatel'stvo sovetskaia entsiklopediia, 1970, 3rd ed.

Dolunts, G. K.. *Kirov v revoliutsii.* Krasnodar: Krasnodarskoe knizhnoe izdatel'stvo, 1967.

Dubinskii-Mukhadze, I. M. *Kuibyshev.* Moscow: Molodaia gvardiia, 1971.

Dubinskii-Mukhadze, I. M. *Ordzhonikidze.* Moscow: Molodaia gvardiia, 1967.

Geroi grazhdanskoi voiny. Moscow: Molodaia gvardiia, 1963.

Gorodetskii, Efrim, and Iurii Sharapov. *Sverdlov.* Moscow: Molodaia gvardiia, 1971.

Haupt, Georges, and Jean-Jacques Marie. *Makers of the Russian Revolution: Biographies of Bolshevik Leaders.* Ithaca, NY: Cornell University Press, 1974.

Ian Gamarnik: Vospominaniia druzei i soratnikov. Moscow: Voenizdat, 1978.

Khrushchev, Nikita. *Khrushchev Remembers.* Boston: Little, Brown, 1970.

Khrushchev, Nikita. *Khrushchev Remembers: The Glasnost Tapes.* Boston: Little, Brown, 1990.

Kirillov, V. S., and A. Ia. Sverdlov. *Grigorii Konstantinovich Ordzhonikidze: biografiia.* Moscow: Gospolizdat, 1962.

Krasnikov, S., *S. M. Kirov v Leningrade.* Leningrad: Lenizdat, 1964.

Krupskaya, Nadezhda. *Memories of Lenin.* New York: International Publishers, 1930.

Kuibysheva, G. V., et al. *Valerian Vladimirovich Kuibyshev: biografiia.* Moscow: Politizdat, 1966.

Lappo, D. *Iuozas Vareikis.* Voronezh: Tsentral'no-chernozemnoe knizhnoe izdatel'stvo, 1989.

Levytsky, Boris. *The Stalinist Terror in the Thirties: Documentation from the Soviet Press.* Stanford, CA: Hoover Institution Press, 1974.

Mikoyan, Anastas. *Memoirs of Anastas Mikoyan: The Path of Struggle.* Madison: Sphinx Press, 1988.

V nachale dvadtsatykh. Moscow: Politizdat, 1975. 989.

O Iakovle Sverdlove: Vospominaniia, ocherki, stat'i sovremenikov. Moscow: Politizdat, 1985.

O Stanislave Kosiore: Vospominaniia, ocherki, stat'i. Moscow: Politizdat, 1989.

Reabilitirovan posmertno. Ed. S. Panov. Moscow: Iuridicheskaia literatura, 1989.

Shlyapnikov, Alexander. *On the Eve of 1917.* London: Allison & Busby, 1982.

Stasova, E. M. *Vospominaniia.* Moscow: Izadatel'stvo mysl', 1969.

Sto sorok besed s Molotovym. Ed. Feliks Chuev. Moscow: Terra, 1991.

Sukhanov, N. *The Russian Revolution: A Personal Record.* Princeton, NJ: Princeton University Press, 1984.

Trotsky, Leon. *My Life: An Attempt at an Autobiography.* New York: Pathfinder Press, 1970.

The Revolution Betrayed: What Is the Soviet Union and Where Is It Going? New York: Pathfinder Press, 1972 [1936].

Stalin: An Appraisal of the Man and His Influence. New York: Stein & Day, 1967 ed.

Zatonskii, V. P. "Iz vospominanii ob ukrainskoi revoliutsii." *Letopis' revoliutsii,* nos. 5–6 (1929).

SECONDARY THEORETICAL AND COMPARATIVE LITERATURE

Almond, Gabriel. *A Discipline Divided: Schools and Sects in Political Science.* Newbury Park, CA: Sage Publications, 1989.

Amsden, Alice. *Asia's Next Giant: South Korea and Late Industrialization.* New York: Oxford University Press, 1989.

Anderson, Lisa. *The State and Social Transformation in Libya and Tunisia.* Princeton, NJ: Princeton University Press, 1986.

Anderson, Perry. *Lineages of the Absolutist State.* London: New Left Books, 1974.

Armstrong, John. *The European Administrative Elite.* Princeton, NJ: Princeton University Press, 1976.

Barkey, Karen. *Bandits and Bureaucrats: The Ottoman Route to State Centralization.* Ithaca, NY: Cornell University Press, 1994.

Barnard, Chester. *The Functions of the Executive.* Cambridge: Harvard University Press, 1937.

Bender, Leonard, et al. *Crises, Sequences and Political Development.* Princeton, NJ: Princeton University Press, 1973.

Blau, Peter. *The Dynamics of Bureaucracy* (Chicago: University of Chicago, 1963).

Brewer, John. *The Sinews of Power: War, Money and the English State, 1688–1783.* Cambridge: Harvard University Press, 1988.

Burt, Ron. *Corporate Profits and Cooptation: Networks of Market Constraints and Directorate Ties in the American Economy.* New York; Academic Books, 1983.

Coleman, James. *Foundations of Social Theory.* Cambridge: Harvard University Press, 1990.

Crozier, Michel. *The Bureaucratic Phenomenon.* Chicago: University of Chicago Press, 1964.

Dawson, Jane. *Econationalism: Anti-Nuclear Activism and National Identity in Russia, Lithuania and Ukraine.* Durham, NC: Duke University Press, 1996.

Downing, Brian, *The Military Revolution and Political Change.* Princeton, NJ: Princeton University Press, 1992.

Eisenstadt, S. N. *The Political Systems of Empires.* New York: The Fress Press, 1969.

Ertman, Thomas. *Birth of the Leviathan: Building States and Regimes in Medieval and Early Modern Europe.* New York: Cambridge University Press, 1997.

Evans, Peter, Dietrich Rueschemeyer, and Theda Skocpol, eds. *Bringing the State Back In.* New York: Cambridge University Press, 1985.

Evans, Peter. *Embedded Autonomy: States and Industrial Transformation.* Princeton, NJ: Princeton University Press, 1995.

Gambetta, Diego, ed. *Trust: Making and Breaking Cooperative Relations.* Oxford: Basil Blackwell, 1988.

Geddes, Barbara, "Building State Autonomy in Brazil, 1931–1964." *Comparative Politics* 22 (January 1990).
       Politician's Dilemma: Building State Capacity in Latin America. Berkeley and Los Angeles: University of California Press, 1994.

Granovetter, Mark. "The Strength of Weak Ties." *American Journal of Sociology* 78 (May 1973).

Hall, John, and G. John Ikenberry. *The State.* Minneapolis: University of Minnesota Press, 1989.

Hall, Peter. *Governing the Economy: The Politics of State Intervention in England and France.* New York: Oxford University Press, 1986.

Hintze, Otto. *The Historical Essays.* Ed. Felix Gilbert. New York: Oxford University Press, 1975.

Huntington, Samuel. *Political Order in Changing Societies.* New Haven, CT: Yale University Press, 1968.

Huntington, Samuel and Clement Moore, eds., *Authoritarian Politics in Modern Society: The Dynamics of Established One-Party Systems* (Glencoe, IL: The Free Press, 1970).

Ikenberry, G. John. *Reasons of State: Oil Politics and the Capacities of the American Government*. Ithaca, NY: Cornell University Press, 1988.

Jackman, Robert. *Power Without Force: The Political Capacity of Nation-States*. Ann Arbor: University of Michigan Press, 1993.

Jessop, Bob. *State Theory: Putting Capitalist States in Their Place*. University Park: Pennsylvania University Press, 1990.

Katzenstien, Peter. *Small States in World Markets*. Ithaca, NY: Cornell University Press, 1985.

Knight, Jack. *Institutions and Social Conflict*. New York: Cambridge University Press, 1992.

Knoke, David. *Political Networks: The Structural Perspective*. New York: Cambridge University Press, 1990.

Krasner, Stephen. *Defending the National Interest: Raw Material Investments and US Foreign Policy*. Princeton, NJ: Princeton University Press, 1978.

Laumann, Edward, and David Knoke. *The Organizational State: Social Choice in National Policy Domains*. Madison: University of Wisconsin, 1987.

Laumann, Edward, and Franz Pappi. *Networks of Collective Action: A Perspective on Community Influence Systems*. New York: Academic Books, 1976.

Levi, Margaret. *Of Rule and Revenue*. Berkeley and Los Angeles: University of California Press, 1988.

Mann, Michael. "The Autonomous Power of the State: Its Origins, Mechanisms and Results." In *States in History*. Ed. John Hall. Oxford: Basil Blackwell, 1986.

Medding, Peter. *Mapai in Israel: Political Organization and Government in a New Society*. New York: Cambridge University Press, 1972.

Migdal, Joel. *Strong Societies, Weak States: State-Societal Relations and State Capabilities in the Third World*. Princeton, NJ: Princeton University Press, 1988.

Migdal, Joel, Atul Kohli, and Vivienne Shue, eds. *State Power and Social Forces: Domination and Transformation in the Third World*. New York: Cambridge University Press, 1994.

Mitchell, J. Clyde, ed. *Social Networks in Urban Situations*. Manchester, UK: Manchester University Press, 1969.

Nee, Victor. "Between Center and Locality: State, Militia and Village." In *State and Society in Contemporary China*. Ed. Victor Nee and David Mozingo. Ithaca, NY: Cornell University Press, 1983.

Nee, Victor, and David Stark, eds. *Remaking the Economic Institutions of Socialism: China and Eastern Europe*. Stanford, CA: Stanford University Press, 1989.

Nordlinger, Eric. *On the Autonomy of the Democratic State*. Cambridge: Harvard University Press.

Oi, Jean. *State and Peasant in Contemporary China*. New York: Oxford University Press, 1989.

Poggi, Gianfranco. *The Development of the Modern State*. Stanford, CA: Stanford University Press, 1978.

Roth, Guenther. "Personal Rulership, Patrimonialism and New States." *World Politics* 20 (January 1968).

Scott, John. *Social Network Analysis*. Newbury Park, CA: Sage Publications, 1991.

Selznick, Philip. *The Organizational Weapon: A Study of Bolshevik Strategy and Tactics*. Gelncoe, IL: The Free Press, 1960.

Shain, Yossi, and Juan Linz, eds. *Interim Governments and Democratic Transitions*. New York: Cambridge University Press, 1996.

Shue, Vivienne. *The Reaches of the State: Sketches of the Chinese Politic.* Stanford, CA: Stanford University Press, 1988.

Skocpol, Theda. *States and Social Revolutions: Comparative Analysis of France, Russia and China.* New York: Cambridge University Press, 1979.

Skorownek, Stephen. *Building a New American State: Expansion of National Administrative Capacities.* New York: Cambridge University Press, 1982.

Solinger, Dorothy. "Urban Reform and Relational Contracting in Post-Mao China: An Interpretation of the Transition from Plan to Market." In *Reform and Reaction in Post-Mao China.* Ed. Richard Baum. New York: Routledge, 1991.

Steinmo, Sven, Kathleen Thelen, and Frank Longstreth, eds. *Structuring Politics: Historical Institutionalism in Comparative Perspective.* New York: Cambridge University Press, 1992.

Tarrow, Sydney. *Between Center and Periphery: Grassroots Politicians in Italy and France.* New Haven, CT: Yale University Press, 1977.

Tilly, Charles. *Coercion, Capital and the Formation of the European States.* Oxford: Basil Blackwell, 1990.

Tilly, Charles, ed. *The Formation of the National States in Western Europe.* Princeton, NJ: Princeton University Press, 1975.

Tismaneau, Vladimir. *Reinventing Politics: Eastern Europe from Stalin to Havel.* New York: The Free Press, 1993.

Walder, Andrew. *Communist Neo-Traditionalism: Work and Authority in Chinese Industry.* Berkeley and Los Angeles: University of California Press, 1986.
ed. *The Waning of the Communist State: Economic Origins of Political Decline in China and Hungary.* Berkeley and Los Angeles: University of California Press, 1995.

Warner, W. Lloyd, and P. S. Lunt. *The Social Life of a Modern Community.* New Haven, CT: Yale University Press, 1941.

Weaver, R. Kent, and Bert Rockman, eds. *Do Institutions Matter? Government Capabilities in the United States and Abroad.* Washington, DC: The Brookings Institution Press, 1993.

Weber, Max. *Economy and Society: An Interpretive Outline of Sociology.* vols. 1, 2. Berkeley and Los Angeles: University of California Press, 1978.

Wellman, Barry, and S. D. Berkowitz, eds. *Social Structures: A Network Approach.* New York: Cambridge University Press, 1988.

White, Harrison. "Where Do Markets Come From?" *American Journal of Sociology* 87 (November 1981).

SECONDARY RUSSIAN STUDIES LITERATURE

Ali, Janice. "Aspects of the RKP(b) Secretariat, March 1919 to April 1922." *Soviet Studies* 26, No. 3 (July 1974).

Armstrong, John. *The Politics of Totalitarianism: The Communist Party of the Soviet Union from 1934 to the Present.* New York: Random House, 1961.

Azrael, Jeremy. *Industrial Managers and Soviet Power.* Cambridge: Harvard University Press, 1966.

Benevenuti, F. "Kirov in Soviet Politics, 1933–1934." CREES Research Papers on Soviet Industrialization, no. 8 (University of Birmingham, 1977).

Bialer, Seweryn. *Stalin's Successors.* New York: Cambridge University Press, 1980.

Brower, Daniel. "The Smolensk Scandal and the End of NEP." *Slavic Review* 45, no. 4. (Winter 1986).

Carr, E. H., and R. W. Davies. *Foundations of a Planned Economy*. vol. 1. New York: Macmillan, 1969.

Chase, William. *Workers, Society and the Soviet State: Labor Life in Moscow*. Urbana: University of Illinois Press, 1987.

Cilaga, Ante. *The Russian Enigma*. London: Ink Links, 1979.

Clark, William. *Soviet Regional Elite Mobility after Khrushchev*. New York: Praeger, 1989.

Cocks, Paul, "The Politics of Party Control: The Historical and Institutional Role of the Party Control Organs of the CPSU." Ph.D. diss. (Harvard University, 1968.)

Cohen, Stephen. *Bukharin and the Bolshevik Revolution: A Political Biography*. New York: Knopf, 1973.

Colton, Timothy. *Commissars, Commanders and Civilian Authority: The Structure of Soviet Military Politics*. Cambridge: Harvard University Press, 1979.

Connor, Walker. *The National Question in Marxist-Leninist Theory and Strategy*. Princeton, NJ: Princeton University Press, 1984.

Conquest, Robert, *The Great Terror: A Reassessment*. New York: Oxford University Press, 1990.
    The Harvest of Sorrow: Soviet Collectivization and the Terror Famine. New York: Oxford University Press, 1986.
    Stalin and the Murder of Kirov. New York: Oxford University Press, 1989.

Crummy, Robert. *Aristocrats and Servitors: The Boyar Elite in Russia, 1613–1689*. Princeton, NJ: Princeton University Press, 1983.

Daniels, Robert V. "Soviet Politics since Khrushchev." In *The Soviet Union Under Brezhnev and Kosygin*. Ed. John Strong. New York: Van Nostran Reinhold, 1971.
    "The Secretariat and the Local Organizations in the Russian Communist Party, 1921–1923." *The American Slavonic and East European Review* 16, no. 1 (March 1967).

Davies, R. W. *The Socialist Offensive: The Collectivisation of Soviet Agriculture*. Cambridge: Harvard University Press, 1980.
    Davies, R. W. *The Soviet Economy in Turmoil*. Cambridge: Harvard University Press, 1989.
    Davies, R. W. "The Syrtsov–Lominadze Affair." *Soviet Studies* 33, no. 1 (January 1981).

Deutscher, Isaac. *Stalin: A Political Biography*. New York: Vintage Books, 1960.

Easter, Gerald M. "Personal Networks and Post-revolutionary State Building: Soviet Russia Reexamined." *World Politics* 48, no. 4 (July 1996).

Elwood, Ralph C. *Russian Social-Democrats in the Underground: A Study of the RSDRP in the Ukraine*. Assen, the Netherlands: Van Gorcum, 1974.

Erickson, John. *The Soviet High Command: A Military-Political History, 1918–1941*. London: Macmillan, 1962.

Fainsod, Merle. *How Russia Is Ruled*. Cambridge: Harvard University Press, 1967, rev. ed.
    Smolensk under Soviet Rule. Cambridge: Harvard University Press, 1958.

FitzPatrick, Sheila. "Ascribing Class: The Construction of Social Identity in Soviet Russia." *Journal of Modern History* 65 (December 1993).
    "The Bolsheviks' Dilemma: Class, Culture, and Politics in the Early Soviet Years." *Slavic Review* 47, No. 4 (Winter 1988).

"Ordzhonikidze's Takeover of Vesenkha: A Case Study in Soviet Bureaucratic Politics," *Soviet Studies* 37, no. 2 (April 1985).

The Russian Revolution. New York: Oxford University Press, 1982.

Getty, J. Arch. *Origins of the Great Purge: The Soviet Communist Party Reconsidered, 1933–1938.* New York: Cambridge University Press, 1986.

Getty, J. Arch, and Roberta Manning, eds. *Stalinist Terror: New Perspectives.* New York: Cambridge University Press, 1993.

Gill, Graeme. *The Origins of the Stalinist Political System.* New York: Cambridge University Press, 1990.

"Political Myth and Stalin's Quest for Authority in the Party." In *Authority, Power and Policy in the USSR.* Ed. T. H. Rigby, Archie Brown, and Peter Reddaway. London: Macmillan, 1988.

Haimson, Leopold. "The Problems of Social Identities in Early Twentieth Century Russia." *Slavic Review* 47, no. 1 (Spring 1988).

"Yuri Petrovich Denike, 1887–1964." *Slavic Review* 24, no. 2 (June 1965).

Henizen, James. "Alien Personnel in the Soviet State: The People's Commissariat of Agriculture Under Proletarian Dictatorship, 1918–1929." *Slavic Review* 56, no. 1 (Spring 1997).

Hough, Jerry. *Democratization and Revolution in the Soviet Union, 1985–1991.* Washington, DC: The Brookings Institution Press, 1997.

Soviet Prefects: Local Party Organs in Industrial Decision-making. Cambridge: Harvard University Press, 1969.

Hughes, James. *Stalin, Siberia and the Crisis of the New Economic Policy.* New York: Cambridge University Press, 1991.

Jowitt, Ken. "Soviet Neo-Traditionalism: The Political Corruption of a Leninist Regime." *Soviet Studies* 35 (1983).

Khlevniuk, Oleg. *In Stalin's Shadow: The Career of Sergo Ordzhonikidze.* Armonk, NY: M. E. Sharpe, 1995.

Kirkow, Peter. "Regional Warlordism in Russia: The Case of Primorskii Krai." *Europe-Asia Studies* 47, no. 6 (1995).

Knight, Amy. *Beria: Stalin's First Lieutenant.* Princeton, NJ: Princeton University Press, 1993.

Kostiuk, Hryhory. *Stalinist Rule in the Ukraine.* New York: Praeger, 1960.

Kuromiya, Hiroaki. *Stalin's Industrial Revolution: Politics and Workers, 1928–1932.* New York: Cambridge University Press, 1988.

LeDonne, John. *Absolutism and the Ruling Class: The Formation of the Russian Political Order.* New York: Oxford University Press, 1991.

"From Gubernia to Oblast: Soviet Administrative-Territorial Reform, 1917–1923." PhD. diss. (Columbia University, 1962).

Lewin, Moshe. *Lenin's Last Struggle.* New York: Monthly Review Press, 1968.

The Making of the Soviet System: Essays in the Social History of Interwar Russia. New York: Pantheon Books, 1985.

Peasants and Soviet Power. Evanston, IL: Northwestern University Press, 1968.

Lieven, Domenic. *Russia's Rulers Under the Old Regime.* New Haven, CT: Yale University Press, 1989.

Mace, James. "Famine and Nationalism in the Soviet Ukraine." *Problems of Communism* (May–June 1984).

Mawdsley, Evan. *The Russian Civil War.* Boston: Allen & Unwin, 1987.

Miller, Robert F. *One Hundred Thousand Tractors: The MTS and the Development of Controls in Soviet Agriculture*. Cambridge: Harvard University Press, 1970.

Mosse, W. E. "Makers of the Soviet Union." *The Slavonic and East European Review* 46, no. 106 (January 1968).

Neuweld, Mark. "The Origins of the Central Control Commission." *The American Slavic and East European Review* 18, no. 3 (October 1959).

Nove, Alec. *An Economic History of the USSR*. New York: Penguin Books, 1969.

Pethyridge, Roger. *One Step Backwards, Two Steps Forward*. Oxford: Clarendon Press, 1990.

Pipes, Richard. *The Formation of the Soviet Union*. New York Atheneum, 1968, rev. ed.

Raleigh, Donald, "Revolutionary Politics in Provincial Russia: The 'Tsaritsyn Republic' in 1917." *Slavic Review* 40, no. 2 (1981).

Rapoport, Vitaly, and Yuri Alexeev. *High Treason: Essays on the History of the Red Army, 1918–1938*. Durham, NC: Duke University Press, 1985.

Reshetar, John. *A Concise History of the Communist Party of the Soviet Union*. New York: Praeger, 1960.

Rigby, T. H. "Early Provincial Cliques and the Rise of Stalin." *Soviet Studies* 33, no. 1 (January 1981).

Lenin's Government: Sovnarkon, 1917–1922. New York: Cambridge University Press, 1979.

Stalin. Englewood Cliffs, NJ: Prentice Hall, 1966.

"Was Stalin a Disloyal Patron?" *Soviet Studies* 38, no. 3 (July 1986).

Rigby, T. H, and Bohdan Harasymiw, eds. *Leadership Selection and Patron–Client Relations in the USSR and Yugoslavia*. London: George Allen & Unwin, 1983.

Robbins, Richard. *The Tsar's Viceroys: Russian Provincial Governors in the Last Years of the Empire*. Ithaca, NY: Cornell University Press, 1987.

Rowney, Don Karl. *Transition to Technocracy: The Origins of the Soviet Administrative State*. Ithaca, NY: Cornell University Press, 1989.

Rutland, Peter. *The Politics of Economic Stagnation: The Role of Local Party Organs in Economic Management*. New York: Cambridge University Press, 1993.

Schapiro, Leonard. *The Communist Party of the Soviet Union*. New York: Vintage Books, 1971, rev. ed.

Service, Robert. *Bolshevik Party in Revolution: A Study in Organizational Change, 1917–1923*. London: Macmillan, 1979.

Sternheimer, Stephen. "Administration for Development: The Emerging Bureaucratic Elite, 1920–1930." In *Russian Officialdom: The Bureaucratization of Russian Society from the Seventeenth to the Twentieth Century*. Ed. Don Karl Rowney and Walter Pintner. Chapel Hill: University of North Carolina Press, 1980.

Sullivant, Robert. *Soviet Politics and the Ukraine, 1917–1957*. New York: Columbia University Press, 1962.

Suny, Ron Grigor. *The Making of the Georgian Nation*. Bloomington: Indiana University Press, 1988.

Tucker, Robert. *Stalin as Revolutionary, 1879–1929: A Study in History and Personality*. New York: Norton, 1973.

Ulam, Adam. *Stalin: The Man and His Era*. New York: Viking Press, 1973.

Urban, Michael. *An Algebra of Soviet Power: Elite Circulation in Belorussia*. New York: Cambridge University Press, 1989.

Viola, Lynne. "Bab'i Bunty and the Peasant Women's Protest During Collectivization," *Russian Review* 45, no. 1 (January 1986).
   The Twenty-Five Thousanders. New York: Oxford University Press, 1988.
Von Hagen, Mark. Review of L. Viola, *The Twenty-Five Thousanders*. *Slavic Review* 48 (Winter 1989).
   Soldiers in the Proletarian Revolution: The Red Army and the Soviet Socialist State, 1917–1930. Ithaca, NY: Cornell University Press, 1990.
Willerton, John. *Patronage and Politics in the USSR*. New York: Cambridge University Press, 1992.
   "Patronage Networks and Coalition Building in the Brezhnev Era." *Soviet Studies* 39, no. 2 (April 1987).
Zaleski, Eugene. *Stalinist Planning for Economic Growth, 1933–1952*. Chapel Hill: University of North Carolina Press, 1980.
Zelnick, Reginald. *Law and Disorder on the Narova*. Stanford, CA: Stanford University Press, 1992.

SECONDARY SOVIET LITERATURE

Abramov, B. A. "Iz istorii bor'by KPSS za osushchestvlenie politiki." *Voprosy istorii KPSS*, no. 9 (September 1981).
   "Kollektivizatsiia sel'skogo khoziaistva v RSFSR." In *Ocherki istorii kollektivizatsii sel'skogo khoziaistva v SSSR, 1929–1932 gg.* Ed. V. P. Danilov. Moscow: Gospolizdat, 1963.
   "O rabote komissi politburo TsK VKP(b) po voprosam sploshnoi kollektivizatsii." *Voprosy istorii KPSS*, no. 1 (January 1964).
   Organizatorskaia rabota partii. Moscow, 1956.
Alampiev, P. M. *Ekonomicheskoe raionirovanie SSSR*. Moscow: Gosplanizdat, 1959.
Beliakov, V. K., and N. A. Zolotarev. *Organizatsiia udesiateriaet sily: razvitie organizatsionnoi struktury KPSS*. Moscow: Politizdat, 1975.
Chigrinov, G. A. "Pochemu stalin, a ne drugie?" *Voprosy istorii KPSS*, no. 6 (June 1990).
Danilov, V. P. *Sovetskaia dokolkhoznaia derevnaia: sotsial'naia struktura, sotsial'naia otnosheniia*. Moscow: Nauka, 1979.
Danilov, V. P., ed. *Ocherki istorii kollektivizatsii sel'skogo khoziaistva v soiuznykh respublikakh, 1929–1932 gg.* Moscow: Gospolizdat, 1963.
Drobizhev, V. Z. *Lenin vo glave sovetskogo pravitel'stva*. Moscow, 1970.
Gimpel'son, E. G. *Iz istorii stroitel'stvo sovetov noiabr 1917 g.–iiuli 1918 g.*. Moscow: Gosiurizdat, 1958.
Ginzberg, S. Z. "O gibeli Sergo Ordzhonikidze." *Voprosy istorii KPSS*, no. 3 (March 1991).
Ikonnikov, S. I. *Sozdanie i deiatel'nost' ob'edinennykh organov TsKK–RKI, v 1923–1934 gg.* Moscow: Nauka, 1971.
Istoriia kommunisticheskoi partii sovetskogo soiuza. vol. 4. Moscow: Politizdat, 1970.
Ivnitskii, N. A. *Klassovaia bor'ba v derevne i likvidatsiia kulachestva kak klassa, 1929–1932 gg.* Moscow: Nauka, 1972.
   "O nachale etap sploshnoi kollektivizatsii." *Voprosy istorii KPSS*, no. 4 (April 1962).

Khrzhizhanovskii, G. M., ed. *Voprosy ekonomicheskogo raionirovaniia SSSR: sbornik materialov i statei, 1917–1929 gg.* Moscow: Gospolizdat, 1957.

Lel'chuk, V. V. "Istoriia sovetskogo obshchestva: kratkii ocherki (1917–1945 gg.)." *Istoriia SSSR*, no. 4 (July–August 1990).

Maleiko, L. "Iz istorii razvitiia apparata partiinykh organov." *Voprosy istorii KPSS*, no. 2 (February 1976).

Moshkov, Iu. A. *Zernovaia problema v gody sploshnoi kollektivizatsii sel'skogo khoziaistva SSSR, 1929–1932 gg.* Moscow: Moskovskogo universiteta, 1966.

Nazarov, S. *Iz istorii sredazbiuro TsK RKP(b), 1922–1924.* Tashkent: Izdatel'stvo Uzbekistana, 1965.

Nemakov, N. I. *Kommunisticheskaia partiia: organizator massogo kolkhoznogo dvizheniia, 1929–1932 gg.* Moscow: Moskovskogo universiteta, 1966.

Ocherki istorii kommunisticheskikh organizatsii urala, 1921–1973 gg. Sverdlovsk: Sredne-ural'skoe knizhnoe izdatel'stvo, 1974.

Ocherki istorii kommunisticheskoi partii armenii. Erevan:Izdatel'stvo aiastan, 1967.

Ocherki istorii kommunisticheskoi partii belorussi, 1921–1966 gg. Minsk: Belorus, 1967.

Ocherki istorii kommunisticheskoi partii gruzii. Tbilisi: Izdatel'stvo TsK KP Gruzii, 1971.

Ocherki istorii kommunisticheskoi partii ukrainy. Kiev: Politizdat ukrainy, 1977.

Ocherki istorii moskovskogo organizatsii KPSS: 1883–1965 gg. Moscow: Moskovskii rabochii, 1966.

Ocherki istorii partii azerbaidzhana. Baku: Azerbaidzhanskoe gosudarstvennoe izdatel'stvo, 1963.

Ocherki istorii saratovskoi organizatsii KPSS, 1918–1937. Saratov: Privolzhskoe knizhnoe izdatel'stvo, 1965.

Ocherki istorii voronezhskoi organizatsii KPSS. Voronezh: Tsentral'no chernozemnoe knizhnoe izdatel'stvo, 1967.

Osipova, A. V. "Bor'ba Dal'biuro TsK RKP(b) za ukrepleniia dal'nevostochnoi partorganizatsii." *Voprosy istorii KPSS*, no. 2 (February 1962).

Pavlovskii, P. S., and M. A. Shafir. *Administrativno–territorial'noe ustroistvo sovetskogo gosudarstva.* Moscow, 1961.

Petukhova, N. E. "Sozdanie oblastnykh biuro TsK RKP(b) i nekotorye storonye ikh deiatel'nosti, 1920–1922 gg." *Voprosy istorii KPSS*, no. 4 (April 1965).

Rosliakov, A. A. *Sredazbiuro TsK RKP(b): voprosy strategii i taktiki.* Ashkhabad: Izdatel'stvo Turkmenistana, 1975.

Selunskaia, V. M. "Kommunisticheskaia partiia v bor'be za kollektiviatsiiu sel'skogo khoziaistva v SSSR." *Voprosy istorii KPSS*, no. 9 (September 1987).

Sharova, P. N. *Kollektivizatsiia sel'skogo khoziaistva v tsentral'no chernozemnoi oblasti, 1928–1932 gg.* Moscow: AN SSSR, 1963.

Shurygin, A. P. "Dal'biuro TsK RKP(b) v gody grazhdanskoi voiny, 1920–1922 gg." *Voprosy istorii KPSS* no. 8 (August 1966).

Startsev, V. I. "Politicheskie rukovoditeli sovetskogo gosudarstva v 1922 nachale 1923 g." *Istoriia SSSR*, no. 5 (September–October 1988).

Teptsov, N. V. "Pravda o raskulachivanii: dokumental'nyi ocherk." *Kentvar* (March–April 1992).

Tulepbaev, A. *Sotsialisticheskie agrarnye preobrazovaniia v srednei azii I kazakhstane.* Moscow: Izadatel'stvo Nauka, 1984.

Vaksberg, A. "Kak zhivoi s zhivyni." *Literaturnaia gazeta* (29 June 1988).

Vasetskii, N. A. "L. D. Trotskii: politicheskii portret." *Novaia i noveishaia istoriia*, no. 3 (May–June 1991).

Zelenin, I. E. "O nekotorykh 'belykh piatnakh' zavershaiushchego etapa sploshnoi kollektivizatsii." *Istoriia SSSR*, no. 2 (March–April 1989).

Zevelev, A. I. *Istoki stalinizma*. Moscow: Vysshaia shkola, 1990.

Zolotarev, N. A. *Vazhnyi etap organizatsionnogo ukrepleniia kommunisticheskoi partii, 1929–1937 gg.* Moscow: Partizdat, 1979.

INDEX

Abramov, B. A., 130
administrative structure, 14, 16, 17, 163, 164, 166, 167, 169, 170
agricultural bureaucracy, 102, 114, 138, 139
Amelin, Mikhail, 101
Andreev, Andrei, 42–5, 80, 81, 99, 112, 115, 116, 120, 135
anti-bureaucracy campaign, 148, 150–3
Antonov-Ovseenko, V., 98
Azerbaidzhan affair, 87

Barkey, Karen, 171
Bauman, Karl, 135
Bazhanov, Boris, 74
Belorussia, 41, 46, 78, 116, 122, 158
Beria, Lavrenti, 80, 81, 137, 148
Berkowitz, S. D., 19
Bolshevik Party, 8, 9, 31, 76, 148, 161
    central committee of, 91
    central party bureaucracy, 68–74, 134
    intra-party cleavages, 35–9
    political bureau of, 90, 91
Brezhnev, Leonid, 169
Bubnov, Andrei, 98
bureaucratic infrastructural power, *see* administrative structure
bureaucratic-absolutism, *see* regime types

cadres policy, *see* personnel policy
center-regional relationship, 11, 12, 25, 34, 76, 101, 109, 110, 159, 160, 173

in conflict, 16, 131, 132, 149, 164
    scholarship on, 26–30
Central Asian (Turkestan) regional bureau, 76, 77, 79
Central Black Earth region, 41, 116, 120–2, 142, 147
central control commission (CCC–RKI), *see* control bureaucracy
central leadership, 121, 122, 124, 139
    Provincial Komitetchiki and, 134–40, 143–50, 153, 164
    territorial administration and, 68–74, 147, 148, 149
Chubar, Vlas, 81, 100, 158
Cilaga, Ante, 59
circular flow of power, 40
civil war, 32, 33, 53–8
civil-military relations, 97–100, 146
class warfare, 113, 115, 120, 127, 128
Cohen, Stephen, 18
collectivization, 87, 92, 109–12
    central leadership and, 112, 115, 124
    famine of 1932 and, 123, 126
    implementation of, 115, 118, 121, 129, 130, 131
    Provincial Komitetchiki and, 115, 121
Communist Party, *see* Bolshevik Party
Conquest, Robert, 145
constraints of power, 3, 15, 16, 17, 89, 90, 133, 134, 140, 141, 143, 159, 160, 164, 168–70